PRAISE FOR *RECOUNTING THE ANTHRAX ATTACKS: TERROR, THE AMERITHRAX TASK FORCE, AND THE EVOLUTION OF FORENSICS IN THE FBI*

"This is an eye opening account of all that goes into an investigation like this, one that is a threat to all of us. As ordinary citizens we never hear about the hard work that is done to protect us from things like the anthrax threat. Scott Decker did an excellent job both with the investigation and writing about it."
—**Marilyn Meredith**, author, *The Deputy Tempe Crabtree and Rocky Bluff P.D.* mystery series; serves on the board of Public Safety Writers Association

"Decker provides a deep and detailed account of how the FBI and other federal agencies used the new field of microbial forensics as well as DNA analysis and other cutting-edge techniques to conduct one of the largest terrorism investigations in the nation's history. His inside knowledge offers something for sleuths and scientists alike."
—**Ed Palattella**, editor, *Erie Times-News*; author, *A History of Heists: Bank Robbery in America* and *Pizza Bomber: The Untold Story of America's Most Shocking Bank Robbery*

"Scott Decker gives an unprecedented look inside one of the most important—but least understood—FBI investigations of the modern era. Every page is a real-life *CSI* episode, a hands-on lesson of what it's like to be inside a cutting-edge, high-profile investigation and the remarkable science the FBI deployed to solve this case."
—**Garrett M. Graff**, author, *Raven Rock and The Threat Matrix: Inside Robert Mueller's FBI*

"With a keen eye for detail, PhD scientist and former FBI agent, Scott Decker, takes the reader deep inside the government's investigation of the 2001 anthrax letter attacks."
—**David Willman**, author, *The Mirage Man: Bruce Ivins, the Anthrax Attacks and America's Rush to War*

"A remarkable scientific whodunnit that peels back some of the biggest mysteries surrounding the case known as Amerithrax. From his own experiences as a lead investigator, Scott Decker paints an intimate and chilling portrait of the hunt for the elusive killer behind history's worst bioterrorist attack."
—**Joby Warrick**, author, *Black Flags: The Rise of ISIS*; winner of the 2016 Pulitzer Prize for General Nonfiction

Recounting the
Anthrax Attacks

Recounting the Anthrax Attacks

Terror, the Amerithrax Task Force, and the Evolution of Forensics in the FBI

R. Scott Decker

ROWMAN & LITTLEFIELD
Lanham • Boulder • New York • London

Disclaimer

The opinions presented in this book are the author's and not endorsed by the Federal Bureau of Investigation or the Department of Justice.

Published by Rowman & Littlefield
An imprint of The Rowman & Littlefield Publishing Group, Inc.
4501 Forbes Boulevard, Suite 200, Lanham, Maryland 20706
www.rowman.com

6 Tinworth Street, London SE11 5AL, United Kingdom

British Library Cataloguing in Publication Information Available

Library of Congress Cataloging-in-Publication Data

Names: Decker, R. Scott, author.
Title: Recounting the anthrax attacks : terror, the Amerithrax Task Force, and the
    evolution of forensics in the FBI / R. Scott Decker.
Description: Lanham : Rowman & Littlefield, [2018] | Includes bibliographical
    references and index.
Identifiers: LCCN 2017038603 (print) | LCCN 2018030172 (ebook) | ISBN
    9781538101506 (Electronic) | ISBN 9781538101490 (cloth) | ISBN
    9781538131480 (paper)
Subjects: LCSH: United States. Federal Bureau of Investigation. | Bioterrorism—United
    States. | Anthrax—United States.
Classification: LCC HV6433.35 (ebook) | LCC HV6433.35 .D43 2018 (print) | DDC
    363.325/30973—dc23
LC record available at https://lccn.loc.gov/2017038603

Without thinking of your own safety and security you responded to the scenes, stayed for weeks and never questioned the hardships, the risks, or conditions and never shirked your duty. . . .

When the first crisis ended and the second one appeared you simply changed directions and charged straight into it. When other people were terrified of the biological terror, you simply stepped up to the plate ready to serve again. . . .

You and I both know that no parade will ever be held in our honor—but that does not lessen your accomplishments.

—Supervisory Special Agent James Rice to members of the National Capital Response Squad, Washington Field Office, FBI, December 2001

Contents

Acknowledgments

There are many people who supported and encouraged me throughout this writing project. Edward Lake, who by keeping his Internet site up to date from the fall of 2001 through the end of 2014, chronicled the investigation. The site is a wealth of information and source of media references. I thank him for agreeing to review my manuscript for accuracy; any mistakes still remaining are completely on me. I also want to thank Tommy Harris Jr., Local 40 Ironworker (retired), for sharing his memory of the days at Ground Zero immediately following the 9/11 World Trade Center attack and for graciously sending me a copy of his excellent book about those days.

I must voice my appreciation for the friendship and support from Tom Reynolds and Greg Meyers over the years. They never turned down any of our ambitious requests as we analyzed and reanalyzed our collection of anthrax samples at Commonwealth Biotechnologies. Their dedication resulted in our first break in the investigation. I wish them all the luck with their new venture at NEXT Molecular Analytics. I am indebted to David Bostwick of Bostwick Laboratories and American International Biotechnology. It was David who first gave me the idea to write this book, and it would not have been possible without his support and encouragement for the past five years.

At the Centers for Disease Control and Prevention (CDC), Rich Meyer, Stephen Morse, and Rich Kellogg have been good friends and great colleagues over the years, especially in the early days of the Laboratory Response Network. They had the vision and put in the hard work to make it happen. The Lab Network saved us on more than one occasion following the chaos of 9/11. Thanks also to Alex Hoffmaster at the CDC for sharing his data and memories of the early days of the anthrax attacks. A thank you also to Segaran Pillai. He unselfishly allowed me use of his data from the sampling and analysis he conducted at the American Media building while he headed up the Public Health Laboratory in Miami. I must of course thank Paul Keim at the Northern Arizona University. He also never said no to whatever our requests, and there were many during the investigation. He showed immense patience and always answered my questions, regardless of how naïve. Finally, my thanks go to Rita Colwell. As director of the National Science Foundation, unfailingly she gave her support to the investigation and offered her friendship. Our meetings were very productive.

I received much encouragement from the writing community as well. Richard Preston, Joby Warrick, and David Willman all shared their wisdom. And thank you to Dean King of the James River Writers for convincing me that my story about Ground Zero should be told. Several people helped me understand the writing process. Linden Gross guided me through the basics, and Lise Funderburg acted as coach and mentor. Jenny Johnston, an excellent writer and editor, taught me about structure, brevity, and keeping it light. A special thanks goes to those at *Creative Nonfiction*: Lee Gutkind, Hattie Fletcher, and their staff. They showed me that nonfiction writing is more than reporting results and documenting history; it can have life. A special thank you goes to Ed Palattella for introducing me to his editor, Kathryn Knigge, at Rowman & Littlefield. Kathryn became my editor, and I am grateful to her for believing in my project. A big thank-you also goes to Elaine McGarraugh, senior production editor at Rowman & Littlefield. Both have been especially easy to work with, consummate professionals, and always have time for my impromptu telephone calls.

At the FBI and Postal Service there are many that supported me. In particular, kudos to Scott Stanley and Richard Langham for doing a fine job in advancing anthrax genetics. And Tom Dellafera for being there and listening, no matter how dumb my ideas might have sounded. To Tom Devlin and Paul Jaskot, who I worked and partnered with in the FBI's Boston office and then again when we drew assignments at Quantico and FBI Headquarters. I learned a lot from them. At the FBI's Washington Field Office Jim Rice and John Perren stand out. Jim is a true patriot and always put his agents first. And as John rose through the ranks to become an assistant director, he always had time to talk.

I must thank my wife, Terry L. Kerns. As a friend she stood beside me when I faced cancer surgery. Later, we married and again she helped me work through a health issue. She found me the best cardiac care at George Washington University Hospital (GW). She has been thoroughly supportive of this writing project and was always there to assist. At GW, a big thanks goes to Farzad Najam, director of cardiac surgery, undoubtedly one of the most caring individuals I have met in the medical arts. And at GW there is also cardiologist Jonathan Reiner, who gave me a new lease on life with his artery stents. Jonathan's book on the history of cardiac care—cowritten with former vice president Dick Cheney—encouraged me to keep writing.

And lastly to my wonderful children, two of the kindest people I know, Kyle and Caleigh, for understanding why I couldn't be with them in the days after 9/11—an uncertain time for all.

List of Figures

1

Beyond Ground Zero

September 11, 2001

The second week of September began hot and humid. I was in day two of a weeklong advanced firearms instructor training at Quantico, along with thirty other FBI agents from field divisions around the country. The day before we had each fired upward of six hundred rounds, carefully watching one another for any small flaw in execution. Tuesday morning we gathered in a classroom overlooking the pistol range to hear the day's agenda. It was close to nine o'clock. We sat silent as a television hanging in one corner flashed news of a commercial airliner tearing into the World Trade Center's North Tower. An unimaginable accident, I thought. How could something so large fly so low and hit the tower so precisely?

The classroom door opened. A range instructor took a half step inside and spoke the unthinkable. "The other one's been hit," he said. "It's intentional. No accident."

For a moment, everything went quiet. Then agents started calling their units and home offices. Our training was over.

I didn't need to make a phone call. I was part of the FBI's Hazardous Materials Response Unit, and the Academy had been our base of operations since the unit's founding five years earlier. We were a mix of agents, scientists, logistical specialists, and first responders—and as FBI units go we were still young, still small, still being incubated. A life scientist by training, I managed our biology program. I worked with infectious disease specialists at the Centers for Disease Control[1] and biological defense experts in the US Army and Navy to prepare for the day our country might be attacked by a living weapon.

I was also one of the unit's five supervisory special agents. Whenever we deployed, one of us would serve as team leader. On September 11, it was my turn.

1

Back at our office, I got briefed. The FBI had already assumed control of the investigation that was about to unfold, though dozens of agencies would be involved. Our Hazmat team would serve multiple roles at the site that quickly became known as "Ground Zero." The first was ensuring the safety of every FBI agent who entered it—issuing them equipment, logging them in, taking their vitals, and making sure they came out. On my team were four FBI Hazmat officers, each one of them a career firefighter recruited by the FBI for their expertise in hazardous materials tactics. All four were also emergency medical technicians, and two were trained in urban search and rescue. They understood collapsing buildings and would escort evidence recovery teams on rooftop searches.

They were also trained in the detection of phosgene, chlorine, methane, sarin gas—and dozens more chemical and biological agents. We didn't know what we might encounter. If someone found a vial or anyone got sick, we would coordinate whatever assets were needed.

In other words, we had to be prepared for anything.

On the way to brief my team and pull equipment together, I stopped at the Academy's gun vault, a storehouse for most of the FBI's service weapons. Its inventory included everything from new Sig Sauer semiautomatic pistols to ten-pound Colt Thompson submachine guns from the 1930s. Walking through the vault's steel doorway, I approached the window, rang the bell, and asked for two extra boxes of pistol ammunition. The armorer looked at me from behind the heavy glass and hesitated. The rule was one box per agent, to be given out only after quarterly qualifications. Rules were rules; he would need authorization.

The vault supervisor—a guy known for adhering to procedure—walked up and nodded hello, towering over me by at least six inches.

"I'm headed up to New York, the World Trade Center, first thing in the morning," I told him.

The supervisor's expression remained impassive as he studied me. "Give him whatever he wants."

Leaving the vault, I walked out to the parking lot and felt an unnatural quiet. Quantico is close to several major airports, but there were no sounds of planes flying above. The Federal Aviation Administration had ordered all commercial flights to the ground.[2] Aside from the occasional military jet, the skies were now silent.

I joined the FBI in 1990, after a brief career in biotechnology. I'd gotten a doctorate in genetics, then used it to study DNA and the diagnosis of disease. The work was interesting, but results came slow. Success often measured itself in years. Investigating crime promised more immediate impact. While

I enjoyed science, the opportunity to help stop a serial killer or thwart operatives from countries deemed a threat to our nation seemed more appealing. I filled out an application.

Written tests, intense interviews, and lots of pushups, pullups, and timed runs followed. So did an eighteen-month investigation into my past and present. Then, in July 1990, my telephone rang. The FBI Academy was forming a new agent training class in Quantico. Could I be there in three days? Without hesitation, I quit my job, bid a temporary goodbye to my pregnant wife, and caught a Sunday flight to Virginia.

Monday morning, thirty fellow trainees and I met our class counselors, field agents on a four-month temporary duty that would see us through training. Next, we stood in unison and swore our oath of loyalty. As I talked with my classmates during breaks, their collective intelligence and strong sense to family and duty impressed me. I thought, *How did I get here?* I felt neither very intelligent nor exactly close with my family (that would change as my siblings and I grew older). I realized the Bureau hired me because of my background. The FBI was building a forensic program in human genetics—my PhD from Michigan had been my ticket in. At that point, I knew my future would involve some role in DNA and its forensics. But for now, I had to learn to be an agent if I wanted to make it.

We began physical training, firearms, and legal tests. I did well on the firing range, but my thirty-five-year-old legs barely kept up in the fifty-yard shuttle dash. Fortunately, I aced the two-mile run. Within months, I was a full-blown agent assigned to the Boston Division, responding to bank robberies, armored car holdups, and money courier waylays—the quintessential work of the Bureau. Experience came fast. I learned to process bank lobbies for latent finger and palm impressions, scan surveillance films for grainy pictures of fleeing robbers, locate stolen and abandoned getaway cars, and testify before judges and juries.

I spent seven years as a field agent. Then a new opportunity came up. The FBI's Laboratory Division had formed a Hazardous Materials Response Unit with openings for agents who had backgrounds in biology, chemistry, and medicine. A position in the new unit would be a promotion. It would also give me the chance to apply my science training and expand into a different kind of investigative work.

That was 1997. The FBI created the Hazmat Unit because of a growing concern that the country was unprepared for large-scale terrorism. The 1995 sarin gas attacks on the Tokyo subway, which killed twelve people and hospitalized nearly one thousand others, were still in the news. Richard Preston's 1994 bestseller *The Hot Zone*—about the threat posed by the highly infectious and deadly Ebola virus, with no known treatments or cures—caused a big stir on Capitol Hill. (President Clinton allegedly read Preston's follow-up biological thriller, *The Cobra Event*, in one night.) After a top Iraqi general—also son-in-law to Saddam Hussein—defected, the extent of Iraq's anthrax weaponization became known. It confirmed a biological attack by Iraq was viable. Near the end of the year, Secretary of Defense William Cohen made a notable TV appearance, holding up a five-pound bag of sugar and saying that if Hussein spread this amount of anthrax over DC, it would kill half the population.

The Bureau gave its new Hazmat Unit a broad mission. We would develop and validate procedures for responding to crime scenes created by weapons of mass destruction. Once at a scene, we would collect and preserve evidence contaminated with biological or chemical warfare agents or fallout from an improvised radiological device. As a new member with a biology background, I anticipated evaluating screening tests for bacteria and viruses and developing protocols for keeping microorganisms alive while getting them to a laboratory. At the time, I had no idea that the procedures and solutions we would develop would become central to one of the largest terrorism investigations in US history.

My team and I spent the evening of September 11 loading five black Chevy Suburbans with essential gear—respirators, hard hats, white paper Hazmat suits, rolls of gray duct tape, evidence recovery equipment, encrypted hand-held radios. The next morning, our caravan headed north on Interstate 95, up through Virginia, then Maryland. I-95's three lanes became four as we approached New Jersey. Above the highway, bright orange words on a black message board warned: *NEW YORK CITY CLOSED*. I picked up my handset and pressed the talk button, breaking the silence. "We keep going," I said.

Soon, the Manhattan skyline appeared through the right side of my Suburban's windshield. The landmark Twin Towers were gone, obliterated. I had known them since childhood road trips from my native New Jersey. In their place, a wide and dense column of smoke rose from the ground. Overhead, two F-16s raced across the sky, flying much lower than usual—so low their pilots were nearly visible.

Normal procedure called for us to report in at the FBI's New York City field office at 26 Federal Plaza. But the building, located just blocks from Ground Zero, had been evacuated. So we made a brief stop at the Newark office. They provided what information they had, but communication with agents in Manhattan was sporadic at best. We called back to Quantico for updates and formulated a crude operational plan. The next stop was New York City.

The commotion and honking horns that make up Manhattan had disappeared. Traffic signals no longer worked, but patience replaced the breakneck pace to get here and there. Drivers paused for one another and for those walking. Looking through dusty windshields, a small nod or wave now meant: *You go first.*

Parking our Suburbans two blocks from the edge of the wreckage, we continued on foot. Heavy smoke, yellow and gray, covered everything. It drifted upward, rising from bent steel and smoldering debris. The ruin went on for blocks. The remains of seven buildings, two of them the tallest in the world, were now one pile, spreading for acres and dwarfing the hundreds of workers who climbed over it, removing dirt and rubble one pail at a time.

I edged my way through dozens of construction workers standing in silence, resting before their turn on the pile. They wore brown, blue, or green hardhats emblazoned with American flags and a blue-and-white seal identifying them as local ironworkers.[3] They held plastic buckets in their hands, and heavy rope and rubber hosing hung from their shoulders. All eyes were turned toward the devastation, following miniature figures of iron and construction workers, police and firefighters, moving among twisted metal and rubble.

Suddenly, an air horn let loose. Nearly everyone, including me, ran. But I'd noticed an older ironworker who had stayed behind.

I asked him what had happened.

"They have a laser on One Liberty." He pointed to the skyscraper directly in front of us. "If it moves a few degrees out of spec, the horn goes off. They think some of these buildings are unstable."

"You didn't run," I said.

"No, it's not coming down, I helped build it." He turned back to the bucket line.

We established our command post two blocks from the perimeter, just below Park Place on Church Street. Inside nylon tents, we set up folding tables, dry-erase boards, laptops, and a satellite phone. Gas-powered generators were our source of electricity. The rising smoke and steel beam destruction was in constant view to our south.

Evidence response team agents from the FBI's New York office and SWAT team paramedics joined our command post—the jumping-off point for all FBI personnel entering Ground Zero. We handed out protective gear as they left to search for evidence, recorded the names of those who went downrange, and added vital health signs to the log sheets.

Our team was on heightened alert for more than shaky buildings and falling glass. Behind the scenes and known only to a few, government officials feared a second attack—one completely different from the violent, earthshaking events of 9/11. An assault so quiet it would not be noticed until its lethal effects emerged days later.

Late on September 11, with the help of Epidemic Intelligence Service investigators from the Centers for Disease Control, the public health department had placed New York City area hospitals under a twenty-four-hour watch. By September 14, they had instituted a citywide syndromic surveillance system, monitoring more than two dozen hospitals for any illness resulting from biological terrorism.[4] The same scrutiny was in place around the Pentagon, the site of the third commercial airliner attack thirty-four minutes after the second World Trade Tower was hit.

Rumors of the hijackers carrying improvised bombs—combined with speculation they might have had biological weapons[5]—prompted scientists from the Department of Defense and the Secret Service to set up air-monitoring stations around the Pentagon and on the roofs of executive buildings in Washington, DC. The sensors pulled air through small filters, trapping minute particles. Day and night, technicians removed samples of those particles, driving them fifty miles north to the nation's premier biological defense laboratory: the Maryland-based US Army Medical Research Institute of Infectious Diseases, known as USAMRIID. On the receiving end of those deliveries was Dr. John Ezzell, a skilled scientist who had spent the prior five years developing methods for detecting and identifying the tiny signatures of biological weapons. Day after day, Ezzell and his team analyzed the trapped dust for indications of aerosolized bioweapons, with anthrax at the top of the list.[6]

USAMRIID also had a fully staffed bacteriology division, much of it devoted to anthrax research, but its members had little to no experience in forensics and weren't asked to assist. But the rumors that al-Qaeda operatives had biological weapons had reached their ranks as well. One of them, anthrax vaccine expert Dr. Bruce Ivins, emailed a colleague: "I just heard tonight that Bin Laden terrorists for sure have anthrax and sarin gas."[7]

The evidence response team made plans to search the roofs of surrounding buildings. In addition to scouring the tops of skyscrapers for evidence of the hijackings, the searches would also uncover body parts and the personal effects of passengers and flight crews. Our two senior Hazmat officers, Steve Rhea, recruited from the Fairfax County Fire and Rescue where he had served as captain and battalion chief, and Mike Cook, a former Colorado State patrolman—both veterans of confined-space rescue missions—led the way. They climbed thousands of steps up dark stairwells. Electrical power would not be restored for many more days.

One afternoon, after assisting with a rooftop search under Cook's careful guidance, I walked alone back to the command post along the edge of the pile. For a moment I just stood and watched. Buckets were being passed down brigade lines, and rescue workers lay flat to look under iron beams and peer through crevices in the debris. Suddenly, motion stopped. A fireman was climbing down from the pile, carrying an orange plastic bag in a white bucket. All around him firefighters, policemen, and ironworkers stood to attention and saluted. The fireman stopped in front of a red, six-wheeled cart—on its side, a blue-and-white six-point Star of Life, symbolic of medical personnel worldwide. All hands held their salute as he carefully placed the bag on the cart. He stepped back, then raised a salute of his own. As the cart moved away, work resumed.[8]

Walking back to our command post, I passed by a small blue nylon tent, its front flaps rolled up and lashed in place. Small orange bags filled the tent—each twisted and tied at the top. They covered a white folding table. Dozens more lay on the tent's grass floor.

FBI agents worked day and night to piece together what had happened on 9/11—and who was behind it. Late in the afternoon of September 14, in a short news conference, the FBI director and the attorney general released the names of the hijackers. They totaled nineteen. They had been living in southeast Florida and belonged to a militant terrorist organization known as al-Qaeda, founded in 1988 by a wealthy Saudi named Osama bin Laden. The organization had made headlines in 1998, when they had used explosive-laden trucks to attack US embassies in Kenya and Tanzania. The September 11 attacks on the World Trade Center and the Pentagon—and the hijacking of a fourth plane, United Flight 93, which crashed into a reclaimed Pennsylvania strip mine—were its latest atrocities.

More details about the hijackers were quick to emerge. Soon, reports of al-Qaeda planning a release of anthrax using crop dusters began to circulate. Mohamed Atta, the pilot hijacker who destroyed the North Tower of the World Trade Center, had inquired about crop dusters in Belle Glade, Florida, just west of Boca Raton, earlier in the year. On September 16, the FBI recommended that the Federal Aviation Administration halt all crop dusting flights. It made instant headlines. The ban lasted one day. But a week later, the government again ordered agriculture pilots to the ground and continued to watch for a second wave of terror.

After more than a week at Ground Zero, I walked into the FBI's evacuated New York City headquarters at 26 Federal Plaza. I found a computer, wrote a memo demoting myself, and sent it to Headquarters. In FBI parlance, it's called a stepdown, and they had no choice but to grant it.

Being a supervisor in a response unit had its upside. But after watching hundreds of men and women work to rectify the damage wrought by nineteen terrorists, I no longer felt productive. I wanted back into full-time investigation. I just wanted to track down terrorists.

I had no idea that less than two weeks later, the country would be confronted with its first deadly bioterrorism attack—an attack that would launch the largest inquiry in the history of the FBI. I did not foresee being part of the team rushing to develop a new field in science—the forensics of microbes—before more attacks could follow.

2

Second Wave

Wednesday, September 26, 2001

Robert Stevens worked late that Wednesday night, hunkered in his third-floor cubicle until well after dark. A veteran photo editor, Stevens had been working at tabloid newspapers since he and his wife, Maureen, emigrated from England in 1974. He'd joined the staff of the *Sun* earlier in the year, at age sixty-three. Before that it had been the *Globe*, and before that, the *National Enquirer*. American Media Incorporated owned all three papers, and they all occupied the same office building in northwest Boca Raton, Florida.

Most of the photos that Stevens sorted through, touched up, and laid out were submitted through the Internet or email. Sometimes, Stevens rifled through American Media's extensive archives—a collection that included the *National Enquirer*'s famous 1977 photograph of Elvis Presley in his coffin. Occasionally, though, photos still came through the mail.

When Stevens left his desk that night, he didn't expect to be back for a while. He and Maureen were heading out on a five-day vacation. Early the next morning, they pulled out of their driveway and a few minutes later joined the northbound traffic on Interstate 95. They drove more than ten hours to Charlotte, North Carolina, where their youngest daughter, Casey, lived. It would be a long day, but they were eager to see their girl.[1]

That same morning, seventy-three-year-old Ernesto Blanco[2] was on his rounds delivering mail throughout the American Media building. He had started the day at his workstation near the first-floor mailroom before winding his cart past hundreds of cubicles and dozens of executive offices on three floors, occasionally stopping to chat with employees. Blanco had been with the company for a few years. Previously, he had run his own carpet installation business. Then he retired, and life got too quiet. Now he looked forward to work again.

Blanco did the same routine the next day—the forty-five-minute commute from Miami, the rounds of mail delivery, the cubicle chats. But this time, something felt off. He felt drained. Maybe it was the flu, maybe not, but something was not right.

On Saturday, the Stevenses and their daughter drove an hour west from Charlotte to Chimney Rock State Park, known for its picturesque trails and its Hickory Nut Falls—at 404 feet, the second highest waterfall in the eastern United States. Chimney Rock itself towered at more than two thousand feet, offering panoramic views stretching seventy-five miles. The family spent the day hiking the park's network of trails, treading up and down steep slopes bursting with flora: fine white Lady Rue blossoms; shiny green fronds of Deer Hair Bulrush; and the green, purple, and brown-striped Jack-in-the-Pulpit, a plant known to be poisonous.

That evening, Stevens skipped dinner and went to bed early, feeling exhausted and nauseated. Maybe the Chimney Rock climb had been too much. Maybe he shouldn't have tasted the mountain water at Hickory Falls, or had gotten too close to the Jack-in-the-Pulpits. On Sunday he was no better. On Monday morning, the couple began the long drive back to Palm Beach County. Stevens was getting worse.

Ernesto Blanco's condition had also deteriorated. As the Stevenses made their way home, Blanco was checking himself into Miami's Cedars Medical Center. On early Tuesday morning, Stevens too was admitted to a hospital.

On the last day of September, I left Ground Zero and drove back to Quantico. Within about one hundred miles of New York City, everyone I encountered was unusually helpful, their sense of solidarity activated by the events of 9/11. Driving south into Delaware and Maryland, attitudes changed. People kept to themselves. They were still polite, but no longer overly so. Also noticeable were the military trucks moving on the roads. The country was preparing for war.

My transfer orders were still in limbo. So I assumed temporary duty with another unit that suddenly needed a lot more agents—the Weapons of Mass Destruction Operations Unit, or WMDOU for short. The unit had the job of handling all WMD aspects of the mounting 9/11 investigation, ensuring that vital information flowed between the many local, state, and federal agencies involved. WMDOU had also started manning a desk in the Strategic Information Operations Center (SIOC)—a forty-thousand-square-foot space located deep inside the J. Edgar Hoover Building in Washington, DC. SIOC serves as the FBI's global watch and communications hub. WMDOU manned its desk 24/7. I was assigned to the 3:00 p.m. to 11:00 p.m. shift.

I had spent plenty of time in the Hoover Building, but I had never seen it so crowded. The attacks of September 11 had triggered seismic changes throughout the US government. Protecting the country from another assault was now everyone's highest priority. Within days of the attacks, the FBI had reorganized. Hundreds of agents were temporarily reassigned, and new operational units sprang up in makeshift offices throughout its headquarters. Conference rooms that had been empty on September 10 were suddenly crammed full of desks, computers, and telephones.

Located in the center of the fifth floor and accessible only to those with the highest security clearances, SIOC bustled with activity. Flat-screen TVs covered the walls, broadcasting breaking events reported by major networks. Agents and analysts sat in long rows, each perched over multiple keyboards and computer screens, many of them typing furiously or talking on the phone, or both. Some of the agents drove in each day from Quantico. Those with unique skills flew in from around the country. Not everyone in the room was FBI. SIOC had become a twenty-four-hour joint operations center: there were also agents detailed from the Secret Service, Immigration and Naturalization, and Customs, as well as officers from the Coast Guard and the Department of Defense. Our new director, Robert S. Mueller, sworn in the week before September 11, moved into a small side room to personally oversee operations.

The director's reorganization of the Bureau included a new multitiered protocol for analyzing every new threat that surfaced. Following 9/11, FBI field offices forwarded thousands of new warnings and potential dangers to SIOC. Each notification circulated among the multiple operational groups established throughout HQ, awaiting recommendations. The other WMDOU agents and I assessed every threat involving chemical, biological, and nuclear materials. Most were unfounded. A few were outlandish. But we treated each one as real, chasing them all down even as new ones came in. The director reviewed every single analysis—numbering in the thousands each week—and our proposed responses. He would not allow a repeat of September 11.

Soon after Robert Stevens was hospitalized, the Florida Public Health Laboratory tested his blood. Initial results indicated that he had anthrax. The lab repeated the tests, getting the same improbable result. They sent a specimen to the Centers for Disease Control and Prevention (CDC) in Atlanta for independent confirmation.

Since 1900, only eighteen cases of inhalational, or pulmonary, anthrax have been documented in the United States—with only two survivors. Most of the victims were workers in the textile and tanning industry that had inhaled dried spores of *Bacillus anthracis* bacteria from contaminated livestock hides.[3] The most recent case, traced to tainted yarn from Pakistan, was reported in 1976. Before that, an epidemic of five cases was reported in 1957, among employees of a New Hampshire woolen mill.[4]

Robert Stevens lived in an oceanside resort in southeast Florida and worked in an air-conditioned office building. He had just returned from the North Carolina Piedmont. Initial interviews with Stevens's wife and co-workers revealed nothing about him coming into contact with infested hides or yarn.

During my four years with the Hazardous Materials Response Unit, I had fielded hundreds of anthrax hoaxes.[5] Police in Florida found a plastic container with *anthrax* written across its side. Eventually, its nineteen-year-old owner admitted that the bottle contained muscle enhancer. He had written *anthrax* on it so that his friends wouldn't use any. In another case, during a single week, thirty letters arrived at abortion clinics around the country. Each bore the same postmark and contained a note reading: "Anthrax. Have a Nice Death." Some contained a small amount of powder. It wasn't anthrax.

Our unit had taken every anthrax-related telephone call and coordinated evidence from each potential crime scene, arranging for the safe transport and testing of materials, reviewing and reporting every result. None of those threats had ever been real.

Within hours of hearing about Stevens's positive blood test, I spoke with a few of my former Hazmat colleagues. They asked what I thought. "A newspaper editor in near-tropical southeastern Florida has anthrax? I think they got it wrong," I said. We all found it difficult to believe.

On October 3—eight days after Robert Stevens had left his cubicle with vacation on his mind—the CDC conducted their own series of tests. They confirmed Florida's results. Separate laboratories at the CDC performed even more tests, some of them so cutting edge that they had been validated only months before. The results proved my skepticism ill founded. On Thursday, October 4, CDC officials announced to the public that Robert L. Stevens, an employee of American Media Incorporated in Boca Raton, Florida, had contracted inhalational anthrax.

That same day, news began circulating that a coworker of Stevens had been hospitalized with similar symptoms. It was Ernesto Blanco. Attempts to culture live anthrax bacteria from Blanco's body fluids had proved unsuccessful, and the CDC could not make a clear diagnosis. But Blanco was close to death. The attending doctor at Cedars Medical Center placed him on extraordinary levels of antibiotics, administered intravenously. A mechanical respirator kept him breathing. Doctors were stymied but continued to hunt for a cause.

The possibility that Stevens—and maybe Blanco—had been infected with anthrax by a natural source seemed unlikely to scientists familiar with the disease. The bacterium *Bacillus anthracis* can infect people through the skin, the stomach, or the lungs—with the last route, inhalation, being the most rare.[6] Nothing in Stevens's life or in his travels suggested that he could have accidentally breathed in the bacterium. But an intentional infection—terrorism—was also difficult to imagine.

For one, virulent anthrax is extremely difficult to obtain. The US military produced weaponized anthrax until 1969, when it terminated its biological weapons program and destroyed all known stockpiles of dry, virulent anthrax. (The Soviet Union likely ceased its production a decade later.) The US government now tightly regulates possession of the bacteria. Since 1996, the CDC has approved all shipments and recorded every instance of anthrax being transferred between laboratories.

Moreover, biological attacks of any kind are notoriously difficult to pull off. Converting anthrax into the fine powder necessary for an airborne attack required talent, training, and equipment—not to mention a level of sophistication that few would-be terrorists possess. Those who have tried have often failed spectacularly. In 1993, members of Aum Shinrikyo—a Japanese religious cult considered a terrorist organization by several countries, including the United States and Canada—sprayed a whole neighborhood in Tokyo with the microbe, sending the organism into the air as wet slurry with a steam-powered aerosolizer. Not a single person was infected. They had mistakenly used a nonvirulent strain of anthrax normally given to livestock as a vaccine that posed no risk to healthy humans.[7, 8]

But on September 11, the world had witnessed a new kind of coordinated terrorist attack that demonstrated considerable skill and planning. The al-Qaeda terrorists had learned how to fly commercial jetliners. If they had gotten hold of a lethal strain of anthrax, they may also have had the patience to learn how to turn it into a deadly powder. And we knew they had access to at least rudimentary equipment. A network of veterinarian laboratories equipped to grow liquid cultures of anthrax existed throughout their Afghan base of operations.

Robert Stevens had contracted anthrax. The diagnosis was now unequivocal, but the source was a mystery. With the 9/11 investigation still in full force, the FBI launched another multistate inquiry, stretching Bureau resources to their limits. Whether we would be hunting down a naturally occurring outbreak to be held in check by public health officials or an intentional release to be halted by law enforcement was unknown.

Quietly, the FBI and the CDC dispatched teams to Charlotte, North Carolina, and Palm Beach County, Florida. Hazmat Response Unit members joined them, heading in both directions and led by my counterparts at Quantico. I remained at SIOC, assessing the barrage of possible terrorist threats still pouring in from around the country, sending back investigative leads, and awaiting my transfer orders.

In the immediate aftermath of September 11, Stevens's employer, AMI, and its *Enquirer* and *Globe* tabloids published numerous inflammatory articles about Osama bin Laden, the infamous leader of al-Qaeda.[9] The *Globe*'s October 2 cover was splashed with the headlines "WANTED! DEAD OR ALIVE," with the last two words crossed out, and "Bin Laden: Inside His Sick, Twisted World." The story asserted that bin Laden's intense hatred of the United States was the result of an American woman laughing at his manhood.[10]

Within hours of the 9/11 investigation's launch, an unexpected connection between AMI and al-Qaeda had surfaced. Late at night on September 11, a call from an FBI agent had awakened the *Sun*'s editor-in-chief, Mike Irish, and his wife, Gloria. Gloria Irish worked as a realtor in Palm Beach County. Four months earlier, in June, she had rented out two apartments in Delray Beach, ten miles north of Boca Raton. Her two tenants were Marwa al-Shehhi and Hamza al-Ghamdi, the hijackers who had flown United Flight 175 into the World Trade Center's South Tower.[11]

Now, in early October, FBI agents in Miami and Washington, DC, wondered how much of a coincidence this could be. The first inhalational anthrax victim in a quarter century worked a few miles from where the al-Qaeda hijackers had lived? Reports of al-Qaeda's interest in crop dusting in southern Florida compounded the concern. What better way for al-Qaeda to gain publicity than by highlighting the United States' vulnerabilities through a second wave of attack? The American news media seemed an ideal target. AMI's tabloids enjoyed a wide readership in the United States, and the *Enquirer* and *Globe*'s unflattering stories about al-Qaeda's leader may have brought unwanted attention to the tabloid.

The presence of al-Qaeda and rare inhalational anthrax in the same Florida county, AMI's critical reporting on al-Qaeda's leader, and Mike Irish's spouse's business association with al-Qaeda operatives suggested this was more than chance. But no one had yet definitively determined whether Robert Stevens's illness had been intentional or a cruel act of nature.

3

Under Attack

October 4, 2001

I arrived at SIOC early, two hours before my assigned 3:00 p.m. to 11:00 p.m. shift. Rumors of Stevens's diagnosis brought me in early, and now the national media outlets were beginning to pick up on them. I needed to find out for myself and placed a call to Doug Beecher, one of the FBI's two full-time microbiologists, a scientist I was proud to say I had recruited for the Hazmat Unit two years earlier.[1] I had a hunch that Beecher would have insight. He did and related what had transpired.

Earlier that day, Beecher had called Dr. Richard Meyer, a colleague at the CDC's new Bioterrorism Laboratory in Atlanta. The two had become acquainted several years earlier when Beecher was studying for his doctorate. They had stayed in contact after the University of Wisconsin's Department of Food Microbiology recruited Beecher for their faculty. At the time, Meyer researched veterinary microbiology at the US Department of Agriculture's Plum Island facility outside New York City.

Taking a senior scientist position at the CDC three years ago, Meyer headed up the new Bioterrorism Rapid Response and Advanced Technology Laboratory—RRAT Lab for short. Meyer placed technology for anthrax testing at the top of his wish list and quickly familiarized himself with what was available and the latest under development. In addition to providing the country with advanced biological weapons testing, the RRAT would also supply the nation's fledging Laboratory Response Network (LRN) with protocols and equipment.

The LRN had been in place since early 1999 and was operational a year later. I had attended the initial kickoff meeting as the FBI's representative in January 1999. The CDC hosted the three-day event at their Atlanta headquarters with prominent state public health and Department of Defense scientists,

including army anthrax expert and North Carolina native John Ezzell in attendance. The concept was simple, elegant, and novel—a national coordinated
response to the never-ending fear of biological terrorism.[2] Each state in the
United States maintained microbiology labs within their public health department. The CDC would validate test protocols and oversee development of
newer testing and then provide tests, reagents, and equipment to each state.
In the event of a suspected biological attack, the nearest public health lab
would begin an immediate analysis of suspicious materials—far better than
shipping samples to the national laboratories—potentially overwhelmed—in
Atlanta and Frederick, Maryland. And the FBI would be a charter member
of the LRN and my biology program at the Hazmat Response Unit would be
responsible for drafting chain of custody procedures.

By the summer of 2001, Florida's public health department had adopted
LRN testing protocols, including those validated by Meyer and Ezzell. It
had performed the preliminary testing of Stevens's spinal fluid and made
the initial anthrax identification. The department had immediately forwarded
samples to Rich Meyer for confirmation.

After Beecher and Meyer spent a few minutes reviewing the Florida test results and Meyer's confirmation, Beecher had broached the reason for his call.
He asked if Meyer could send a sample of the anthrax grown from Stevens's
spinal fluid to Dr. Paul Keim at the Northern Arizona University.

The proposal took Meyer aback. Meyer knew Keim and was very familiar
with Keim's cutting-edge genetic techniques for testing the identities of individual anthrax cultures. Meyer countered Beecher's request with the CDC's
own intentions to conduct specialized genomic testing on Stevens's isolate.
In fact, a newly hired CDC scientist, Dr. Alex Hoffmaster, had spent a week
in Flagstaff learning the ins and outs of a new DNA-based test that Keim had
developed. Keim coined the term *Multiple Locus VNTR Analysis*[3] (MLVA)
to describe his invention. A test comparing eight genes—also known as *loci*
(singular being *locus*) in genetic parlance—of the anthrax DNA genome,
MLVA could identify nearly one hundred strains of anthrax, many bearing
unusual and arcane names: Vollum, Sterne, Zimbabwe, Porton Down. Each
strain contained small differences in its DNA sequence making it unique and
distinct. By the fall of 2001, Hoffmaster had implemented MLVA technology
in his own Atlanta laboratory.

Meyer knew Hoffmaster was preparing to test Stevens's isolate. Its strain
should be identified in a day or two. Beecher also knew that the tenets of the
FBI laboratory and criminal forensic procedures in general did not condone
duplicative testing. By asking Meyer to transfer a sample to Keim for MLVA
analysis at the Northern Arizona University, Beecher risked criticism—it

might be construed during future legal proceedings that neither the Atlanta nor Arizona testing was fully trusted.

Beecher continued to press. Keim was one of the world's experts on anthrax. The Flagstaff scientist had not only developed the original MLVA test but also was working toward an expanded version capable of examining fifteen loci. He maintained the largest compilation of anthrax in the United States. While the CDC maintained its own library of anthrax strains and isolates dating back to the 1950s, in recent years the CDC had curtailed researching the collection.[4]

Meyer listened; Beecher was making sense. An independent confirmation by Keim would only strengthen any identification by the CDC. Meyer would immediately prepare an isolate for shipment to Arizona. He even offered an airplane—a corporate jet to ensure speed and a CDC representative to guarantee a chain of custody. If American Media had been intentionally targeted, the Stevens specimen represented critical evidence.

After he and Meyer hung up, Beecher made a second call. Over the past two days Beecher and Keim had discussed the possibility of obtaining an isolate from Robert Stevens to test with Keim's MLVA procedure. Beecher left a message on Keim's voicemail and waited impatiently. In less than an hour Keim was on the telephone.

"It's coming your way," Beecher said. "We need the answer as fast as possible."

Keim agreed. Par for the course when he worked with the FBI, it was always: *We need it yesterday.* And adding to the pressure, he knew the FBI would only be satisfied if they were convinced the results were solid and unquestionable. But he understood. Members of the press and Congress had a habit of second guessing the Bureau. And yet Keim admired that, fully aware that they would be doubted, they still led the charge to find answers. Keim was proud to be asked.

The faster Beecher and his colleagues could determine whether Stevens's anthrax was caused by a well-known laboratory research strain, a defunct biological program weapon, or an isolate from nature never before seen, the sooner the investigation could find direction. But the test results they would pass on had to be conclusive. One erred test procedure, a single misunderstanding during rushed telephone conversations, could have tremendous impact. Beecher laid down the telephone and prepared to brief Headquarters on the plan he had put in motion.

While Beecher filled me in on his discussions with Meyer and Keim,[5] Dr. Segaran Pillai's telephone was ringing in his Miami office. Pillai directed one of Florida's five Public Health Laboratories, and his staff had been recently certified in the new LRN testing protocols. His was also the closest network lab to Boca Raton. Pillai listened as the caller from the CDC described Robert Stevens's symptoms, the laboratory test results, and the diagnosis. Pillai agreed with the finding of inhalational anthrax. The caller asked if Pillai could assist in testing areas that Stevens frequented in Palm Beach County. A CDC team of Epidemic Intelligence Service (EIS) specialists was already on the way down from their headquarters on Atlanta's outskirts. Would Pillai meet them in Palm Beach County?

Pillai was convinced that this case of inhalational anthrax could only be intentional. The disease was rare in humans and, in general, unheard of in the southeastern United States. As far as anyone knew, Stevens, an employee of a newspaper company, did not work with livestock—the most common victims of anthrax. Pillai also wondered if there might be additional anthrax casualties. Before leaving his office for Boca Raton, he alerted the area hospitals to be on the lookout for patients with symptoms similar to Stevens's.

The next morning Pillai began the hour-long drive north to meet the CDC team; barely into the drive, his cell phone rang. The Cedars Medical Center in Miami called to report a patient in critical condition. The patient, an elderly man named Ernesto Blanco, had checked in with pneumonia-like symptoms, but the symptoms could not be attributed to either bacterial or viral pneumonia. The doctors at Cedars Medical continued to test for various pathogens but had found nothing yet. State health and CDC officials were requesting that nasal swabs be taken. An uncharacteristically large buildup of fluid between his lungs—pleural fluid—further complicated a diagnosis. Finally, the caller mentioned Blanco's employer, AMI, and Blanco's job, delivering the mail.

It was too much of a coincidence for Pillai. The pleural fluid buildup, the pneumonia symptoms, the lack of either a bacterial or viral identification, and the connection to AMI in Boca Raton—it all convinced Pillai. *It must be anthrax. The source must be the AMI building. Probably the mail*, ran through his mind as he arrived in Boca Raton.

On the opposite side of the country, early Friday morning on October 5, Paul Keim was tired; his voice trailed off slightly when he spoke. He and his staff had worked straight through the night, from early Thursday evening when Keim met the CDC's twin-engine jet on Flagstaff Pulliam Airport's runway to now. Keim had barely noticed the rising sun shining through the small lab windows that looked out over the northern Arizona mountains. His lab consisted of three small connecting rooms on the third floor of the campus's Living Science Building. An oversized, double-sided workbench filled each room. The latest microbiology equipment crowded the black Formica bench tops. Three tiers of shelves ran down the center of each bench. Bright rolls of red, blue, yellow, pink, and green tape; large and small glass flasks with different colored labels; and blue boxes of stretchable opaque gray Parafilm and rows of color-coded pipettes and disposable plastic tips crowded every shelf. Each student and technician had staked out an area on the benches for their experiments, not leaving much room to spread out test results and data for a final review. Food and drinks were also forbidden inside the lab, and Keim was ready for some fresh coffee.

Keim collected all the data from the prior night's analysis of the anthrax isolate from Robert Stevens's spinal fluid. The isolate had arrived as a long, gray streak of growing bacteria in a thin glass tube filled with yellow gelatin agar. The agar—supplying needed nutrients and produced from algae—had been allowed to harden at an angle, or slant, allowing the bacteria more surface area to grow. Enough anthrax had grown in the tube that Keim could simply heat the tube for a few minutes, killing and breaking open the bacterial cells, without additional culturing and growth.[6]

He immediately extracted the DNA. Now, at the end of a long night, he walked out of the lab and down the hallway to his office. Away from the hum of laboratory equipment, ringing telephones, and students and lab assistants shouting across the workbench, Keim carefully checked and double-checked the MLVA data.

The results startled him. He checked the protocols that his technicians had used to perform their tests, and most importantly, he made sure that all the necessary controls were included and had performed correctly. The data looked accurate. But still he hesitated before picking up his telephone receiver and dialing Doug Beecher's number. Keim knew what the results would mean.

Only three-and-a-half weeks after the September 11 attacks, Keim had identified the infecting anthrax as a well-known strain, a strain grown only under controlled, contained conditions in secure, certified laboratories. There was almost no chance the anthrax bacteria could have leaked out of a laboratory by accident. The laboratories' rooms were ventilated by a negative air pressure system—when a door opened, air passed into the lab, but not out. Any air leaving the lab first passed through high-efficiency particulate air filters—HEPA filters. They captured any bacteria that, on a rare occasion, managed to escape a microbiologist's culture plate or flask. A second set of outer doors created air locks at the laboratory room entrances to further guard against an accidental release. Keim's first reaction to his nightlong testing was that the victim in Boca Raton had been infected on purpose—someone had intentionally removed deadly anthrax from a laboratory.

But in the back of his mind, Keim's scientific training was constantly in play. The key to science and investigation is to remain objective. He realized that he really didn't know whether Stevens's infection had been intentional or naturally caused. Keim still had several hundred anthrax samples in his freezer that had not been tested for their strain identity. The samples had been collected from dead livestock at various locations and were waiting to be analyzed. If the anthrax strain that Keim now saw in the Stevens specimen was also found in one of the untested samples—matching the laboratory strain that he had identified—that would change the conclusion he was certain would be reached by his FBI counterparts once he called back East with the previous night's results. Still, in his heart he knew what his results meant. He dialed Doug Beecher's cell phone.

Beecher's phone rang, and an Arizona area code lit up on its small screen. Keim sounded exhausted, excited, and apprehensive. He immediately told Beecher that a well-known laboratory strain of anthrax called Ames had infected Robert Stevens.

"Well, we know what that means." Beecher penned *Ames* on a notepad.

Keim thought that the strain was widely used by research laboratories in the United States, maybe even around the world. Research using the Ames strain had been written up in scientific journals. But neither Keim nor Beecher knew exactly how widespread Ames was or how easy to obtain. During his career, Keim had analyzed several hundred isolates of anthrax infecting livestock from around the world, and he had seen only one isolate close to a genetic match with the Ames strain—one sample from a single dead goat in Texas. But Keim's MLVA procedure could still distinguish between the Texas goat isolate and Ames. So in Keim's opinion, an anthrax strain with a DNA pattern identical to the Ames pattern suddenly appearing in nature was too much of a coincidence. Even though a natural infection could still not be definitively ruled out, Stevens's anthrax most likely came from inside a research laboratory. Beecher agreed.

Seated back at my desk in SIOC, I began my shift by sorting through the week's WMD-related threats: an oddly shaped package tied underneath propane cylinders in Seattle, a weaving eighteen-wheeler bearing Hazmat placards, an unfamiliar car parked beside a Midwest crop dusting hanger. I read through leads written and responding interview notes attached for each; all seemed innocent enough, but each would still be catalogued and entered into a Rapid Start database for cross referencing. Suddenly, my desk telephone rang with the SIOC switchboard number appearing on the screen.

"Hello."

"Yes, please hold for a conference call with FBI Lab." In a few seconds the sound of talking came through the receiver, and I recognized the voices of Doug Beecher and Rich Meyer.

"Hello, Decker on."

"Hi, Scott." Beecher and Meyer spoke in unison, and Meyer took over. "Been a busy twenty-four hours, hasn't it?"

Before I could answer, more voices arrived on the call: an FBI supervisor from the WMDOU at Headquarters, more CDC representatives, and three agents assigned to the Miami FBI office.

Beecher spoke up. "Paul Keim has identified the isolate from Stevens as Ames. It is a research strain originally isolated by the USDA lab in Ames, Iowa—we think."

"How many labs have they sent it to?" a voice interrupted.

"Miami should be getting a list of anthrax labs from CDC today," answered one of the Florida agents.

Beecher started again. "With a laboratory strain, it is likely intentional, an attack, but we still can't say with absolute certainty. We need to locate the method of delivery, first."

A Miami agent spoke up again. "We are working on that also." He began summarizing: FBI agents and CDC's EIS specialists had begun interviewing Robert Stevens's family. They learned that Stevens might have visited several outside locations around Palm Beach County before his trip to North Carolina, including the Lake Worth Inlet Park and the Loxahatchee Wildlife Preserve. Stops he potentially made included an Indian grocery store, a greeting card store, and a pastry shop. The interviewers worked on the theory that Stevens had inhaled deadly anthrax spores a few days before he fell ill.

Samples would have to be taken at each outdoor location and store Stevens had frequented, and, of course, at Stevens's home and work and his cubicle and desk in the AMI building. The FBI agents and CDC specialists paired off into four groups, joined by Pillai and his laboratory technicians from Miami. They headed off in separate directions to take air, soil, and surface samples.[7]

The team worked throughout the day, carefully collecting and cataloging samples at Inlet Park, the wildlife preserve, shops, and areas around Stevens's home. After 5:00 p.m. they arrived at the AMI building. They had saved Stevens's workplace for last so that most of the employees would be gone for the weekend. They also decided to forego using the protective gear commonly worn by Hazmat specialists since the sight of white paper suits, masks, and overshoes would unduly alarm any remaining employees. It made sense. The epidemiologists from the State Public Health lab and the CDC were used to working in outside settings, often with deceased animals, settings in the eastern part of the United States that were damp and exposed to the environment and well ventilated.[8]

Word quickly spread among the team that Stevens had died that afternoon, just before they had arrived at AMI. The news caused them to pause for a moment and consider the possibility of a terrorist nearby, on the loose, spreading deadly anthrax. They redoubled their efforts and committed themselves to finding the source of Stevens's fatal disease.

Several of the team went to AMI's third floor and began to wipe areas on Stevens's desk: his computer keyboard, mouse pad, Rolodex, and tape dispenser. They used small, sterile squares of white cotton cloth and placed each wiped square in its own sterile screw-capped plastic tube. Each tube was carefully labeled with the time and location, followed by a team member's name and initials.

Pillai remembered the earlier telephone call from Cedars Medical Center, that a second possible victim delivered mail in the building. Logically, if anthrax had been sent in the mail, then Stevens's mail should be contaminated. Pillai found his way to the AMI mailroom on the first floor, located a mailbox labeled "Robert Stevens," and carefully wiped a square of cotton around the inside of the small box.

The combined FBI, CDC, and Miami laboratory team tried to finish sampling without disturbing the few remaining employees. But the meticulous wiping of Stevens's desk, keyboard, and mailbox did little to calm the handful of employees who remained behind that Friday afternoon.

The collecting and cataloging of samples went on into the night, past midnight, until 2:00 a.m. on Saturday. The team collected air samples from the Inlet Park and Pier and the Wildlife Preserve Visitor Center in Lake Worth, soil samples from around Stevens's home in Lantana, and wipe samples from the AMI building in Boca Raton. They agreed that the fastest way to test the samples for anthrax would be at Pillai's lab in Miami. Using the new LRN test protocols, Pillai could get a DNA identification of anthrax in hours. Pillai headed back south with fifty-six critical samples; by 8:00 a.m. he would have an answer.[9]

Pillai and his technicians worked through the night. They tested each sample three times.[10] In a few hours, results from Friday's sampling began to appear. Two of the fifty-six contained anthrax DNA. Virulent anthrax contaminated Stevens's computer keyboard from his desk in the AMI building. Anthrax also contaminated the sample Pillai took from the inside of Stevens's mailbox. The other fifty-four samples—from Stevens's home, the various shops, the Park Inlet and the Preserve Visitor Center—were all negative for anthrax.

Pillai's first thought was al-Qaeda; it was well known that many of the 9/11 hijackers had been in Palm Beach County only five or six weeks earlier. Pillai recalled a large, framed, front-page photo of Osama bin Laden prominently displayed in the front lobby of the AMI building. *Maybe the anthrax attack was retaliation for the bad publicity bin Laden had received at the hands of the National Enquirer*, Pillai thought. He picked up his telephone to tell the FBI, CDC, and Palm Beach County officials his results.

That weekend, I participated in conference call followed by conference call. Everyone involved in the growing investigation tried to make sense of the information coming in. A day after Paul Keim reported that Ames anthrax infected Robert Stevens, Alex Hoffmaster reported the identical result. Ames anthrax also contaminated Stevens's mailbox at AMI.[11, 12] The mail seemed to be the route of infection, but no letter had been found yet. Test results for a second possible victim, Ernesto Blanco, were still inconclusive. While Blanco's nasal swab contained a small bit of anthrax DNA, his blood did not contain live anthrax, and the CDC standard for an anthrax diagnosis required the live bacteria be found. Whether Stevens was intentionally infected or not, and whether Blanco even had anthrax, were both hotly debated. But one thing became clear that weekend—the AMI building contained live anthrax bacteria spores. By the end of Sunday, October 7, the Palm Beach County Public Health Department ordered the AMI building closed.

During the weekend, FBI agents in Miami also began to trace possible sources of the Ames strain. They requested the CDC's database of recorded transfers and shipments of anthrax.[13] In coordination with the US Attorney's Office, they drafted subpoenas for the laboratories on the CDC list. Once issued, the orders would ask: Which scientists used Ames in research, where and when had they gotten it, had they shared it with anybody, and if so, with whom? But foremost, in the back of everyone's mind, and in discussions between Director Mueller, the attorney general, and White House staff: *Had the Ames strain found its way overseas? To Iraq weapons scientists, or into crude al-Qaeda laboratories?*

4

Denial
October 8, 2001

Segaran Pillai returned to Palm Beach County early on Monday. At 8:00 a.m., he arrived at the offices of the Palm Beach County Health Department, poised to assist with a massive intervention and prevention campaign. By approximately 9:00 a.m., more than one thousand people had lined up outside the Public Health offices in Delray Beach. The throng included AMI employees, their families, and anyone who had visited AMI in the past two months. Within the next days—allowing time for adequate bacteria growth in culture incubators—Pillai and his public health colleagues would find out if anyone else had inhaled anthrax.

The events of the past weekend weighed on everyone's mind while they waited patiently in the early morning of Columbus Day as rain fell from the gray South Florida sky. The shocking attacks of 9/11 were less than four weeks prior, and there was the startling revelation that many of the hijackers had been living among them. The bombing of Taliban strongholds in Afghanistan was only just yesterday.[1] Two days prior to that, after the grounding of crop dusters, amid the speculation of looming biological or chemical attacks, their colleague had suddenly died of a rare disease. News broadcasters speculated Stevens's death had a connection to bioterrorism, in contrast to the nation's leaders urging calm and arguing that Stevens's death was not related to the attacks of September 11.[2]

One by one, each person moved forward as medical staff carefully wiped inside noses using sterile, long-stemmed Q-tips. Laboratory technicians then took each nasal swab, and in a single fluid motion, wiped it back and forth across the hard, glossy surface of red, gelatin-like agar that filled a small culture plate. After replacing the plates' clear plastic lids, they carefully put each plate, one by one, into a small portable incubator. Each incubator maintained a constant temperature of 98.6 degrees, human body temperature. If a swab contained live bacteria, it would begin to grow on the agar's surface. When the plates arrived at Pillai's lab in Miami, the growing bacteria had already formed tiny, round, gray colonies, ready for precise identification. Further testing by Paul Keim or Alex Hoffmaster could be done to determine the strain, Ames or otherwise.

The testing of the AMI employees served several fronts. First, additional anthrax victims would need close supervision and monitoring for signs of infection. Second, individuals contaminated with anthrax possessed valuable information. Their activities, the places they worked, the places they visited, and the places they lived would all need scrutiny for information that might provide an insight as to the source of the anthrax. The widespread testing of employees would complement the testing inside the AMI building and that ongoing in the hills of North Carolina.

Before the employees, family members, and visitors left the public health office, the staff handed each a sixty-day supply of small, white, oblong ciprofloxacin tablets, commonly known in shorthand as Cipro. While taking the potent antibiotic carried with it some risk of adverse effects,[3] the Florida Department of Health chose to err on the side of caution.

Doug Beecher had arrived in Boca Raton the day before, late on Sunday, October 7. An FBI Hazmat officer and several FBI Hazmat specialists had accompanied him. They had flown down from Quantico in the Bureau's well-used de Havilland Dash 8 twin turboprop airplane. After landing at Boca Raton's World War II–era airport, the team located a rental car office and requested the Suburbans reserved in their names. An area map pinpointed the nearby hotel being used as a makeshift command post. They unloaded Hazmat gear and personal protection equipment from the Dash 8 and packed it into the rentals, pulled off the runway, and drove off into southern Florida's hot, humid evening.

Early the next morning, Beecher pulled up to the office complex containing the AMI building. A silver chain link fence had been erected around the AMI building and its adjoining parking lots. Security guards verified identification cards and credentials at the fence's single entrance.

Opposite the checkpoint, high-energy spotlights glared down. In the background stood wide, circular, multipaneled fluorescent umbrellas reflecting clean, white illumination. News reporters and camera crews had quickly staked a claim in an adjacent parking lot. White panel trucks marked with colorful advertising—CBS, CNN, and similarly familiar names—surrounded the bright lights and white umbrellas. Crews from smaller news outlets were also arriving from nearby Miami and as far away as Milwaukee. Thin antennas, wrapped with spiraling white cable, towered above the bright media logos and disappeared among tree branches. Electric generators hummed a constant, distant noise, gradually becoming white noise for most of those within earshot. The media group resembled a campground, so much so that it became known as "Camp Anthrax." The encampment grew to the point that the City of Boca Raton was obliged to truck in sanitary facilities before camera crews and news anchors abandoned the site a week later.[4]

Once through the checkpoint, Beecher immediately recognized the Miami FBI Evidence Response Team. Its members wore the familiar tan Royal Robbins 5.11 cargo pants, the same ones that Beecher wore. By 2001, the pants had become so much of a trademark for the FBI that they couldn't be worn in public without announcing "Fed."

Together, FBI Miami's Evidence Team, Beecher and the FBI Hazmat officer, the CDC specialists, and the Boca Raton Fire Department Hazmat Team planned how to trace the source of the anthrax. They studied the floor plans of the AMI building and marked the two spots in the building that contained live anthrax spores—the desk of Robert Stevens on the third floor and his assigned mailbox on the first floor. The group selected the mailroom as the first testing location for Monday morning; the second- and third-floor mail sorting areas would immediately follow.

Finding live anthrax spores in the AMI building meant that from here on out only full hazardous materials protective gear and protocols would be used—sealed white Tyvex suits, rubber boots, battery-powered respirators, fitted black rubber masks, a decontamination line with buckets of diluted bleach separating the hot zone—the term given to an area contaminated with hazardous material—from the cold, hazard-free zone, and a strict time limit for operating inside the building. The group divided themselves into smaller teams and waited their turn to go down range.

Weighed down by the sealed, white encapsulating suits, respirators and batteries, full masks and heavy boots, the operators walked slowly and deliberately past the front of the decontamination area and into the hot zone. They carried white five-gallon buckets filled with clear plastic bags of sterile blue-capped soft plastic tubes and sterile individually sealed six-inch wooden Q-tips. One team member carried a small vacuum cleaner with interchangeable filters that fit over the suction nozzle. Another carried waterproof log sheets, permanent ink markers, and a waterproof camera.

They worked with concentration, focusing on every detail—swiping across a surface with a single Q-tip, handing off to a team member, placing the Q-tip in a blue-capped tube, labeling each tube with initials, time, date, and location. A third member recorded each sample's identifying information on a log sheet and assigned an evidence number; a fourth took a photograph of each item's location. Later, the camera would be washed with bleach to remove any contaminating spores before the film was removed.

The operation's Hazmat officer also doubled as safety officer, and he imposed strict health and safety guidelines. The constant motion in the sealed and taped white suits, breathing filtered air, the lack of ventilation in the closed building, and the focused attention all worked together to raise blood pressures and core body temperatures. Double layers of purple nitrile rubber gloves made writing and recording information tedious and added to the exertion. Each team worked continuously for thirty minutes, then walked outside and back to the decontamination line. Boca Raton Fire Department members washed off the Tyvek suits and rubber boots with bleach, discarded the nitrile gloves, and helped unhook the respirators. A second team finished suiting up and entered the AMI building before the first team finished its decontamination.

The teams made multiple entries into the building and collected hundreds of samples. They labeled several samples from the mailroom and from each floor's mail sorting cabinets *very high priority*, and rushed them off to Pillai's Miami lab. The team took samples from a construction area on the first floor that they also labeled *very high priority*. While everyone's instinct pointed toward Stevens's death being the result of an intentional act, possibly by the al-Qaeda operatives who, until recently, had lived in the area, the team still considered the possibility that the new AMI building was a sick building, accidently contaminated with anthrax during construction.

The FBI's Evidence Team was thorough—it was their trademark. One member collected all the video surveillance tapes from the first-floor security office. Possibly the tape recordings would reveal something suspicious, maybe a lead to follow up or something incriminating, perhaps an image or even the identity of the culprit. They searched for trash compactors containing discarded mail, correctly assuming that AMI received a lot of mail from its many devoted tabloid fans. But this line of inquiry proved to be a dead end. AMI incinerated its mail, and there was none left to test.

A few miles north, the testing of AMI employees and others at the Delray Public Health offices dragged on. By the end of the first day, Pillai's lab identified another victim. One nasal swab sample, accession number 2002008301, was found contaminated with anthrax.[5] The sample belonged to Stephanie Dailey, an AMI employee whose daily duties included opening mail. Her desk stood fifty feet away from Robert Stevens's desk on the third floor of the AMI building. Pillai's laboratory rated the bacteria growing in the clear plastic culture plate containing Dailey's sample as 4+ on a scale of one to four. During the incubation step, the pale gray anthrax colonies had grown to the point of being confluent. Instead of single isolated circular colonies, thousands of growing anthrax colonies had merged together—a gray lawn covering the red blood agar that filled the palm-sized plate.[6]

Dailey broke down in tears when she was told.[7] Earlier in the day, she had started taking her sixty-day prescription of Cipro, but in October 2001, many in the public health and research communities doubted that taking antibiotics after exposure would prevent anthrax. The accepted thinking was that only vaccination prevented someone from contracting anthrax. And complete immunity required a series of injections over a period lasting eighteen months. Aging production equipment coupled with concerns of the US Food and Drug Administration plagued the vaccine's only licensed manufacturer, BioPort, a privately held firm in Michigan, and demand for the vaccine had outstripped the supply by 2001. So, the medical staff prescribed antibiotics—estimating the required dosage—as the only viable course.[8]

Now, Dailey could only wait to see if the same suffocating disease that had killed Robert Stevens would infect her. But she never developed an infection or an illness related to anthrax; in fact, she experienced no ill effects at all other than the extreme emotional distress.

Outside the AMI building, the news of Dailey's test results brought a sense of urgency—more victims could be expected. The Hazmat team quickly suited up in full protective gear, put together sterile Q-tip swabs, cameras, and vacuum filters, and prepared to test Dailey's work area. The sooner the team uncovered how and where the anthrax spores had gotten into the AMI building, the faster the spread could be contained. Spores contaminated the mailroom, possibly the AMI mailman, and now a third person, one responsible for opening AMI mail.

The Hazmat team entered the building and climbed the stairs to the third floor, stopping in front of a desk with items bearing Stephanie Dailey's name. The location agreed with the description that Dailey had provided to interviewing FBI agents earlier that day. The team went straight to work. One team member took a sterile six-inch Q-tip and scrubbed the cotton tip back and forth across the top of Dailey's desk. A second member sealed it in an opaque plastic tube. Another prepared the vacuum by placing a fresh filter over the suction nozzle and then set out extra filters, each in an individual cellophane package. They vacuumed the floor around Dailey's desk, replacing the filter with a new one before moving on to vacuum the surface of Dailey's chair. The team didn't stop working until they had vacuumed four separate areas around the desk.

The Hazmat team drove the swab and vacuum samples to Miami, and within hours Pillai's laboratory had the answer—live anthrax covered Dailey's desk, chair, and floor. The sampling team had even found spores coating the vents of the air duct in the ceiling above Dailey's desk.

The FBI agents, public health specialists, and postal inspectors working at the AMI building came to a conclusion as they looked at the sampling results. The AMI mailroom, mail sorting cabinets, and mail workers were all "hot"—exposed and contaminated with anthrax spores. By midweek all the results pointed to the mail as the source of the deadly bacteria. It was difficult to imagine how anthrax in the mail could be an accident. But others in the government held out for more proof.

I kept abreast of the events in Boca Raton during twice-daily conference calls. As the avalanche of threats began to subside, my duties in SIOC became less pressing, and I assumed a larger role in the developing anthrax case. The WMDOU asked me to sit in on the calls; I was one of the few agents in the Counterterrorism Division with a biology background, and during my time in the Hazmat Unit I had come to know many of the players involved in biological threat defense on a first-name basis.

Every day at 10:00 a.m., and again at 4:00 p.m., we—a collection of agents, analysts, and senior executives—convened around a secure telephone hooked up to a speaker. One of us dialed a number that connected with a recorded voice, then typed a pass code into the keypad of the heavy beige telephone, and finally turned a black plastic key inserted into its side. Within a few seconds, *SECRET*, in black letters, appeared on the phone's small gray screen. Often, a discussion already in process greeted us, which then paused as one of our executives would say, "FBI is on."

Officials from the National Security Council, Department of Defense, and CDC dialed in. Many of the voices became familiar, and frequently the conferences went on for an hour or more. At times the well-known White House spokesman Ari Fleischer joined in. Every time a participant rang in, a faint *ping* sounded over the noise of the speaking voices, pausing the dialog until the new participant identified himself or herself. Several participants, notably White House staffers, pressed for any connection of the anthrax crisis to Saddam Hussein, but most of the participants were in agreement that not a shred of evidence made that link. After one such debate and the end of the call, the leading FBI executive in our room, thinking out loud as we stood to adjourn, "They sure want to go after Iraq for this."

Leading executives and scientists of the CDC's National Center for Infectious Diseases, NCID, sat around the large table in the conference room outside of the CDC director Jeffrey Koplan's office. Robert Stevens had died just a few days earlier, and now the group discussed Ernesto Blanco, whose illness still did not have a clear-cut diagnosis, which left the group divided.

During prior meetings the group had disagreed about the Stevens case. CDC's associate director of epidemiologic science, Dr. Stephen Ostroff, had voiced the opinion that Stevens's anthrax was naturally caused, a chance infection. Dr. Stephen Morse, associate director of science and deputy director of the CDC's new Bioterrorism Preparedness and Response Program, countered, emphasizing that naturally caused inhalational anthrax had never been seen in Florida. On occasion the differences in opinion became more noticeable; once a fist slammed the conference room table to add emphasis to a point being made.[9]

Some of the stress in the room originated from events occurring much earlier in the year and unrelated to the current anthrax case. Proposals had been circulated within the CDC's parent organization, the Department of Health and Human Services in Washington, to reduce funding for the NCID's epidemiology programs. On the other hand, funding for the NCID's bioterrorism program had increased dramatically during the past three years.[10] And historically, the experience of the Epidemiology Intelligence Service—considered an elite group within the CDC ranks—had always been with illnesses stemming from natural causes.

The scientists went around the room one by one and described their testing of Blanco's specimens. None of the scientists in the room had been successful in growing anthrax from any of the clinical specimens that had been taken from Blanco. The group also discussed the fact that Blanco's clinical symptoms did not match those expected for inhalational anthrax. But then, no one had seen an inhalational victim until Robert Stevens appeared at the hospital only days before.

The group next turned to Dr. Richard Meyer. Meyer and his team had developed a new process for detecting anthrax spore particles.[11] The new test, an immunoassay called Time-Resolved-Fluorescence (TRF), was extremely sensitive. It consisted of antibodies, proteins produced by the body's immune system capable of recognizing, binding, and neutralizing pathogens, such as bacteria. Meyer's new assay used antibodies specifically targeting one of the several proteins produced by anthrax during an infection. He had also modified the antibodies so that when they bound to anthrax proteins fluorescent light was generated. New instruments in Meyer's Rapid Response and Advanced Technology (RRAT) Lab detected fluorescent light with extreme precision. The TRF assay not only detected the presence of anthrax proteins, it also measured their concentration—the more anthrax proteins binding the antibodies, the brighter the fluorescence. Meyer had spent the better part of the past year conducting exacting validation studies on the new immunofluo-rescence assay.[12]

Meyer described the results of his advanced testing on Blanco's specimens in simple laboratory jargon: "The TRF assay is hot, red hot! My assay says its anthrax." His lab had detected a high concentration of inert anthrax proteins in Blanco's pleural fluid, but not live bacteria.

The majority of the group, under the leadership of Dr. Julie Gerberding, the acting deputy director of NCID, disagreed with an anthrax diagnosis. Again, they emphasized that Blanco did not exhibit all of the symptoms expected for inhalational anthrax. And in 2001, the CDC's definition of an anthrax infection required the presence of growing bacteria in a clinical specimen such as blood or in the chest cavity and spinal fluid. Since live anthrax had not grown out of any of Blanco's specimens, either in Pillai's Miami Public Health lab or at the CDC, Blanco could not be diagnosed with anthrax. The fact that Blanco had been put on extremely high doses of antibiotics before diagnostic specimens were taken—decisive action that undoubtedly saved his life by killing the live bacteria, leaving behind only bacterial protein—ironi-cally now complicated a clear diagnosis.

The internal disagreements at the CDC spilled over into its communica-tions with other agencies. Near the end of another meeting that same week, Gerberding relayed an unexpected request from the CDC's parent, the De-partment of Health and Human Services (DHHS). She addressed the room quietly, but with authority, and asked that everyone be careful not to discuss the developing anthrax investigation outside the CDC; all communications about test results should only come from the front office of the CDC or the CDC's parent organization in Washington. And the group was reminded "not to talk to the FBI."[13]

Every day CNN reported more information about the anthrax case than the CDC received from other government agencies. At one point earlier in the week FBI representatives had briefed White House staffers on CDC test results without the prior knowledge of CDC officials. Health and Human Services had decided to formalize the flow of information and directed the CDC's leadership to follow suit.

The members of the CDC's Bioterrorism Preparedness Program did their best to remain calm and to comprehend the new directive. The FBI had col-lected samples at the AMI building and then shipped many of them up to the CDC laboratories for testing. Now the group was being told not to report the test results back to the FBI. The RRAT Lab, through Meyer and Morse, together with Richard Kellogg, the CDC's Liaison Coordinator for the Labo-ratory Response Network, had spent the last two-and-a-half years building a partnership with the FBI.

Meyer immediately began to picture the FBI's reaction to this latest change and quickly countered, "But we've built a strong relationship with the FBI through the LRN, our Laboratory Response Network. There will be repercussions if we don't share information," trying to be as tactful as he could and not let his emotions get the better of him. "We've built up an excellent rapport with the folks in the FBI's Hazmat Unit." But the leadership would not yield.

The decision reached the evidence teams on the ground in Boca Raton. They needed to continue getting test results as soon as they could. The teams drove their wipe and vacuum samples to Pillai's lab in Miami, and Pillai, who was on the state of Florida's payroll, continued to provide both the FBI and the CDC with his results. But Pillai's lab struggled to keep up, and soon backlogs developed. The lab had just finished testing nasal samples from over one thousand potential victims, working twenty-four hours a day as fast as humanly possible to get the results.

Meyer, despite being a CDC employee, also continued to provide the FBI with test results in an unofficial capacity. His stance came with risks; it could place him in a precarious position with upper management. Meyer was new to the CDC, which had hired him only two years before to run their Viral Special Pathogens biosafety level-4 laboratory, and then to direct the new RRAT Lab. He had given up his job at USDA's Plum Island laboratory and left his native New York City to move to Atlanta. He had enjoyed his research job at the USDA and had spent many a weekend kayaking along Plum Island's isolated shores at the eastern tip of Long Island during the New York summers—mild in comparison to urban Atlanta's steamy months. But Meyer had taken the CDC job to help defend the country against what he saw as a very real and looming threat—bioterrorism. And now, in early October 2001, Meyer believed the threat was being realized.

Meyer had believed it the previous Saturday when he and his wife had taken a quick trip back home to attend a family wedding. Meyer knew that his RRAT Lab at the CDC had received Robert Stevens's computer keyboard from the Public Health Lab in Miami earlier that same day with a request to confirm a test result for anthrax spores. While Meyer and his wife were leaving the evening reception, one of the laboratory fellows telephoned him. The scientist relayed the RRAT Lab's immunoassay results—they were blazing hot; anthrax spores covered Stevens's computer keyboard. *This is it*, Meyer immediately thought. *Bioterrorism!*[14]

5

A Zillion Spores

October 12, 2001

Rich Meyer walked into his office early Friday morning just as his telephone began to ring. The past week had been full of developments. But the source of the anthrax infecting the Florida victims had still not been found after seven days of sample collection. The Miami FBI suspected the US mail as the source. This morning testing was scheduled to begin at the Boca Raton area post offices that served the now-closed AMI building.[1]

Meyer picked up the telephone receiver to hear an urgent request. "Rich, can you fly to New York City? Right now?"

Earlier in the week, New York City's Mount Sinai Hospital had reported a case of cutaneous anthrax[2] in a young woman, Erin O'Connor, who worked in the NBC building as an assistant to news anchor Tom Brokaw. The day before the call, Mount Sinai had sent skin biopsies to the CDC, and the presence of anthrax had been confirmed.[3] CDC director Jeff Koplan and New York City mayor Rudolph Giuliani had just finished a 6:00 a.m. conference call during which Koplan verified O'Connor's anthrax diagnosis.

The call from his boss, Stephen Morse, asking him to fly to New York did not come as a complete shock. He had been helping with the New York case. A suspicious "white powder" letter from Brokaw's office had also been sent to the CDC, and Meyer had just finished the testing. To Meyer's surprise, however, the NBC letter did not contain anthrax.

Meyer rolled the events over in his mind: *The third anthrax case in seven days, and still we don't have a source. And this time New York. The Florida case looks like it's from the mail, but the NBC letter was negative. Maybe New York City Public Health has some answers.*

Meyer drove fifteen minutes north to the DeKalb Peachtree Airport and climbed up the short row of steps leading into the CDC's leased corporate jet. The small airplane grew crowded as Steve Ostroff and several other CDC epidemiologists, along with two industrial hygienists, joined Meyer. Ninety minutes later they touched down on a runway at New York's busy LaGuardia Airport. A dark blue-and-white NYPD van met them in front of the terminal. Without getting out, the officer driving the van told the group to jump in. They pulled away from the curb as blue-and-red lights flashed back and forth over the top of the windshield and a siren blared from somewhere in front.

They first drove through lower Manhattan and stopped to pick up Marci Layton, New York City's assistant commissioner of public health. Four weeks earlier, the World Trade Center towers had stood only blocks from Layton's office. Now faint smoke drifted up from the towers' wreckage as men and cranes removed its twisted steel.

With lights and siren still flashing and blaring, the van pushed back into the congested flow of the city's morning traffic and headed to midtown. When the group pulled up to the NBC building at 30 Rockefeller Center, Meyer turned to Layton. "So, Marci, what do you think? They made a diagnosis of anthrax, but the letter doesn't contain any anthrax powder."

"I'm confused too, Rich. We tested the letter also, before you did, and I agree, it's negative for anthrax." Meyer shook his head, trying to make sense of it.

Large crowds had gathered outside Rockefeller Center and inside the building's lobby, but otherwise everything appeared to be normal. The negative test results of the suspicious white powder letter had given everyone a sense of safety. The CDC group was led up to a large conference room and greeted by officials from the New York Department of Health and the director of security for NBC. Meyer pulled the two hygienists aside and told them, "I'm going to try to follow the letter."

Meyer turned to the security director. "Can you take me through the building and show us the path of the letter—how it would get to Brokaw's office?"

The two men took an elevator down to the NBC mailroom. At the mailroom the director showed Meyer a row of cubbyholes and mail slots, then the cart used to deliver the mail. Meyer learned that a courier distributed the building's incoming mail to the offices above. The two made their way upstairs to Tom Brokaw's office. Meyer asked several people standing around the office about any recent suspicious letters. One of the office assistants mentioned that a letter with powder had arrived earlier. They had put both the letter and the powder into a plastic bag and called the security office. Meyer asked the director, "Where would the letter go after they called security?"

"My guy came up and got it. He put it in another plastic bag and brought it to our office."

Leaving Brokaw's office, the two made their way back downstairs to the security office. Meyer walked into the office and nodded hello to a security guard sitting at a desk. The guard quietly ate a sandwich while Meyer asked, "Where did you put the letter from Tom Brokaw's office?"

"I put it in that drawer." The guard pointed to an empty drawer.

"What happened to it?"

"A Hazmat guy took it. I'm not concerned about it; we heard it wasn't anthrax," finishing his sandwich.

Meyer considered Brokaw's assistant and the diagnosis of anthrax, *So, what happened? If there wasn't any anthrax in the letter, we still need to find another letter.* Meyer thought through the possibility of another letter not yet found and turned again to the security director. "Do you get any other suspicious letters sent to Tom Brokaw?"

"Yes, they're in my office." He turned and led Meyer down the hall. In his office the director pulled open a desk drawer and showed Meyer a clear plastic bag. The bag, top open, was full of letters and envelopes.

Meyer looked closer through the side of the bag and saw one of the envelopes leaking powder. Meyer looked at the address on the leaking envelope. It began: TOM BROKAW . . . "Let's seal this and get it to the health department immediately!"

Meyer arrived at his hotel a little after midnight. The day had been exhausting, but at least an anthrax letter, the source of the NBC employee's infection, might have been located.

Meyer's cell phone rang. The number for the New York City Laboratory Response Network Lab appeared on the telephone's screen.

"Rich, there's a zillion spores here in this powder! In the Brokaw letter you sent over!" said John Kornblum, the primary scientist at New York City's Response Network Lab. "We'll have the DNA tests done soon, and we'll call you with the results."

So, that's it, we have an anthrax letter. Finally, Meyer thought. He tried to get a couple of hours sleep, but it was no use. He waited for the DNA confirmation. Saturday would be a full day, especially if the testing showed the powder was anthrax, and not one of those anthrax cousin bacteria used as insecticide powders commonly available in hardware stores.[4]

Early Saturday morning Meyer went to the NBC building. Members of the FBI's Hazmat Unit from Quantico had arrived, and Meyer gave them a quick update on the recent events. While Meyer briefed the FBI, his cell phone rang.

"Rich, the PCR test is positive,"[5] Kornblum said. "The spores in the Brokaw letter are anthrax, fully virulent."

"Okay. Can you put some of the powder in a vial so I can take it back to CDC with me? And, also some in another vial for John Ezzell at USAM-RIID? I'll be right over."

When Meyer arrived at Kornblum's lab near chaos greeted him. Police officers and detectives carried piles of different items either filled or covered with various types of powders into the lab for testing. Boxes stuffed with letters and suspicious powders lined the hallways. Word had spread that an anthrax letter had been found, and alarm was spreading rapidly.

Inside the public health lab, the staff worked amid the commotion, preparing a package for Meyer containing a small amount of the Brokaw powder. Once back at the CDC, Meyer would attempt to confirm Kornblum's DNA results and begin growth cultures. The cultures would be sent to Hoffmaster's lab for crucial MVLA strain typing. If the spores in Brokaw's letter were the Ames strain, it would be a link to the Florida investigation. And Meyer would be sure to include the FBI Hazmat Unit scientists in the test planning. The discovery of the letter now put the FBI in charge of the investigation.

Meyer prepared to leave and was about to inquire about the status of the powder he had requested. Alex Ramon, the laboratory director, greeted him as a police van pulled up to the curb outside. "Rich, can you take another package with you? New York University Hospital just sent over a skin biopsy from a second possible anthrax case. This time it's a baby."

"Okay, sure, but I need to hurry. They sent the jet back up this morning. It's waiting at La Guardia for me right now. I need to get back to CDC with the powder as soon as possible to start analyzing."

The NYPD van's blue-and-red lights flashed across the front windows of the public health building. The officer didn't bother to turn them off as he waited; the van had several more trips to make around the city and Dr. Meyer was holding things up. Finally, one of the laboratory scientists handed Meyer a large package wrapped in wide packing tape. Meyer jumped in the van, and they began the race to LaGuardia Airport and the waiting jet. Meyer guarded the precious package as best he could, bouncing back and forth in the passenger seat as the officer hurtled through Saturday midday traffic.

Meyer walked back into his lab at the CDC late on Saturday. He stood in the same spot where he had stood only a day-and-a-half ago when he had gotten the call to fly to New York. The scene in New York had shocked him to his core. Al-Qaeda's attacks of four weeks earlier had left lower Manhattan in ruins. Now, someone had attacked Manhattan with anthrax by mailing a spore-filled letter.

From somewhere in the lab he heard yelling, "Rich, the FBI is calling! They've been calling all night. They want to have a conference call. They're furious!"

The trip had exhausted Meyer. He had very little rest, had gotten to his hotel after midnight, and the commotion at the New York public health lab had taken its toll. His patience had worn thin.

Meyer reached across the desk and grabbed the telephone. "Hello, this is Richard Meyer. Who's this?!"

Meyer could hear talking in the background and sensed more than one person on the call. A special agent, after identifying himself as the head of the FBI's New York Evidence Response Team, spoke. "You took the evidence! You took the Brokaw letter! Why'd you take the letter?!"

FBI or not, team leader or otherwise, Meyer was in no mood to be screamed at. "What are you talking about? No, I didn't. I only have powder!"

The agent persisted. "Yes, you did!"

They hollered back and forth, both men tired and each convinced the other wrong. Finally, Meyer lowered his voice as he realized the agent was not going to give up. Then Meyer began to wonder, *Maybe the public health lab did make a mistake when they handed me the powder from the Brokaw letter. Things were chaotic.*

"Okay, okay, I'll look in the package," Meyer said. He put the telephone receiver down and walked back into the lab, first pulling on a white lab coat followed by purple nitrile rubber gloves. One of Meyer's scientists had arranged sterile tubes and vials inside the lab's glovebox in preparation for testing the Brokaw powder. The glovebox, made of clear plexiglass and tightly sealed, making it airtight, would prevent leakage of potentially deadly powder.[6] The scientist pulled on a fresh pair of tan latex gloves, put his hands into a second pair of heavier black gloves attached to round holes in the box's front, and unscrewed the orange top of an opaque, polyethylene bottle. Looking inside, the two saw the top of a clear plastic bag. Meyer knew the bag should contain a sealed glass vial—a small amount of Brokaw letter powder should be in the vial.

The younger scientist pressed the outside of the bag awkwardly with his black-gloved fingers and gently pulled it out through the wide mouth of the bottle. A small vial was visible in the bottom of the bag. Then, turning the bag over, the scientist turned to Meyer and nodded. *Uh-oh,* thought Meyer as a sinking feeling flooded his stomach. The feeling turned into a flush of embarrassment as the scientist pulled out the bag and the two men stared through the clear plastic. There was the envelope, the same one that Meyer had taken from the NBC security guard twenty-four hours ago. It bore an address, handwritten in block letters at a slight angle, to the right of the envelope's center:

TOM BROKAW
NBC TV
30 ROCKEFELLER PLAZA
NEW YORK NY 10112

Meyer ripped off his rubber gloves, removed the lab coat, and rushed back to the telephone. "Look guys, OK, I do have the letter. They did give it to me. I'll get chain of custody forms ready and repack it. I'll ship it back up to you right away. We're testing the powder now."

"Don't worry, Rich, we'll take care of it. I'll get a plane down there first thing in the morning. Again, don't worry, I'm just glad we have it. The way things were today, we're happy we found it intact."[7]

The lethal bacteria were being sent through the mail, and the investigation had come closer to a solution. The Brokaw letter and envelope might hold valuable clues: handwriting for future comparison, ink for chemical analysis, a postmark to trace the origin, and faint bar codes—understood only by the US Postal Service—for interpretation.

The following Monday, October 15, the National Center for Infectious Diseases' scientists gathered again in the large conference room. Their discussion returned to Ernesto Blanco. They went around the room; each scientist and doctor took his or her turn, giving the latest test results and relaying new developments at the Cedars Medical Center. The doctors from Miami had reported on possible nonanthrax causes for Blanco's illness. One by one, each possible cause, either bacterial or viral, had been ruled out. Additional testing at the CDC identified traces of anthrax DNA in fluid drained from his chest. The group discussed the nasal swab taken from Blanco on October 5. The swab contained enough spores to grow a colony of anthrax—proof of exposure, but not proof of the cause of illness. MLVA DNA testing[8] of the colony clearly showed it was the lethal Ames strain, the identical strain that had killed Robert Stevens.[9, 10]

Finally, it was Rich Meyer's turn to speak. The overnight trip to New York City, supervising the testing of the Brokaw letter's powder during the weekend, and meeting the two FBI agents to return the misplaced anthrax letter had left him drained, but he pushed through his exhaustion and repeated his earlier report—the Rapid Response and Advanced Technology Lab immunoassay results remained the same—anthrax proteins filled Blanco's lung fluid. Meyer felt the group's stare. He thought he could read their minds: *Why does he keep saying the same thing, meeting after meeting?* Meyer knew repeating the same results annoyed the other scientists, but he stuck by his test results even though he risked alienating the rest of the group.

A medical infectious disease specialist from neighboring Emory University, recently invited to sit in and join them, spoke up, "You have all the information. Rich's test result is positive. Why are you hesitating to call this anthrax?"

There was no reason to wait for more testing. The answer, already obvious to some, became obvious to everyone. Again the question was put before the group: Did Blanco have anthrax? One by one, in turn, they agreed. Finally, Meyer looked over at Gerberding. Gerberding looked back at Meyer and nodded, *Yes*.

A wave of relief swept through Meyer—finally, validation of his long hours of work and persistence.[11, 12] The investigation could move forward. There was no doubt now; the country was under attack by a silent killer, using mail as the weapon. Three victims were ill or dead, a fourth exposed, and possibly a small infant now infected.

6

Floating through Air

Friday, October 12, 2001

The arriving mail in Senator Tom Daschle's office lay in two piles—one from his home state of South Dakota and from around the nation, a much larger stack. An intern began to sort through the pile of national mail and noticed an envelope addressed in a child's handwriting; the words written in even block letters. He picked up the letter, felt a slight lump through the paper, and gently shook the small envelope. He held it to his ear and shook again, but heard no sound. Curious, he looked at the address a second time when he heard the office manager announce that training for the new mail security procedures would be starting. He put the letter back in the pile; opening the mail would have to wait until Monday.[1]

Capitol Hill had been in fast motion. For the past four weeks, ever since three hijacked airplanes had destroyed the World Trade Center towers and the west side of the Pentagon, and a fourth had crashed into a reclaimed field covering a coal strip mine outside Shanksville, Pennsylvania, fears of a second attack preoccupied thinking on the Hill. The press speculated the airliner that had crashed in Pennsylvania had been heading for Washington—possibly the White House or the US Capitol Building[2]—only a block away from where interns and staffers answered telephones, greeted visitors, and responded to constituent's mail. United Flight 93 had been forty-six minutes into its daily route from Newark International to San Francisco when al-Qaeda operatives overpowered the crew. The hijackers turned the airplane to head southeast and were twenty minutes from the nation's capital when heroic passengers stormed the cockpit and the hijackers sent the jet hurtling into the ground. Legislators on the Hill now worked nonstop on a future USA Patriot Act designed to prevent a reoccurrence of September 11.[3]

Monday morning, a little before 10:00 a.m., Grant Leslie joined her fellow interns in Room 612, a small office they used when sorting Senator Daschle's mail. A native Georgian, Leslie had studied political science at Boston University. Her Senate intern assignment now gave her a chance to see the political process in action. As she looked over the pile of mail, one letter—addressed in a child's handwriting—stuck out. The return address indicated a fourth-grade class had sent it from Franklin Park, New Jersey. The letter was thicker than normal. Opening mail could be tedious, and a letter containing drawings or messages from grade school children offered a fun distraction.[4] Leslie picked up a letter opener and started to insert the tip under the envelope's flap, but transparent tape sealed both its sides and edges. She picked up a pair of scissors and began to cut across the top. She had opened a slit about an inch long when she froze—powder spilled out of the small cut. The powder dropped into her lap, light in color against her black skirt. Then it fell on her feet, a pale gray on her black shoes, before splashing across the carpet. A faint cloud drifted up and filled the air, followed by a pungent odor.

Senator Daschle's staff had just completed training on how to handle mail containing suspicious powder, and Leslie did exactly as she had been taught. Holding the envelope upright and remaining motionless, she announced, "I have a problem."

"Dial 911!" a voice called out.

FBI agent James (Jimmy) Rice glanced out of his office window at the US Capitol in the distance. Things were finally beginning to calm down. His agents had just wrapped up processing the crime scene left in the wake of al-Qaeda's attack on the Pentagon. At the end of the week he had made an inventory of the supplies his evidence team had expended, as well as gear they acquired during the three-week operation; items that might be needed again in the near future. Rice believed that al-Qaeda had more attacks in the planning. He made a mental note to have all the equipment organized as soon as possible when his telephone rang.

"Hello, Supervisor Rice? This is US Capitol Police dispatch. Can I put you through to our sergeant at the Hart Senate Building?"

"Sure, I'll stand by."

"Jim Rice? Hi, we have a situation here. I'm at Senator Tom Daschle's office in the Hart Building. We've been testing some powder that was in a letter they opened this morning. It's positive on the SMART tickets.[5] I think we have some anthrax here."

"What makes you think it's real? We get a lot of false positives with those tests," said Rice.

"You don't understand. We repeated the test over and over. Each time the tickets turn dark red fast—a fast positive—not slow, or pink, like the false ones," said the sergeant.

"Ok, I'll roll some people. Thanks for letting us know," said Rice. He hung up the telephone, picked up the response list for the week, and walked out into the squad area where he found the standby agent typing at a computer.

"You're next on the list. Get over to Capitol Hill, here are the details I wrote down."[6]

Rice thought for a second and decided they might need more. He paged the Hazardous Materials Response Team leader and then looked across the fourth floor to his sister squad, the Joint Terrorism Task Force. Walking over, he found the task force supervisor. "Who's on for this week? You should probably send them."

The two looked at the standby list—agents Scott Stanley and Gary Vienna were at the top.[7]

Rear Admiral John Eisold walked into the Office of the Attending Physician to the US Congress early on Monday morning. He had been the attending physician since 1994 and oversaw medical care for congressional members and their staff. Originally from Cleveland and growing up in Baltimore, he had served as a nuclear submarine officer, been assigned to the Navy Surgeon General's office at the Pentagon, and was appointed chair of internal medicine at the Naval Medical Center prior to his present duties at Congress. Like his counterparts in other areas of the federal government since the late 1990s, Eisold and his team of three dozen doctors, technicians, pharmacists, and therapists regularly trained in responding to a weapon-of-mass-destruction attack. Eisold took the training seriously; it included dressing out in Hazmat suits and using chemical and radiological detection equipment. It was no secret the airliner that had crashed in Shanksville might have been headed for the US Capitol.

In the aftermath of 9/11, the news of crop dusters being grounded around the nation, and last week's death in Florida, Eisold's team now focused their preparations on responding to an anthrax attack. Stocks of antibiotics and sterile Q-tip swabs that had been purchased and put in storage were brought to his Capitol Building clinic. He had recently presented his protocol for examining and treating anthrax victims to an interagency meeting, and the attendees, which included experts in biological threats, agreed with his approach. And just the previous Friday afternoon, Eisold tested a US Senator for anthrax exposure. The senator had been in New York City when news of a case of cutaneous anthrax at the NBC Building was announced. The Naval Hospital performed the anthrax culturing flawlessly, which fortunately had proved negative.[8] If al-Qaeda attacked the Capitol with anthrax, Eisold and his team were ready.

Down the hall from Eisold's office, Norman Lee, a senior medical officer to Congress and lieutenant commander in the US Navy, organized his desk for the coming week of patient visits. Suddenly, a bell in the hallway began clanging, just like the school bell he used to listen for that signaled the end of a day's classes. Lee, next in line on Eisold's rapid response rotation list, jumped up, grabbed his medical supplies, ran into the hallway and to the designated rally point in front of the clinic pharmacy. The rest of his team—a pharmacist, lab technician, and a physical therapist—arrived at the rally point the same time Lee did. As Lee made a roll call of the team members, loudspeakers broadcast the reason for the alarm—white powder in the Hart Senate Office Building.

"OK, we know how to handle this," Lee said as he grabbed a large bottle of Cipro pills from the pharmacy and led his team to a waiting ambulance. Within minutes they had raced five blocks across Capitol Hill and braked to a halt in front of the Hart Building.[9]

Lee ran to the office suite of Senator Daschle and entered through the outer door. Inside two US Capitol Police officers greeted him. They were dressed in full Hazmat protective gear: rubber boots, white Tyvek suits, latex gloves, and black masks. The two looked at Lee with question. Why wasn't the doctor concerned, they seemed to ask—should he be entering the premises without protection? But Lee just nodded hello and kept walking into the office. He had received at least six anthrax vaccine shots over the past eighteen months, and his last booster had been on schedule—by now he should be immune to any anthrax spores he might encounter.

"Is it anthrax?"

The police officers nodded, "Yes."

"OK, where's the victim?"

One of the officers pointed to a young woman. She sat beside a desk, holding an envelope upright in her hand, perfectly still. Her face was expressionless, and she seemed to be in shock.

"Are you OK?" Lee said. "Don't worry, we have medicine for you."

Lee motioned for the woman to hand the envelope to one of the officers and then to stand up and follow him. He gathered together all the other people in the office, more than ten in all, and led them down the hall and away from the contaminated room.

The young woman seemed to grow more and more concerned as she walked. A stream of questions began to pour out. "Should I be quarantined?"

"Absolutely not," Lee answered.

"Should I stay away from my family?"

"Absolutely not."

"Should I burn my clothes?"

"Absolutely not."

Lee and his team began to wipe out the noses of the office staff using long-handled Q-tips and handed each person a three-day supply of Cipro tablets. The swabbing was not pleasant; each Q-tip not only went around the inside of their noses but also reached for the back of their throats as their eyes began to tear. No one complained.

Agent Scott Stanley's pager began to vibrate; it was already midway through Monday morning. Only the past week Stanley, a new member of the FBI's Washington Evidence Response Team, had finished working twelve-hour shifts sifting through the wet ashes and jet fuel at the massive Pentagon crime scene created by American Flight 77. Yesterday, he and his partner, Capitol Police agent Gary Vienna, had assumed on-call duty for the Washington National Capital area. Any incident with a possible nexus to terrorism was theirs to handle—they would be the tip of the spear for the next seven days. Stanley anticipated a busy week.

The pager's message directed them to go to the Hart Senate Building and meet with the Capitol Police who had a suspicious white powder letter. No more details were available, but the message did not worry Stanley. He had handled hundreds of these calls in the past—each one had been a false alarm. At the worst, an occasional letter contained a commercially available insecticide, *Bacillus thuringiensis*, Bt for short. Bt is a close bacterial relative of *Bacillus anthracis*, and both bacteria form spores capable of surviving outdoor conditions. Similar to anthrax and its Ames strain, Bt also exists in multiple strains. The Kurstaki strain is deadly to leaf-eating caterpillars, such as tent caterpillars and those that grow to become gypsy moths. The strain of Bt known as *israelensis* is effective against mosquito larvae.[10] This difference in toxicity lies in the bacteria's genetic code. *Thuringiensis* DNA contains genes that encode poisonous crystalline proteins, known as Cry proteins. The Cry proteins are produced as the bacteria form spores. Caterpillar and larvae feed on the spores, and once ingested, the Cry crystals damage the insect's digestive system, with death resulting in a day or two. Changes in the DNA encoding the Cry proteins account for the ability to target different insect species. Many gardeners favor the environmentally friendly Bt over harsh chemical insecticides because it does not harm humans, wildlife, or beneficial insects, such as pollinating honeybees or ladybugs that feed on plant-eating aphids.[11] Widely available, Bt is sprayed as a dust over vegetable crops to prevent caterpillar infestation. At first glance a microbiologist might not be able to distinguish Bt insecticide from anthrax spores until tests analyzing the suspect powder's DNA or using selective antibodies are performed.

Stanley's training made him ideal for responding to these white powder calls. Before joining the FBI, he earned a PhD in Biomedical Sciences from the State University of New York in Albany. After graduation he remained in his home state and conducted microbiology and immunology research at the New York State public health laboratories. And in his spare time, he volunteered on his local fire department's emergency medical service and special operations team. He was also a member of New York State's Urban Search and Rescue.

In 1997, Stanley applied to the FBI, filling out an application to be a special agent. While waiting for an opening in new agent class, FBI Headquarters offered him an intermediary job. The Laboratory Division had just started to staff its new Hazardous Materials Response Unit at Quantico and needed people with his exact qualifications: a doctoral-level scientist with microbiology experience as well as Hazmat training and certifications. Stanley joined me in the Unit, and together we made up its fledgling biology program. Tasked with developing procedures to collect evidence of biological weapons and protocols for their identification, he hit the ground running, first designing a training course in the use of hand-held immunoassay tests.

The US Navy had invented the tests—sophisticated strips of white nitrocellulose coated with highly specific antibodies that recognized only anthrax spores. The navy chose nitrocellulose for its affinity in binding protein antibodies while still allowing the immobilized antibodies to recognize and bind anthrax spores. They fixed the fragile strips of cellulose inside three-inch-long rectangles of rigid white plastic. The UN Special Commission, known as UNSCOM, had used the tests when its teams inspected Iraq for biological weapons following Operation Desert Storm. With the growing awareness of biological terrorism in the United States, the assays were in high demand by the first-responder community. Applying spores—first diluted in a weak salt solution—to the small white strips resulted in a brilliant red line of color—similar to a positive over-the-counter pregnancy test. While simple to use, they were not foolproof and could give both false positive and false negative answers; test results required confirmation in a laboratory.

In addition to developing training courses, Stanley responded to crime scenes around the country involving hazardous materials.[12] Within a short time FBI executive management noticed Stanley's enthusiasm and dedication—matched by his scientific acumen—and in May 2000, they offered him a seat in new agent's class. Upon graduation in September, the Transfer Unit sent him to the Washington Field Office (WFO). There, the front office assigned him to conduct background investigations, to learn as much as possible about someone applying for a job with the FBI and to talk to the applicant's neighbors, friends, landlords, coworkers, and supervisor and to look at transcripts, civil and occasionally criminal court records, traffic violations, and the fines paid. For many new agents graduating from the Academy, the assignment was not exactly their first choice, but Stanley thrived on the work. Year 2000 was a presidential election year, which meant SPINs, Special Inquiry Investigations. These are the FBI's background investigations of presidential appointees, and the deadlines are very short, measured in days, not weeks. Scott seized the opportunity. He viewed SPIN assignments as a once-in-a-lifetime opportunity, a chance to meet and interview some of Washington's most powerful and successful.

By winter's end, Stanley finished his SPIN assignments, meeting all the short deadlines, and earned a spot on the Joint Terrorism Task Force.

Stanley and Vienna parked their beige Ford Crown Victoria in front of the Hart Building and rode an elevator up to the sixth floor. A Capitol Police officer greeted them and pointed down the hall to Senator Daschle's office. They walked toward the office suite but stopped short as they reached an open door. Looking inside, Stanley saw two police officers dressed in familiar white Hazmat suits, boots, and latex gloves. The officers were each on one knee and looking at two small, white plastic strips lying on a sheet of cloth spread over the office carpet. Stanley recognized the white field tests; they were the hand-held immunoassays he had developed for the training course almost three years ago. In the center of each strip, Stanley saw a bright red line. As he watched the officers, a pungent odor jolted his sinuses, catching him off guard for a moment. Memories of the microbiology laboratory in graduate school hit him as he recognized the smell: *culture broth used to grow bacteria.*[13]

Stanley felt the tension in the office. Everyone was on edge, September 11 still foremost in their minds.

"What do you think?" one of the officers said, looking up at Stanley and Vienna.

"I think we have a problem here," Stanley replied. At that moment a uniformed naval officer walked up and introduced himself as Dr. Lee, an attending physician for the US Capitol. Lee told Stanley that the office staff, including the young woman who had opened the envelope, was being tested and given Cipro. The group would also shower before leaving. Stanley asked to interview them before they left and then leaned closer to Lee, so no one else could hear. "I have a really bad feeling about this."

"I know. I have a bad feeling about this too," Lee said.

Several members of the WFO Hazardous Materials Response Team arrived and collected items from the Capitol Police officers as Stanley and Vienna began their interviews. The team placed Leslie's clothes in plastic bags, along with her letter opener and the scissors she had used. They rinsed the outside of the bags with diluted bleach and then passed it all into the hallway, where everything was packed inside a second, larger bag. The letter, in its envelope, and the remaining powder were placed in a separate bag, the outside rinsed off and then passed out into the hallway for overpacking. It would all be rushed north to John Ezzell at the US Army Medical Research Institute of Infectious Diseases, USAMRIID, for more testing. The light aerosol quality of the powder, the way it floated in the air, and the positive field test results meant confirmatory testing had to be completed quickly. The tests would also address the question of antibiotic resistance. Resistance might arise naturally or be the product of intentional genetic engineering. Any resistance exhibited by the spores released in Daschle's office might mean adjusting the ongoing and future treatment of those exposed.

Lee and his team continued to test the Senate staffers for contamination, distributing Cipro tablets at the end of each exam. The team collected all the information about the workers' locations that morning, where they had been and how long they had been there. Lee told them to come to the Capitol's Health Clinic in three days—sooner if they felt ill—and their test results would be available. By that evening, his team had taken nasal samples from three hundred people: Daschle's office staff, Capitol Police officers, FBI agents, and personnel assigned to Wisconsin senator Russ Feingold, whose two-floor office suite adjoined Daschle's.

Later that night, Stanley worked at his desk filing notes and typing interviews; it was nearly 10:00 p.m. He had just participated in a conference call between scientists from USAMRIID and agents from FBI Headquarters and the Washington Field Office. He had listened intently as USAMRIID's Ezzell relayed the first set of test results for the powder collected from the Hart Building. Ezzell used terms like *puff of smoke* to describe how the powder behaved in his sealed glovebox. Ezzell then said, "I've never been this scared in my life,"[14] and the call's participants became quiet for a few seconds before talk resumed.

After the call ended, Stanley wanted to speak with Ezzell one on one and get some of the technical details of the testing. He really wanted to confirm the information he had just been told, to make sure he heard what he thought he had—Ezzell's description of the powder could have far-reaching implications. He dialed Ezzell's number; after three years in the Hazardous Materials Response Unit he knew it by heart.

"John, hi, it's Scott Stanley. I was on the conference call. This is unbelievable; it's really BA?"[15]

"Yes, definitely. I've never seen anything like it."

Stanley listened as Ezzell reviewed the testing in scientific terms. Ezzell's voice sounded frightened, but calm—more like stunned, almost speechless astonishment. He had first examined the powder under a microscope. In a single tiny sample, Ezzell saw thousands of individual spores with little to no debris mixed among them. Ezzell then tested for the presence of the three different DNA molecules the anthrax bacteria needed for its lethality—all were present. His antibody test again confirmed the spore powder as anthrax. Ezzell had started cultures on blood agar plates that would be incubated overnight and provide additional confirmation the following day, but at this point Stanley did not need any more test results. He thanked Ezzell for his work and placed the receiver back on the telephone. Then he began to send page messages to all the FBI personnel who had been at Daschle's office suite. The hand-held immunoassays had a reputation for false positive results, but now that Ezzell had confirmed the release of anthrax—a potentially lethal strain—those exposed had to be told, and it would be better in person, because there would be a lot of questions. At the same time he sent a message to the FBI's medical officer at FBI Headquarters. Hopefully, HQ had enough Cipro on hand.

Rear Admiral Eisold's telephone rang early Tuesday morning. The Naval Hospital had results ready for the three hundred people that had been tested on Monday. Twenty-eight had very high levels of anthrax on their nasal swabs. The bacteria had grown quickly; the cultures plates had reached confluency—individual white colonies almost completely covering a plate's surface to form a single layer across the blood red agar—in less than twelve hours. The results surprised Eisold. He did not expect growth to be that concentrated for at least forty-eight to seventy-two hours. Most of those contaminated worked in Daschle's office, but two were from Senator Feingold's office, and two responding police officers had also been exposed. The implications of the test results immediately struck the admiral as he said to himself, "This is big!"

Eisold, like his counterparts in the other health and government agencies, would be learning as they worked. They knew little about preventing and treating anthrax and had never seen a case of it before. They used their best judgment and what experience they had accumulated treating more common infections. And they would rely on colleagues who specialized in infectious diseases for advice.[16]

Eisold called his staff together and quickly gave his directive, "Anybody who comes in for testing, test them and treat them. Get all the information they have. Where did they go yesterday, what time they came and went, every detail about their travels on Monday. We will test and treat anyone who is worried."

His staff set up an impromptu clinic in the auditorium of the Hart Building and opened the doors just before 7:00 a.m. Mayhem greeted them. People pushed forward in lines that ran out of the building and onto the street. Agitation and anxiety pervaded the crowd; people were scared. Eisold immediately realized he would run out of testing supplies and protective equipment in short order. The surge of people anxiously waiting looked like just the tip of the iceberg of what he could expect in the coming days. *Wednesday is going to be a huge problem*, he thought. He made telephone calls to alert all of the area military hospitals for an influx of test samples. He advised them to locate additional laboratory equipment and asked for technicians and doctors to help staff his impromptu clinic. By the end of the day, Eisold and his staff had tested and treated 1,500 people.

That evening, Eisold met with Tom Daschle and brought the senator up to speed. Daschle then picked up his telephone and placed a call to President George W. Bush. As Eisold listened, Daschle relayed Tuesday's events to the president. Eisold heard the president reply, "Whatever you want, we will provide it."

Eisold then made a call to Rear Admiral Bob Knouss, his friend and counterpart at the Department of Health and Human Services' Office of Emergency Preparedness. Eisold explained the situation as he had done for Senator Daschle. Knouss simply answered, "John, what do you need?"

Knouss's immediate offer to help took Eisold aback; he had been prepared to discuss the situation in greater detail in order to convince his counterpart of the urgency. He calculated quickly, "Three hundred thousand Cipro, one hundred and fifty thousand Doxy,"[17] then went on to list testing supplies and protective equipment such as latex gloves and disposable masks.

"I'll call you back," said Knouss. Within an hour, Knouss returned to the telephone. Everything Eisold had requested would be at the makeshift clinic before 7:00 a.m.

By the end of Wednesday, 3,500 more people on Capitol Hill had been tested and treated, thanks to Eisold's herculean efforts. The testing continued into Thursday for another 1,500. Behind the scenes, the CDC's Epidemic Intelligence Service doctors, dispatched from Atlanta on Tuesday, had been analyzing Eisold's testing results. They identified a hot zone, the approximate area in which someone could expect to have been exposed to a lethal dose of anthrax spores. By comparing each individual's location at the time Grant cut open the envelope with that same person's test results, the epidemiologists identified one hundred that had likely inhaled a lethal dose[18]—some as high as one thousand lethal doses.[19] The epidemiology team leader conferred with Eisold, and together they decided to follow those exposed in the hot zone for the next one hundred days. While the standard practice would be to monitor the one hundred people for only sixty days, Eisold chose to be conservative and err on the side of caution; he frequently reminded himself that they were all in unfamiliar territory—standards and guidelines were only that. Further, at the seventy-five-day mark, Eisold would offer the one hundred victims the anthrax vaccine; taking the vaccine would guard against the possibility that the inhaled anthrax had developed antibiotic resistance over the course of the seventy-five-day regimen or that spores still lingered deep in airways.

The Sergeants-at-Arms for both the Senate and House of Representatives halted mail delivery, and sessions in the House were adjourned as the contamination spread. Elite Hazmat teams from around the country began to arrive, including the Coast Guard's Strike Teams and the US Marine Corps' Chemical Biological Incident Response Force, joining the FBI's Hazmat Response Unit to assist with sample collection from the Hart and neighboring Capitol Hill buildings. The teams sent their samples to USAMRIID for analysis; there, the army scientists set up an operation and command center, manning it around the clock.

On Tuesday, October 16, the front office of the Counterterrorism Division contacted the US Postal Inspection Service for assistance, and by day's end several postal inspectors had joined the growing team at FBI Headquarters. Dr. Mitch L. Cohen, a graduate of Duke University School of Medicine and officer in the US Public Health Service at CDC Headquarters, also became part of the group. Cohen, an infectious disease expert, was friendly and diplomatic. He would later rise to the rank of rear admiral in the Public Health Service's Commissioned Corps, a high distinction. The earlier lack of coordination with the CDC quickly resolved itself; Cohen made a perfect addition. He would remain at FBI Headquarters for the next four months.

FBI and government scientists held additional meetings to determine which forensic tests would be most valuable in predicting exposure risk, areas of contamination, and, ultimately, in developing clues as to the attacker's skill, sophistication, and his or her identity—always with the understanding that only a tiny amount of powdered anthrax spores had been recovered and many forensic tests under consideration were destructive; the material being analyzed would be destroyed and lost for future examinations. Together, scientists at the FBI's laboratory and agents with science backgrounds at the Washington Field Office sought out the best forensic resources and institutional capabilities in the country—from the Department of Defense, the Department of Energy, universities and colleges, and industry. Expertise in carbon dating, chemistry of agar and other bacterial nutrients, trace metals, and electron microscopy would all be needed.

The postal inspectors analyzed the postmarks and barcodes on Daschle's envelope. The letter had traveled through the Trenton Processing and Distribution Center in Hamilton Township, New Jersey, where it was postmarked during the early evening of October 9. The timing of the postmark stuck out—it occurred four days after the highly publicized death of Robert Stevens in Florida.

The same postal Trenton Distribution Center had postmarked the Brokaw letter three weeks earlier on September 18. Agents and postal inspectors compared the two envelopes; they were identical in size, and both bore blue, preprinted Eagle stamps. The mailer had written both addresses in a virtually identical hand—all the words in block-style capital letters; the first letter of each word twice as large as the ones following. One difference stood out. Senator Daschle's envelope contained a new addition—a return address.

The path the letters had taken through the mail system particularly concerned the postal inspectors. They began to wonder if anthrax contaminated postal facilities in New Jersey, New York, and Washington, DC. They knew the contamination in the Boca Raton post offices had been minimal, and no postal workers were found exposed when tested.[20] Several post offices that processed mail for Boca Raton had just undergone testing, and only three samples were found to contain anthrax of more than five dozen taken.[21] Hopefully, that would be true for the post offices of the mid-Atlantic.

During Wednesday's midmorning conference call, the inspectors' fears were realized. The New Jersey Department of Health reported anthrax might have infected Richard Morgano, a mechanic at the Trenton Distribution Center. A skin biopsy was flown to the CDC. The next day, October 18, the CDC confirmed the health department's suspicions—Morgano's lesion, black and deepening, was anthrax. And then, the same day, a second postal worker in New Jersey—Theresa Heller, a mail carrier for the Trenton area—was also reported to have cutaneous anthrax. She had gotten sick in the beginning of October, the same day Robert Stevens died. After a day in the hospital, she had been sent home with antibiotics. Fortunately, before being released, Heller's doctor had taken a biopsy of the lesion on her lower arm and preserved the material at his office. The lesion had started out as a red sore on the inside of her arm above the wrist. A couple of days later it turned brown, then black. By the time she saw her doctor, the lesion had become deep and taken on a purplish hue.[22] After watching the news story about Erin O'Connor's anthrax at the NBC building, Heller's physician alerted health authorities, and the CDC tested the biopsy, confirming anthrax. His foresight saved Heller from a disfiguring disease and may have even saved her life. She would soon recover and be back at work before Thanksgiving.

Thursday's conference calls continued to bring bad news. In New York City, the CDC confirmed two additional anthrax victims: Claire Fletcher, an assistant to Dan Rather at CBS News, and editorial associate Johanna Huden at the *New York Post*, making a total of four cutaneous cases in Manhattan.

In New Jersey, the situation also grew worse. By Thursday evening, four postal employees in the Trenton area had been diagnosed with or suspected of having contracted anthrax. Three—George Fairfax had now been added to the list[23]—had the cutaneous disease and a fourth, Jyotsna Patel, had been infected with the inhalational form. The New Jersey Department of Health acted swiftly. By the time the second victim was confirmed, the department ordered the Processing and Distribution Center shut. Within hours an Epidemic Intelligence Service team deployed from Atlanta. The next day testing began on the closed facility with the help of the FBI's Hazmat Team from Newark; the Department of Health recommended Cipro for all Center workers.

Postal authorities now realized their employees were at greater risk than earlier believed. In Florida and again in New York, no infections had been seen in postal workers. Postal inspectors traced the route of the Daschle letter from the Trenton Processing and Distribution Center to the Brentwood Processing and Distribution Center in northeast Washington, DC. The Postal Service located a private contractor able to take samples for anthrax testing, and work began at Brentwood. Just after midnight, early Friday morning, they shipped off twenty-nine samples, including one swab each from the display panel and electrical box of Delivery Bar Code Sorter Machine #17, and pieces of air ventilation filters above sorters #18 and #19. Before the laboratory could complete its analysis, the crisis grew deadlier.

The number of anthrax infections among Trenton Distribution Center employees continued to increase. Throughout Friday, the status of these new victims dominated the conference calls. The CDC confirmed a cutaneous infection in Patrick O'Donnell, a Hamilton employee. A second employee, Norma Wallace, who worked on the same bar code sorter as Jyotsna Patel, had checked into a Mount Holly hospital where the attending infectious disease physician, aware of the anthrax cases appearing in the news and circulating through medical alerts, suspected the inhalational form of the disease. He ordered an intravenous cocktail of potent antibiotics—a powerful combination of drugs immediately flowing into her bloodstream to combat the multiplying bacteria, harsh treatment reserved for the most severe infections—and contacted New Jersey's health department.

The final conference call on Friday began late, fifteen minutes before midnight. The FBI's Hazmat Team in Manhattan had just gotten back from the

New York Post, where they had recovered another letter suspected of containing anthrax—a duplicate of the NBC letter. The six-and-one-half-inch envelope contained a small amount of brown powder and bore a blue, preprinted Eagle stamp and the postmark: Trenton, NJ PM 18 Sep 2001—all identical to Brokaw's. The slanting handwritten address was made of small and large capital letters, and the sender did not include a return address. Comparing the *Post* envelope with Brokaw's of a week earlier and Daschle's from the prior Monday convinced the New York agents they had recovered another letter containing anthrax spores—this one the source of Johanna Huden's skin lesion. An obvious question lingered as the midnight conference call ended: *Who would be the next victim?*

7

Assault on Brentwood

Saturday, October 20, 2001

In less than a month since Robert Stevens's death raised the specter of bioterrorism, the growing investigation evolved into a model of interagency coordination. Early instances of friction were put aside as government groups joined forces, each applying their individual areas of expertise to stem the first widespread bioterrorism attack in the nation's history. Postal inspectors assigned to FBI Headquarters streamlined the flow of information. The addition of Mitch Cohen made sharing victim diagnoses and environmental test results effortless. Cohen's colleagues at the CDC worked around the clock testing samples, and they contracted with outside diagnostic laboratories for additional testing, building a tremendous surge capacity for handling the flood of samples expected from Capitol Hill, Florida, New York, Trenton, and Brentwood. The nation's elite in hazardous materials mitigation converged on the Capitol to assist with sample collection and testing, as the House of Representatives adjourned its sessions and Senate and House office buildings closed.[1] Finished helping John Eisold determine the extent of the hot zone in and around the Daschle office suite, the Epidemic Intelligence Service doctors moved to the Brentwood Processing and Distribution Center as the Postal Service began testing the five-hundred-thousand-square-foot facility.

Sample collection continued nonstop in Boca Raton—at its post offices, the AMI Building, even in the September 11th hijackers' apartments and cars. A sample of the Brokaw anthrax had been flown to Arizona, and Paul Keim confirmed it as Ames strain. A sample of the anthrax from the newly recovered *New York Post* letter would soon be on its way to Arizona as well. The CDC diagnosed anthrax in the seven-month-old infant in New York City, but the child had no visible connection to either the Brokaw or *Post* letter. Antibiotic resistance had been everyone's fear, but the day before New York agents recovered the *Post* letter, John Ezzell reported that the anthrax in both the Brokaw and Daschle letters was susceptible to common antibiotics—the one piece of good news for the week.

From a hospital bed in Fairfax, Virginia, Leroy Richmond struggled to talk. Agent Scott Stanley gently tried to get details of Richmond's routine for the days leading up to his admittance to Inova Fairfax. The postal worker had arrived at the hospital the day before. He had started feeling ill on Tuesday, with fever, headache, and tightness in his chest. By Friday, he knew he needed help, and after seeing an internist he and his wife drove to Inova Fairfax. The physician on duty reviewed his symptoms, recalled an alert sent to Washington-area hospitals about the Daschle letter, and suspected inhalational anthrax. The doctor ordered antibiotics, started blood cultures, and contacted authorities.

Now, hooked up to an intravenous drip of potent life-saving drugs, Richmond tried his best to relay to Stanley his daily work schedule and any unusual letters he had come across at his workplace, the Brentwood Processing Center. Richmond reported to work at 4:00 a.m. after a fifty-five-minute drive from Stafford, Virginia, ahead of the rush hour traffic that would follow an hour later. By 5:00 a.m., he was usually on his way to the Baltimore airport to pick up Express Mail, reviewing each piece for its address and zip code. At 9:00 a.m. he was back at Brentwood. As Richmond related how the rest of his day usually went, the Intensive Care Unit's head nurse appeared and cut the interview short. She saw that Richmond had difficulty speaking; the agents would have to come back.

While Stanley talked with Richmond and his wife and daughter, Qieth McQureerier,[2] a supervisor at the Brentwood Center, checked into the Inova Fairfax Emergency Room. For the past four days, McQureerier had endured unrelenting headaches; aspirin and Tylenol provided no relief. Two days earlier, his vision had become blurred, and that did not go away, either. So on Saturday, McQureerier sought help at the emergency room. The staff, now aware of Richmond's case, suspected anthrax. Wasting no time, they contacted the infectious disease specialist on duty, who did what had been done for Richmond. McQureerier was placed on intravenous ciprofloxacin, additional antibiotics, and his case was reported to the CDC and the FBI.

The next day, another Brentwood employee, Thomas Morris, telephoned 911 to report severe flulike symptoms. He had been ill off and on for the past five days and had gone to see a doctor, who ran tests. The results were negative, but now, back home on Sunday, he was in trouble—great difficulty in catching a breath now compounded the aches and pain, and for the first time, he began to vomit.

The dispatcher sent an ambulance to take Morris to the emergency room, where hospital staff checked him into the intensive care unit and began blood cultures. Throughout the day, his condition deteriorated, and that evening, Morris became the second person to succumb to the anthrax attacks. Anthrax bacteria teemed through his blood.

Also on Sunday, a Brentwood coworker, Joseph Curseen, drove to a Maryland emergency room. The staff made a diagnosis of gastroenteritis and he was discharged. Early the following morning his wife found him doubled over on their bathroom floor. He could barely draw a breath, unable to speak in complete sentences. Mrs. Curseen drove her husband to the hospital, but anthrax already streamed through his blood system. Six hours later, at ten minutes past noon, he became the third fatality.

The letter sent to Senator Daschle on Capitol Hill brought a new and far-reaching dimension to the investigation. Two government postal employees in Maryland had been killed, mail workers in Washington, DC, and New Jersey were sent to hospitals, a leading member of the US Senate was targeted, and federal law enforcement officers—US Capitol Police officers and FBI agents—were attacked. In its wake, it left a crime scene rarely encountered. The collection, processing, and testing of samples quickly reached unprecedented proportions. To assess the extent of contamination as quickly as possible, the Capitol Police turned responsibility over to the Environmental Protection Agency (EPA), who in turn brought in a private contractor to oversee and maintain logs of the massive collection effort. Ideally, a police agency would not delegate evidence collection to a non–law enforcement group, but safety was now the paramount concern. The crime scenes at the AMI Building and nearby post offices in Florida, the NBC and *New York Post* buildings, and the Brentwood and Trenton Distribution Centers stretched police, Hazmat, and our own FBI resources beyond capacity.

Even so, the FBI required that records of the sample collection, matched with test results, be saved and some form of chain of custody preserved. I was designated to take control of the records of the Capitol Hill cleanup.

By the third week of October, the array of threats being reported by FBI offices around the country subsided, and we stopped the twenty-four-hour coverage of telephones in SIOC. I returned to a cubicle at the Weapons of Mass Destruction Operations Unit (WMDOU). After checking in and getting what little information was available on the cleanup efforts, I headed over to Capitol Hill.

I drove down Constitution Avenue, busy with pedestrians and other vehicles, past the US Capitol and up a narrow street with a gradual rise, past the Ford and Dirksen Senate office buildings, finally approaching the rear of the Hart Building. I stopped in front of a white barrier and identified myself to a Capitol Police officer. Further up the street, yellow crime scene tape surrounded a tall, white stone building. Government cars and black cargo trucks crowded together on white-lined black macadam. Blue-and-orange nylon tents stood on manicured grass lawns. Gas generators droned in the distance. Hazmat responders wearing white, paperlike Tyvek suits, holding black masks connected by a hose to wide belts and battery packs, rested on small folding stools and chairs inside the tents.

Inside a large black box truck, labeled with the round blue-and-gold FBI seal, I found Steve Rhea and Mike Cook, the same Hazmat officers that had traveled with me to Manhattan six weeks prior. Back from New York only days before, they now led the FBI's Washington Field Office's Hazmat Response Team on a search of the Hart Senate Building. Other agencies pitched in as coast guard sailors, EPA personnel, and Chemical Biological Incident Response Force marines spread out to surrounding buildings. Rhea explained that the EPA contractor had overall coordination of the site and was located three blocks away.

Ten minutes later, I pulled up to the address Rhea had given me, a small, red brick building trimmed in marble cornices. I introduced myself to the several people working at folding computer desks. Floor plans and Capitol Hill street maps spread across tables. A strange stillness circulated around the large room as everyone concentrated on entering test results into the computers, collecting sampling numbers from the Hazmat teams, and printing out updated schematics. Red dots covered the floor plans of the Hart and Dirksen buildings in clusters; each dot the result of a positive laboratory test for live anthrax spores that had escaped from the envelope held by Grant Leslie. For the next three weeks, I would visit the EPA's operations center, once in the morning and again in the afternoon. Each time, a new floor plan appeared and the number of red dots increased. Hundreds became thousands as the days went on, and the test locations continued to expand outward and further across and beyond Capitol Hill.

Anthrax contaminated buildings, cars, and people. The response teams found spores in the cars of the Capitol Police and on their bomb detection dogs. It contaminated Scott Stanley's FBI car that he had driven to the Hart Building on October 15. Before the Hazmat specialists finished their work, they would collect samples from twenty-six buildings, many of which contained contamination and would require monthslong reclamation before reopening. Cultural and historical significance complicated the task. The Russell Senate Office Building, adjacent to the Hart Building, dated to 1909. Polished white marble made up its floors and stairways. Delicately carved marble Corinthian columns rose to support its rotunda's dome. The Caucus

Room, lined with carved benches and settles that dated to 1910, had hosted hearings on the sinking of the *Titanic*, Senator Joseph McCarthy's accusations of communism, and President Nixon's role in the Watergate break-ins. Remediation would be slow and tedious.[3]

During the fourth week of October, Dean Fetterolf, a forensic chemist from the FBI Academy, visited us at the WMDOU.[4] Pulling me aside in the hallway, he excitedly described his recent work. The sudden onset of anthrax in multiple postal workers had sparked alarm in the Forensic Science Research Unit at Quantico. They searched the scientific literature in publications going back to the 1940s and found research into porosity and paper.[5]

Deciding on a simple experiment, they cut a small section from an unused envelope, placed it on a glass slide, and covered it with a second, thinner piece of glass. Clamping the glass slide to the stage of a powerful microscope—the movable black tray underneath the lens—they slowly adjusted the field of view by turning the large focusing knob, then the smaller knob, and watched as the image sharpened. They saw what they had been expecting—not a smooth, solid surface, but an irregular crisscross of thin fibers, each varying slightly in diameter along its length.[6] Gaps of different sizes separated the fibers; some spaces were as narrow as a single fiber's width, others as large as the width of five and even ten fibers. The scientists made calculations based on the magnification strength of the microscope's lens and estimated that each fiber was approximately ten microns[7] wide; they estimated the larger gaps must measure as much as fifty microns wide. And they knew that one anthrax spore measured one-and-one-half microns in diameter.[8]

But the presence of gaps and irregular passages in the paper's fiber mesh did not mean the gaps formed pores in the paper that spores could pass freely through, and they devised a second, simple experiment, filling an ordinary mailing envelope with a gram of Amido Black, a fine black staining powder[9] common in biochemistry labs. Sealing the envelope and placing it in an improvised vice, they applied pressure on both sides. The black powder began to appear, forming tiny dots on the outside of the envelope. As they increased pressure, the dots grew and became more frequent. The more pressure they applied, the more powdery dye worked its way through the paper, and they reasoned the same must hold true for dry bacteria spores. It explained the sudden appearance of anthrax in the postal workers; the machines sorting incoming mail at the Hamilton and Brentwood mail centers used pressure to push thousands of pieces of mail along every hour.

The Brokaw letter had been recovered with very little powder, but when the FBI Hazmat team recovered the unopened *Post* letter, it contained a much larger amount of spores. The material was gritty, a mix of brown debris—dried anthrax made up a minor percentage of the total material. In contrast, the Daschle letter contained only spores—pure, fine, and a light tan.[10] During the three-and-a-half weeks that had passed between the New York and Capitol Hill mailings, as reflected by the September 18 and October 9 postmarks, the anthrax attacker had honed his—or her—skills.

Investigators at FBI Headquarters quickly realized what the refinement in spore preparations and the porosity of paper envelopes meant for potential victims. The anthrax infections in New York had been limited to the skin form, and postal workers in New York City had not been affected. This was in stark contrast to the ensuing situations in Hamilton, New Jersey, and Washington, DC. The route taken by the Daschle letter, first through Hamilton, then Brentwood, was marked with anthrax victims, many with the inhalational disease caused by a fine powder aerosolizing into a vapor of minute particles.

Postal inspectors looked closely at the Brentwood operations for an explanation of how its four victims became infected. One of the victims, Joe Curseen, had worked on Delivery Bar Code Sorter #17 during the time the Daschle letter had passed through, and Leroy Richmond had cleaned the area around #17 on the same day. Thomas Morris sorted the Senate's mail by hand. But Qieth McQureerier was a supervisor, and his office was not near Sorter #17 or the area where Morris worked.

The same day the FBI scientists reported their observations of paper porosity, analysis of the preliminary samples taken inside Brentwood Center was completed. Of the twenty-nine samples taken, fourteen contained live anthrax. Both samples taken from #17 were hot, but samples from Sorters #16 and #18 were not contaminated. Eight of the fifteen samples taken from the sorting cubby and pigeonholes used for mail bearing zip codes beginning in "205 . . . ," indicating Senate mail, contained anthrax.

The results finally provided an explanation for Qieth McQureerier's infection. Of the only two overhead air filters tested—above Sorters #18 and #19—both were contaminated.[11] The Brentwood employees cleared their machines of accumulated paper dust using high-pressure air hoses two or three times a day. The bursts of air had likely aerosolized spores from the Daschle letter that found their way into McQureerier's lungs.

The ever-widening areas requiring anthrax testing exhausted the resources available to the FBI, federal partners, and local hazardous materials teams. In addition to the crime scenes left behind in the AMI building, NBC building, *New York Post* building, and across Capitol Hill, post offices and mail distribution centers throughout the mid-Atlantic region and Florida needed to be examined. And at the same time one more crisis, this one largely hidden from the public eye, spread across the country and again threatened to exhaust law enforcement and public health resources.

The day after Daschle's letter had been opened, FBI Director Mueller and Attorney General John Ashcroft went public with a guarantee to the American people.[12] Persons who preyed on the county's fears and pulled a prank communicating a biothreat would pay a price. Since October 1, hoax investigations, those involving anthrax threats and packages containing suspicious white powders, conducted jointly by the FBI and the Postal Inspection Service, totaled over 2,300. Mueller stressed that his resources were needed to locate a real killer. At least 500 of the 650 agents assigned to his Washington Field Office were working solely on either the 9/11 or anthrax attacks.[13] In the National Capital region alone, law enforcement resources could not respond to every call. Fire department trucks carried buckets of bleach to decontaminate suspicious letters and packages, risking potential evidence. During October, postal inspectors would locate and arrest eighteen people for mailing hoax threat letters. Fourteen more individuals would come under investigation.

The plea had little effect. In the week to follow, the number of hoaxes continued to soar. In the WMDOU, at first we attempted to coordinate testing of each suspicious white powder with a conference call from Headquarters and a formal threat assessment, as I had done for the past four years while in the Hazmat Unit at Quantico. Each telephone conference included an FBI Hazmat officer and agent, one of us at the WMDOU and a field agent who had responded to the scene of the threat. We reviewed the screening protocol conducted by the local Hazmat team in partnership with the field agent. The procedure required separate testing for explosives, radiation, and chemical hazards; all were sources of danger that a public health lab—designed to work with infectious diseases—could not prepare for. Once declared free of nonbiological hazards, the suspicious powder could be delivered to the nearest CDC Laboratory Response Network member lab and tested for the stated threat—usually anthrax.

By the end of October we had reached fifty thousand hoaxes nationwide. In November, the number would rise to almost one thousand per FBI office, on average. Each of the FBI's fifty-six field divisions around the United States experienced the same flood of suspicious letters, packages, and threats. And in each field division, the FBI had the assistance of the Laboratory Response Network.

Eventually, the Response Network's laboratories around the country felt the crush of incoming samples, at times becoming temporarily overwhelmed. Several of the Network labs, such as those in Baltimore and Richmond, refused any more white powder letters for short periods until they could clear their backlogs.

The white powder letters also besieged the postal system. By the beginning of November, the Postal Service had evacuated nearly three hundred of its offices around the country for varying amounts of time due to over seven thousand hoaxes, threats, and suspicious pieces of mail.

Outside the United States the situation also escalated. By the end of October, more than two dozen of the FBI's overseas legal attachés were involved in investigating anthrax threats. In London, England, New Scotland Yard requested our assistance with letters mailed to addresses in Scotland that threatened anthrax. Suspicious letters containing white, gray, or brown powders arrived at US embassies as far away as Sri Lanka, Bogota, Dhaka, Malta, and Moscow. FBI agents posted at the embassies struggled to arrange testing by local facilities.

At FBI Headquarters, a whirlwind swirled. As the number of anthrax casualties grew, the Bureau reviewed its resources. On Sunday, October 21, Director Mueller named the Washington Field Office as Office of Origin, OO in FBI jargon, for the growing investigation, consolidating efforts by the offices in Miami, Newark, and New York. Washington Field Office agents would now coordinate all aspects of the case.

The investigation was then designated a Major Case, MC #184, and given the codename AMERITHRAX. The new title was significant. The Bureau specified the 1932 kidnapping of Colonel Charles Lindbergh's twenty-month-old son as its first major case. AMERITHRAX would be the 184th investigation complex enough to necessitate major case status. In practical terms, it meant AMERITHRAX would receive top priority at Headquarters for resources.

By mid-October, the prospect of an attack by al-Qaeda-flown crop dusters began to fade, but the Daschle letter's New Jersey postmark brought back memories of al-Qaeda-associated terrorism from eight years before. The convicted terrorists of the 1993 World Trade Center underground bombing lived in Jersey City. The van they had used to carry their explosives into the basement parking deck of the Trade Center had been rented in Jersey City. The group's members were associates of current al-Qaeda operatives, including Khalid Sheikh Mohammed, the mastermind of 9/11.[14] Within the WMDOU and around FBIHQ the suspicion prevailed that al-Qaeda had a hand in the anthrax attacks, but still no proof had surfaced. But our thinking was to change.

On October 24, the Behavioral Analysis Unit requested a meeting to share their preliminary assessment. The profilers described the anthrax mailer as a loner, an individual domestic to the United States—in short a Ted Kaczynski, Unabomber type,[15] but well versed in microbiology. They did not see an al-Qaeda operative as the killer this time; mentions of Allah in the letters and the misspelling of penicillin seemed, to them, an attempt to mislead.

Upon designation of the Washington Field Office as OO, coordinating the bulk of the investigation mostly fell to FBI Supervisory Special Agent Jimmy Rice and his National Capital Area Response Squad. In between answering the calls reporting white powder letters—calls that came into his office at a rate of one every hour or two—Rice, a former state trooper from nearby West Virginia, studied the test results I had been collecting on Capitol Hill. Air circulation, powered by the Hart Building's nineteen-year-old ventilation system, appeared to have spread the powder throughout the two-floor office suite of Senator Daschle, then to the adjacent suite of Senator Russell Feingold and beyond. As the powder settled, foot traffic spread it further, through the Hart Building and then to neighboring buildings. But a pattern not associated with foot traffic also appeared in the sampling results—it followed the direction of the mail; the Daschle letter had traveled from Brentwood to the US Capitol warehouse on P Street. From P Street, it traveled to the Senate mailroom in the Dirksen Building and then to the adjacent Hart Building and Daschle's office; anthrax contaminated each mail facility along the route. A third pattern emerged. The bacteria also contaminated a mailroom in the Ford Building, seven blocks from the Hart Building.

Rice assessed the contamination. Its trail split into dual streams, seeming to connect mailrooms along different routes. Both the Longworth and Ford buildings contained anthrax, but the Daschle letter should never have been in either of those structures. Rice reasoned that while it was possible the House's contamination came from cross-contamination—contact with the Daschle letter or the contaminated machines at Brentwood—the amount of contamination seemed too high. He recalled at least two letters had been mailed to media outlets in New York City: the NBC letter and the *New York Post*'s. Both had been postmarked on the same day. Thinking that there might be one more anthrax-filled letter among the unopened, quarantined mail on Capitol Hill, he placed a call to the US Capitol Police. Would they collect the mail that was being held in the congressional office buildings? Then he met with Washington Field Office Executive Management and described his plan. He needed to locate a place where thousands of letters could be sorted and examined, letters that might leak anthrax spores with only a slight amount of pressure.

On October 24, the same day the behavioral profilers from Quantico met with agents at the Washington Office and WMDOU, an eighth individual, David

Hose, was hospitalized with inhalational anthrax. Hose's case differed from the others; he worked at the Department of State (DOS) mail facility in Sterling, Virginia, an hour drive from District of Columbia's Brentwood facility. When agents interviewed Hose, he told them he had never been inside the Brentwood Mail Center. A review of the route taken by the Daschle letter discounted any contact with Hose's workplace at the DOS facility. The agents discussed two possibilities: a second letter existed and had been mailed to the Department of State, or Hose had contracted anthrax from mail that had passed through Brentwood and come in contact with the Daschle letter before being delivered to the DOS mail center. But the trace levels of cross-contamination expected to remain on mail that traveled from Brentwood to Sterling seemed unlikely to cause a full-blown case of inhalational anthrax in an otherwise healthy person. Hose's infection reinforced the suspicion that at least one more anthrax letter existed.

8

The Springfield Operation

Saturday, October 27, 2001

Across the country, the Postal System faced massive disruption. With the anthrax mailer at large and still no identification made, government agencies, concerned about becoming the attacker's next target, quarantined their incoming mail until methods could be devised to sterilize it. Credit card statements and bills lay dormant and undeliverable, utility bills did not make it to their recipients, and check and money order payments already placed in the mail did not reach their destinations. The economic impact of the anthrax attacks began to escalate at an alarming rate.[1] Compounding the disruption, thousands of threats and hoaxes continued to besiege the country and required testing, tracking, and conveying results to victims.

The investigation intensified as forensic efforts pushed forward on multiple fronts.[2] As expected, the anthrax in the *New York Post* letter matched the strain of the earlier attacks—all were Ames, indistinguishable from one another. In a small office outside John Ezzell's lab, I joined two FBI Laboratory scientists to discuss how to pry forensic information from an envelope coated with a volatile and lethal powder. We needed to begin looking for fibers, ink, human DNA, and latent finger and palm impressions. Finding a print would be a big step forward. Its pattern could be fed into the Automated Fingerprint Identification System for a possible match. But before we could pursue traditional forensics, the anthrax spores had to be neutralized. The Armed Forces Radiology Research Institute in nearby Bethesda had the single cobalt radiation source in the Washington, DC, area. With the Institute's scientists, we planned a series of short experiments to determine the minimum time and dose of radiation necessary to inactivate the spores lying within the fiber lattice of our three envelopes and letters.

During the month of October, close to eight hundred interviews were conducted in Florida. Public health authorities in Palm Beach County examined over a thousand AMI employees and associates and dozens of postal workers for exposure to anthrax. Similar investigations took place around Trenton, New Jersey. Testing had been completed or was pending at the Trenton Distribution Center, the residences of postal employees, and nearby schools and businesses. The Postal Inspection Service in New Jersey had identified almost fifty post offices that fed mail to the Trenton Center and in turn had located 183 collection mailboxes, any one of which might have served as the drop point for the letters. By the end of October, the collection boxes would be placed under surveillance.[3]

FBI agents and postal inspectors continued to cast an increasingly wide net. Hazmat teams from public health, the FBI, EPA, CDC, and private contractors collected thousands of samples from dozens of post offices, buildings, vehicles, and people throughout Trenton, New York City, and Washington, DC. Agents and inspectors—on the lookout for the slightest lead—interviewed mail carrier Theresa Heller's customers, nearly five hundred in all, and talked to post office employees, Trenton-area pharmaceutical scientists and sales representatives, and local police. The interview teams contacted colleges and universities throughout New Jersey and neighboring parts of Pennsylvania, asking about anthrax research, missing laboratory equipment, safety violations, and questionable behavior. Veterinary hospitals in New Jersey were quizzed about recent anthrax cases—all inquiries met with negative results.

The refined nature of the spores mailed to Senator Daschle also provided a potential lead. During the three weeks between mailing letters to New York and Capitol Hill, the attacker had improved the production process. The ability of the powder to spread through the Hart Building as an aerosol and then across Capitol Hill suggested a milling step had been added. Milling—grinding a solid material into particles of a small, uniform size—could be crudely done with a small, hand-held mortar and pestle. But finer grinding required innovative machinery. The United States' former biological weapons program had implemented milling for weapon production and refined several methods to advanced levels. More recently, the pesticide industry had further refined milling technology to produce its eco-friendly Bt, or *Bacillus thuringiensis*, insecticides.[4]

Analysts at FBI Headquarters and the Washington Field Office worked to identify makers of milling machines. They found several companies that built equipment capable of producing particles under two microns and sent investigative leads to the FBI offices nearest the manufacturing plants. Agents requested customer lists, inquired about the number of mills made each year, and whether the machines came with options such as airflow and protective filters. They also asked about recent unusual requests and names of competing manufacturers.

The ease with which the Daschle spores seemed to float through air and seep from the envelope raised another question: Why hadn't the mailer become infected? The answer seemed simple. The mailer had been vaccinated, had self-medicated with antibiotics—or both. Working with New Jersey's Division of Medical Assistance and Health Services, FBI agents from Newark contacted two thousand pharmacies in New Jersey and Pennsylvania and issued subpoenas for Cipro prescriptions written since April. The Division then set up a hotline and staffed it with licensed pharmacists to screen incoming calls about unusual Cipro purchases. All information was immediately passed on to agents stationed at the Trenton Command Post in New Jersey State Police Headquarters. The calls generated over two hundred interviews, but none provided a viable lead. The Miami FBI followed suit and subpoenaed south Florida pharmacies.

In Washington, DC, a request went to the military for its vaccine records. The Department of Defense contracted production of the anthrax vaccine, but production problems had limited the supply. Outside of active military personnel, the Department restricted distribution to its own civilian scientists and select emergency responders and operatives within the federal government, including my former Hazardous Materials Response Unit. If inoculation had protected the mailer, he or she was among a select group.

At the Washington Field Office, Supervisor Jimmy Rice continued searching for a building large and secure enough to sort through thousands of potentially contaminated pieces of unopened mail. Since his call to the Capitol Police, Hazmat teams had collected several hundred trash bags of unopened mail from the contaminated House and Senate office buildings. Using the tents on Capitol Hill to sift over the assortment was not an option. The weather, the humidity, and the wind were all too variable and unpredictable. The place had to have a system to control environmental conditions and containment— allowing no chance for volatile powder to escape. Rice began placing calls to large laboratories with containment rooms. He tried the CDC, USAMRIID, and the US Department of Agriculture's Plum Island. Each laboratory denied his request. Rice began to feel abandoned. He was in the middle of a national emergency, and he needed their help. But after days of unproductive requests, the reason became clear. Each institute needed to maintain a clean lab; they could not risk cross-contamination inside their facilities. If that happened, their laboratories would be shut down, followed by weeks of cleaning and revalidating protocols. That's exactly what had happened at the New York City Public Health lab after powder from the Brokaw letter had escaped.[5] Or if the cross-contamination went undetected, suspicious samples sent in for testing, originally free of anthrax, might be mistakenly contaminated. The laboratories would run the risk of misleading investigators by reporting false positive results.

Rice's search for a secure containment facility continued, but he kept getting turned down. For a brief moment senior executives in the office considered sorting the mail on a floating barge.[6] It could be anchored far enough from land to avoid contaminating other buildings and people, and when the mail had been sorted, it would be sunk. In the meantime, the office management agreed they should keep looking.

Rice made one more call, this time to the General Services Administration (GSA) in Washington, DC, and explained his request.

"Sure," the administrator said. The immediate and positive response shocked Rice. The GSA maintained a group of large warehouses in Springfield, Virginia, within sight of one of the busiest commuter routes in the country, the mixing-bowl intersection of Interstates 95, 395, and 495.

"Let me get my notebook. Ok, here it is, you need a Number 14," the administrator said.

"What's a Number 14?"

"That's what we use for asbestos mitigation. It should work fine for what you need. We'll build the containment room out of plywood and then test the seals and ventilation—it'll take ten days, maybe two weeks, tops. When do you want to start?"

"Immediately."

Rice's success in locating a mail sorting facility came not a moment too soon. Within days the CDC confirmed Jyotsna Patel, who operated a Delivery Bar Code Sorter at the Trenton Center, had contracted inhalational anthrax. Patel had been in the hospital for six days—she became the nineteenth confirmed case of anthrax in three weeks.

In Quantico, Virginia, the Hazardous Materials Response Unit began its planning. Just back from Capitol Hill, Steve Rhea was assigned the job of writing the operations and safety plan for Springfield. He worked with the GSA to design a temporary laboratory. He then coordinated with Doug Beecher, who had been called back from Boca Raton to design testing protocols. The two drove to Springfield and surveyed the empty warehouse. They agreed it would be perfect.

Rhea studied the plans for a Number 14. Primary on his checklist were multiple provisions for safety, not only for the agents who would search through the mailbags but also for neighboring buildings and their inhabitants. In addition to the main laboratory room, there would be a separate room for decontaminating the Hazmat specialists following rotations in the hot zone, and a third, smaller isolation room for emergency decontamination in cases of accidental exposure. The main laboratory used for opening the mailbags would be ventilated under negative pressure. Powerful exhaust fans would pull air from the room at a high rate. This would ensure that each time a Hazmat technician opened the entry door, air would rush into the room rather than out. Loose spores could only leave the room through the fans, where they would be trapped by twin sets of HEPA[7] filters. As a safety check, Rhea's operations plan included testing the outermost set of HEPA filters for contamination on a regular schedule.

Construction began on Saturday, October 27. The General Services employees first erected a 5,900-square-foot plywood laboratory inside the vacant warehouse. They carefully sealed each seam joining the sheets of wood with heavy, white silicon caulk. At eye level, they sawed two eighteen-inch square holes and installed clear plexiglass windows, sealing the edges with extra layers of silicon. They added a powerful ventilation system. Fluorescent light fixtures were hung inside and wired into the warehouse's electrical system. Finally, the workers carried in two new blue-and-silver biological safety cabinets. Weighing five hundred pounds each, the cabinets had a six-foot-by-two-foot stainless steel work area faced with a glass door that opened by sliding up twelve inches. Each cabinet contained its own fan-driven ventilation system pushing air through dual HEPA filters. Only in the biosafety cabinets would individual pieces of mail be opened.

The day after construction started, anthrax claimed another victim. Kathy Thi Nguyen, a sixty-one-year-old hospital supply clerk, checked herself into the emergency room of the Lenox Hill Hospital on New York City's Upper East Side. A few hours later, after ruling out heart trouble and reviewing chest X-rays, the physician on duty suspected inhalational anthrax. The emergency room staff contacted Marci Layton at the Department of Public Health. Nguyen deteriorated rapidly and three days later succumbed, the fourth fatality at the hands of the anthrax mailer. Nguyen had no known connection to the *New York Post*, NBC, or any media outlet. A search of her apartment and workplace turned up no suspicious mail or connections to the other nineteen anthrax victims. Layton, FBI agents, and the CDC epidemiologists stationed in New York could only wonder if a new attack was underway.

While the GSA built their Number 14, the Hazmat crews on Capitol Hill continued to collect quarantined mail. By the time they had finished, 642 large plastic trash bags had been filled with envelopes. The teams sealed the bags into 230 fifty-five-gallon drums and drove the barrels fourteen miles south to the Springfield warehouse.

Rice had originally planned to have his Hazmat team sort through the collected mail by hand, one envelope at a time, confident that by now an additional letter would be fairly easy to identify—the distinct envelope, stamp, and handwriting immediately recognizable. It would be a tedious process, further slowed down due to the team members being required to wear full Hazmat gear. The FBI had a limited number of Hazmat-trained agents to draw on, and most of them had been committed to work at the massive crime scenes up and down the East Coast, or were responding to threats and hoaxes across the country. The team estimated the sorting would take several weeks. The EPA, which had been given overall responsibility for the operation on Capitol Hill, offered its own Hazmat-trained personnel from its Criminal Investigative Division, but even with this extra assistance, the work would be extremely time consuming. And there was always the possibility that the mailer might change the type of envelope and writing. Included in the behavioral profile from Quantico was a statement that the attacker had the ability to modify his methods as circumstances dictated.

Doug Beecher studied the operations plan from Rhea and added a scheme elegant in its simplicity. Rather than looking for an envelope, Beecher reasoned it would be more efficient to look for spores. The experiments showing the porosity of the envelope had all but proven that spores leaked through the paper. The spread of contamination along the path taken by mail as it moved through the US Capitol office buildings strongly suggested that the spores had continued to leak after being pressurized by the sorting machines at the Brentwood Center. If a trash bag contained another letter similar to Senator Daschle's, spores would very likely contaminate the bag's interior. Beecher estimated that by testing for spores rather than manually searching for a single letter, the work would take several days instead of weeks. He began devising a method to test the air both inside and outside the trash bags for spores.[8]

Beecher first connected air sensors to vacuum pumps and had them placed inside the main plywood containment room. As the pumps pulled air into the sensors, water inside each sensor would filter the air. At regular intervals, water samples would be taken out and applied to agar culture plates. Beecher and Rhea also introduced a sampling step at the decontamination line. Each FBI and EPA Hazmat specialist who went into the hot zone would be under a strict time limit—standard for any Hazmat operation.[9] At the end of the designated time in the hot zone, each specialist would walk to the second room to be washed down with soap and water.[10] But before being decontaminated, the surface of a culture plate would be pressed on the surface of the specialist's white Tyvek suit and then incubated. Beecher reasoned that by comparing the time of a culture plate giving rise to anthrax colonies with the time each mail bag was sliced open, he would be able to pinpoint which of the 642 bags contained anthrax spores.[11]

Near the end of the construction phase, while GSA technicians tested the biosafety cabinets' air flow, workers laid down the last seams of caulk and fabricators fit the ventilation system's final ductwork, Rhea and Beecher were called to a meeting. As they walked to the rear of the warehouse, the commotion of construction work and din of overlapping conversations grew distant. Reaching the back wall, a relaxing calm and reassuring quiet greeted them, a welcome relief from the day's commotion and bright overhead lights. In the corner, the head of the FBI's Laboratory, Acting Assistant Director Allyson Simons, greeted them. The three sat down on folding chairs, and Simons began.

"You are doing something that has never been done before in the FBI," Simons began. "This is our chance—an example to show how operations and science can work together—how things have evolved and grown in our organization."

Simons's short pep talk energized Rhea. Two long months before, on the morning of September 12, Rhea had been on his way to New York City. It seemed that everything that had been accomplished since that time was new, for the most part untested and requiring on-the-spot assessment and validation. Rhea's operations plan for Springfield was no exception. It contained several novel approaches. The anthrax investigation had grown to vast proportions, and by early November there was no end in sight. Simons, a former hair and fiber examiner who had led a body recovery team to Kosovo two years earlier, had hit the nail on the head. This is what he, Beecher, and the rest of the agents, specialists, and scientists in the Hazardous Materials Response Unit had spent the past four years preparing and training for.

The enthusiasm and support did not stop at the executive level. Rhea received votes of confidence and support from all the FBI's specialized response units based at the FBI Academy complex. One backing came from the elite of the Bureau's special weapons and tactics program—its Hostage Rescue Team (HRT).[12]

Team members were familiar with the basics of handling biological and chemical hazardous materials, having been trained in the past by Rhea and his fellow Hazmat officers from the Hazardous Materials Response Unit. The team offered to man the decontamination line, considered the least glamorous of duties in a Hazmat operation, but critical. Rhea welcomed the new addition.

After ten days of construction, the GSA completed the three-room ply-wood containment suite. Two days later, they tested the ventilation system and certified the temporary laboratory safe to use. On November 10, GSA turned the warehouse over to Rhea. As they had done in Boca Raton, the Hazmat-trained FBI specialists, along with their EPA counterparts, proceeded methodically and with careful deliberation. One by one they wheeled fifty-five-gallon drums of mail into the main containment room and unpacked the trash bags. They numbered and photographed each bag. Taking a single bag at a time, one of the Hazmat specialists shook the bag and placed a small piece of gray duct tape on the outside of the bag's plastic side. A second specialist recorded the time on an evidence log sheet. The first specialist cut through the tape along a line less than half an inch in length and inserted a long-handled Q-tip. The specialist wiped the white Rayon tip, moistened with sterile water, back and forth across the inside surface of the plastic bag. The specialist then withdrew the Q-tip, now a faint gray, and in a practiced, fluid zigzag streaked it across the surface of a blood-red culture plate while the second specialist resealed the cut with gray tape. The two moved to the next bag and repeated the process.

By the morning of Tuesday, November 13, the team had taken a sample from each of the 642 bags and test results had returned from the Naval Medical Research Center. Beecher compared his three sets of data: first the results of directly wiping the inside of the bags; then the times of the air samples being drawn through water onto culture plates; and finally the contact agar surfaces pressed against the Tyvek suits of the Hazmat specialists. The results suggested twenty of the bags contained significant amounts of anthrax spores.

Beecher again used his water filtering and culturing technique and took an air sample from each of the twenty contaminated bags. The air in three of the bags contained high levels of spores; one of the three held almost one-hundred-fold more bacteria than the other two. Its two-minute air sample produced approximately twenty thousand bacterial colonies. Beecher's team of specialists began to sort through the twenty suspect bags, leaving the one-hundred-fold bag until last.[13]

One by one they laid out the envelopes, comparing them to pictures of the Daschle and New York envelopes. Three-quarters of the way through a familiar envelope appeared—almost a perfect match to Senator Daschle's. It had been addressed to Senator Patrick Leahy with the same block hand printing; the first letter of each word was twice the size of the remaining letters. Also similar to the Daschle letter, Senator Leahy's address had been written on a slant across the front of the envelope. The return address matched that on the Daschle letter. A Hazmat specialist walked over to the plexiglass window and held the letter up. As Beecher read the address and mentally compared it to the Daschle letter, a faint puff of dust appeared—the envelope had a tiny hole in one corner, allowing minute amounts of deadly powder to escape.

By 8:37 p.m., Leahy's letter had been delivered into the hands of John Ezzell at USAMRIID and safely locked away. The envelope would not be opened until the volatile nature of the dry powder expected to be inside could be neutralized. Saving every bit of the powder was vital to the investigation. At almost the same moment Ezzell was accepting possession of the letter, FBI Director Mueller placed a telephone call to Senator Leahy. The director detailed the work that had taken place that week in Springfield and explained that the Vermont senator had become a terrorism target.

As construction was getting underway in Springfield, duty agents in the Command and Tactical Operations Center at the Washington Field Office had been answering telephones; many of the callers reported tips about who could be the anthrax mailer. By the end of October, a list of eleven individuals who might possibly have knowledge of the mailings had been developed.

On October 29, an anonymous caller reported on one individual who quickly moved to the top of the list. The caller named Steven Jay Hatfill, a doctor with an extensive knowledge of both US and Russian biological weapons. Hatfill fit the profile of the mailer—not yet released to the public—that had been developed by the agents at Quantico's Behavioral Analysis Unit.

Hatfill's resume was impressive. He was both a medical doctor and a doctor of molecular microbiology, with claims of expertise in wet and dry biological weapons and large-scale production. Adding to the agents' interest, Hatfill cited service in the famed C Squadron of the Rhodesian Special Air Service during the late 1970s—a time when Rhodesian Special Forces were suspected of involvement with an anthrax outbreak that killed nearly two hundred people. Then, the FBI learned that the US government had suspended Hatfill's security clearance just six weeks before Robert Stevens's death.[14]

The anonymous caller also provided information about where Hatfill worked. Agents from the Washington Field Office quietly paid a visit to Hatfill's employer in the northern Virginia suburbs.

9

Persons of Interest

November 19, 2001

My orders finally came through, effective for the third Monday of November. As expected, the Transfer Unit was sending me to the Washington Field Office, where I would report to the National Security Branch and the Iraqi Squad. Not the anthrax case. I cleaned up my temporary desk at Headquarters, turned over the sample collection logs from Capitol Hill, and got ready to go back to the field. But I was not sure what to expect. National security work would be far different from the violent crime investigations of my Boston days.

Early Monday morning, I walked into the Washington Field Office, identified myself to the front lobby security post, and was greeted by Scott Stanley. He had worked for me when we were both assigned to the Hazmat Response Unit in Quantico, but now we would be on an even footing.

Before being introduced around the office, we found a seat in the first-floor break room, where Stanley could bring me up to speed on his year since graduating the FBI Academy. We reminisced about our days together in the Hazardous Materials Response Unit at Quantico. A particular case in Los Angeles came to mind. The Los Angeles Division had called the Hazmat Unit to request help with searches that would accompany an arrest for murder. The killer and his victim had been partners in a medical practice or medical business; that was all that was known at that point. The LA Division needed a rapid response; the arrest was imminent and search warrants were being written when we took their call. Stanley raised his hand to go; I was committed to stay in Quantico and finish reports on recent case deployments.

The next day a photographer for *Time* magazine captured him on film carrying large vinyl pipes across a parking lot to a waiting Suburban. The caption under the photograph identified an FBI Hazmat specialist recovering tubes of ammunition from a concealed underground bunker.

As we talked, Stanley reminded me that the munitions were only half of what had been found that day in southern California. After securing the munitions and several seized weapons, he had spent the afternoon and most of the night inventorying a hoard of vials and tubes containing potential pathogens and toxins. By daylight, he had nearly one hundred small containers safely packed and ready for the trip back East. He loaded it all on the Bureau's Citation jet and six hours later touched down at Peachtree Airport outside Atlanta and the CDC. Minutes later Stanley had his package of bacteria, viruses, and poisons at the door of Rich Meyer's laboratory, and they began to analyze for potential bioweapons.

Our discussion returned to the anthrax crisis. Stanley filled me in on the developing case and the new task force being set up to solve it. The Field Office had been scrambling to get a grip on the rapid sequence of events since intern Grant Leslie opened the Daschle letter. Most of the agents in the office either followed up on leads stemming from the 9/11 Pentagon attack or responded to white powder scares and hoaxes. The growing anthrax squad had spent the past month screening white powder calls for ones that might be related to the Daschle and Leahy letters. Also, since the investigations in Florida, New York, and New Jersey had been consolidated into a single major case at the Washington Field Office, they also rushed to learn the investigative steps initiated by their counterparts in the other divisions.

Since responding to Senator Daschle's Capitol Hill office, Stanley had been working nonstop on anthrax. His experience in microbiology and understanding of hazardous materials placed him directly in charge of the primary evidence in the case—a new form of evidence for the FBI—live, growing bacteria.

The application of forensic science to bacteria was in its infancy. Recent investigations involving biological weapons in the United States had been limited to a few isolated instances of making and possessing the poison ricin. Unlike the anthrax bacterium, which requires growth in the human body for its lethal effects to be felt, ricin acts as an inert toxin. It is a protein isolated from beans of the castor plant, much the way cyanide can be isolated from almonds. The plant grows to heights of six feet or more and often it is cultivated for its ornamental appeal. After its large yellow and red capsule-like flowers have finished their bloom the beans can be harvested. Occasionally, ricin poisoning is suspected in a mysterious death, but proof is difficult to obtain. The lethal toxin is not detectable once the victim has succumbed, making it a deadly weapon leaving no trace.

One such case in London has become a textbook example. In 1978, operatives of the Bulgarian Secret Police were suspected of assassinating dissident and fellow countryman Georgi Markov, who had defected nine years earlier, using poison injected from the tip of a modified umbrella. Doctors considered a range of toxins in Markov's death but could find no trace of poison. Markov's autopsy did, however, uncover a minute, silver-colored metallic ball. The tiny sphere had been hollowed out with what appeared to be a thin drill bit passed through the pellet in opposite directions. But when the examiners tested the sphere they again found no telltale chemicals. The physicians then reviewed the physical damage that had been done to Markov's tissues. Symptoms of ricin toxicity and the resulting injuries to internal organs had been studied in animals. The damage seen in the studies mirrored what the medical team found in Markov. These findings led a majority of the Scotland Yard investigators to speculate that ricin had filled the tiny hollow sphere.[1] Years later, during the early 1990s, a former Soviet spy and KGB general confirmed their suspicions. The Russian defector revealed that Markov had been targeted using pinhead-size ricin pellets, and further implicated KGB scientists with supplying the pellets to the Bulgarians.[2]

While ricin has occasionally served as a tool for assassins, it is not suited for fine powder floating in the air. The toxin has a limited life span in the open. Sunlight, heat, and humidity work together to degrade ricin at a rate that makes it impractical for uses other than isolated poisonings and assassinations.[3] Biochemists have developed simple tests for the presence of ricin, but its limitations as a weapon of widespread destruction made more sophisticated advances in ricin forensics of debatable value. Anthrax—with its ability to rise effortlessly in the air, find its way deep into lungs, and survive harsh environments—is a different story.

The post-9/11 anthrax crisis presented new challenges in forensic science. In contrast to ricin, which consists of a single protein,[4] *anthracis* contains thousands of unique proteins, many made up of multiple peptide chains. The bacterium also requires three separate and distinct strands of DNA to fully function. It produces lipids for its cell wall, incorporates different isotopes of chemical building blocks, and contains traces of various elements.[5] All these components represented potential sources for unique forensic signatures.

Coordinating the analyses performed by state public health laboratories from New York to Florida, private contract labs located around the country, Atlanta's CDC, Keim's lab in Flagstaff, and John Ezzell in Maryland consumed Stanley's days. When not on the telephone inquiring about test results or asking when the next set of samples was scheduled for testing, he studied. He reviewed the growth requirements of anthrax; the types of culture media the bacteria needed for a food source and the conditions necessary for efficient spore production. And then, what methods are used for converting wet spores into a powder? Understanding the process would add specific scientific skills to the profile developed by the behavioral analysts in Quantico. I offered to help with the coordination, especially in the area of genetics and DNA, my area of experience, but first I had to get the office to agree to transfer me to the growing task force. Stanley suggested that I submit a request to the special agent in charge, Art Eberhart.

Leaving the break room, we walked into the hallway past a row of three elevators and down a short corridor. As we turned a corner and approached an open door a mix of ringing telephones, tapping keyboards, and spirited conversations greeted us. Stepping through the doorway, we entered what had been a training classroom only a month before. Special agents and analysts now filled the small room. They sat behind rows of narrow, brown cafeteria-style folding tables. Keyboards, computers, and flat-screen monitors crowded together on tabletops. An endless array of orange fiber-optic cables, black power cords, and gray wires ran across the floor between table legs and under chairs. Telephones rang constantly, and agents, postal inspectors, and analysts shouted questions back and forth.

We edged our way between the rows and to the back of the room. Stanley introduced me to Tom Dellafera, on loan from the US Postal Inspection Service. He stood and offered his hand with a wide smile. A third-generation postal employee originally from Connecticut, he had supervised a squad of postal inspectors headquartered in the Brentwood Processing and Distribution Center. When testing revealed contamination throughout the Brentwood facility, postal management had quarantined the facility, including Dellafera's office and everything—papers, files, equipment, and personal items—it contained. So, the Postal Inspection Service had assigned, or detailed, the seasoned investigator to the FBI and the new anthrax task force. For the indefinite future he would provide coordination with the postal inspectors. He smiled again as we said goodbye. He seemed like a perfect addition to our expanding team.

As we turned to leave, I glanced up at the white dry-erase board covering the front wall. The victims of the anthrax attack had been listed on the left side, both those surviving and the ones deceased. In the center of the board, written at the top in black, was a term I had never heard before, *PERSONS OF INTEREST*. Underneath, two names topped a handwritten list: *BioPort* and *Steven Jay Hatfill*.[6] Notes scribbled next to his name indicated that in spite of having his security clearance suspended, Hatfill had left the country for the United Kingdom to attend a two-week training course in weapons of mass destruction inspections. He was due back at the end of the week. The squad had requested authorization from the US Attorney's Office to review his bank statements, credit card records, and telephone logs. Hatfill's employment file placed him at work in Northern Virginia prior to each of the mailings. The reason for suspending his personal security clearance added further to the suspicion—he had failed at least one polygraph examination in the preceding months.

BioPort, the troubled manufacturer of the anthrax vaccine, also raised suspicions. The profit factor stood out as prime motivation. The squad learned that its German-born CEO had spent his childhood in the Sudan and recently worked in Saudi Arabia. The company kept anthrax spores on hand to test vaccine efficacy.[7] Further adding to the interest, BioPort's General Counsel was under a federal indictment for a variety of offenses. Investigators realized that it might all be coincidence, but BioPort had to be examined closely. Agents quickly drafted requests for court authorizations seeking bank statements and credit reports. The case against the General Counsel was reviewed and the company's Internet provider identified in preparation for court-authorized access to electronic mail.

Also taped to the white dry-erase board was a four-page press release. Following their October 24 briefing on the preliminary assessment and sending a final assessment to the task force five days later, the Behavioral Analysis Unit in Quantico had drafted a carefully worded public version. It described several peculiarities in the way the addresses and content of the letters had been written, oddities potentially recognizable as belonging to a friend, coworker, or family member. Comparing unique phrases and writing style had been successful in identifying mathematician and Montana hermit Ted Kaczynski as the infamous Unabomber six years earlier.[8]

On November 9, FBI management had authorized the release of the Behavioral Unit's linguistic assessment of the anthrax letters:[9]

Previous high-profile investigations conducted by the FBI involving writings were solved with the help of the public in identifying the author by either how he wrote, or what he wrote. We are asking for the public's help here again in the same way.

While the text in these letters is limited, there are certain distinctive characteristics evident within the writing style of the author. They may have been used in other letters, greeting cards, or envelopes written by him. Perhaps someone has received a correspondence from this person and will recognize some of these characteristics:

A. The author uses dashes ("-") in the writing of the date "09-11-01."
B. In writing the number one, the author chooses to use a formalized, more detailed version. He writes it as "1" instead of the simple vertical line.[10]

A psychological profile of the anthrax mailer accompanied the writing analysis. The appraisal contained descriptors such as *adult male, loner, nonconfrontational*. The profilers stressed the mailer's knowledge of science and the ease of working with hazardous materials. They also mentioned the allusions to "Allah" and "Israel" in the letters—they were of the opinion that both terms were meant to mislead, and the misspelling, "penacilin," was intentional. Our suspicions of al-Qaeda being responsible for the anthrax mailings began to fade.

The press release prompted several individuals to call with information about who the mailer might be. Dr. Bruce Ivins telephoned the tiny FBI office in Frederick, Maryland, with one of those tips. In response to Ivins's telephone call, the Frederick office dispatched its two agents to talk to him about his suspicions. Ivins told the special agents he was a senior member of the US Army's Bacteriology Division at USAMRIID, and had been instrumental in anthrax vaccine development and production. Until recently, the army had viewed his vaccine work as critical. In December 1997, Secretary of Defense William S. Cohen went so far as to mandate that all US soldiers, sailors, and airmen receive the inoculation. However, claims of the vaccine being connected to Gulf War Syndrome in veterans, an illness characterized by fatigue, headaches, and memory problems, made Cohen's directive controversial. Severe criticism by the media followed.[11] Compounding the health and safety concerns, officials at the Pentagon began to view a widespread battlefield attack with anthrax as unlikely. Further, problems plagued the vaccine's manufacturing process, making an adequate supply difficult to maintain. BioPort, the sole licensee for making the vaccine, had lost FDA approval. Last year, the army had directed Ivins and his coworkers to assess BioPort's capabilities. Also in year 2000, Ivins had coauthored a patent application for a new generation of vaccine developed through genetic engineering, which Ivins clearly hoped would replace the decades-old, controversial BioPort product.[12]

Ivins wanted the FBI to be aware of one of the coinventors on the patent filing. The researcher, Joseph Farchaus, had left USAMRIID for a pharmaceutical company in New Jersey sometime in the past. Farchaus now resided a short drive from the recently closed Hamilton mail center. Ivins described Farchaus as very bright but controversial, an intimidating person who exhibited a bad temper when the two had worked together. Farchaus hated "anyone in green," referring to army personnel, and "had access to *B. anthracis*, (and) the knowledge about how to disseminate it." As the agents thanked Ivins and stood up to leave the cluttered office he shared with his two technicians, he made a request. He asked the agents to conceal his identity when they interviewed Farchaus. Farchaus had "made comments threatening several associates"—often enough to worry Ivins.[13, 14]

The following morning, the task force added Joseph Farchaus to their Persons of Interest list. Two criteria had to be fulfilled in order for an individual to be added and remain on the list: (1) the ability to be in the Trenton, New Jersey, area at the time of both mailings, and (2) access to the Ames strain of anthrax at some point in the past. The first criteria would be straightforward to substantiate. Cell phone records, credit card usage, time sheets from workplaces—all could establish a person's whereabouts during the windows for the mailings. The second criteria would be more difficult. We had no idea—nor did those running the nation's top anthrax research programs, including Paul Keim[15] and John Ezzell—which laboratories contained Ames.

The next day, a fifth name was added to the list of deceased victims. Ottilie Lundgren, a ninety-four-year-old resident of rural Oxford, Connecticut, succumbed to inhalational anthrax. A team of epidemiologists departed Atlanta to meet with Connecticut Department of Public Health counterparts. Three weeks had passed since the last known anthrax infection. Concern was high that Lundgren's infection could be the harbinger of a new attack.[16] The epidemiologists descended on the town of Oxford and began taking samples. Postal inspectors scoured the area's post offices. The teams learned that due to Lundgren's age, she had depended on friends and relatives to get around town and to help with errands such as shopping. During interviews, the investigators quickly determined Lundgren's activities and the people and places she had visited during the past sixty days.

The success in being able to determine recent activities had not been possible in the case of Kathy Nguyen. Nguyen had also lived alone but had no known relatives in New York City, and she had commuted to work by herself.[17] The interviews in Oxford confirmed, as with Nguyen, that Lundgren had no known connections to media outlets or politicians. At the CDC laboratory, genetic testing identified Ames as the strain of anthrax that had coursed through her blood, firmly linking Lundgren to the casualties in Florida, Washington, New Jersey, and New York.

The following week the front office called me—they agreed with my request and transferred me to the anthrax task force. I would be partnering with Scott Stanley, and together we would work with the scientists in the Forensic Science Research Unit at Quantico to tackle a new discipline we began calling microbial forensics.

Stanley and I sat down to divide up the work. We had already outgrown the classroom, so we commandeered a small room attached to the office's Command and Tactical Operations Center (CTOC). We were joined by another agent[18] with a chemistry background and began to identify our future work. My duties would include staying in contact with the outside scientists, such as Paul Keim, and begin to coordinate a genetic analysis of the mailed Ames anthrax. I would also take up what agents in Miami had begun—tracing the travels of the Ames strain. Once I had identified all the places that maintained stocks of Ames, we would collect samples from each facility. Each sample, known as an exemplar, would be traceable to its location, time of collection, and attached to a specific person's identity.

Our plan was to eventually use the collection of Ames to trace the origin of the mailed spores. It would require first identifying a genetic difference between the mailed Ames and the majority of Ames anthrax used in laboratories such as Keim's and Ezzell's. If the mailed anthrax were identical to every sample of Ames we hoped to collect, it would do nothing to pinpoint from which lab the mailed Ames originated. In essence, we needed to separate the strain known as Ames into substrains. Keim was already hard at work fine-tuning his MLVA testing system—he had added seven additional genetic loci to the original eight also in use at the CDC. But he was having no luck finding a unique feature distinguishing the mailed Ames. Then, late in November, he telephoned me with surprising news.

A Maryland-based company that had pioneered the science of whole genome DNA sequencing in the late 1990s told him they could distinguish Robert Stevens's Ames isolate from a common laboratory isolate of Ames. They claimed the Stevens's isolate differed in at least seventeen DNA locations compared to an Ames isolate they had acquired from the large national public health laboratory located in Porton Down, England.

Keim's news alarmed me. When I told Scott Stanley, he was also shocked. We had no knowledge that the company, The Institute for Genomic Research in Rockville, known by its acronym TIGR and pronounced "tiger," had gotten a sample of the Stevens isolate. Ideally, we, and law enforcement officials in general, keep a close hold on evidence—it's not made available to outside groups without prior consent of the collecting department and only with a compelling reason. But in the wake of the anthrax attacks on the heels of 9/11, normal evidentiary controls and procedures sometimes took second place as safety and security became the foremost consideration. However TIGR had gotten access to the Stevens's anthrax DNA,[19] and if what they had found held up, it would be a huge breakthrough for us.

I asked Keim if he could begin to reproduce the TIGR results, but I didn't need to; he had already started. I made a mental note to contact him frequently and report his progress in our weekly science briefings to Headquarters. I also realized that we needed to visit with TIGR's scientists in nearby Rockville.

10

A Forensic Strategy

December 2001

While I began planning the genetics with Paul Keim, Scott Stanley coordinated the opening of the Leahy letter. He had seen firsthand the volatility of the powder from its forerunner, Senator Daschle's letter. Opening the envelope had allowed its contents to contaminate more than two dozen buildings. John Ezzell, the US Army's anthrax expert in Frederick who examined the traces of powder remaining, had gasped when the spores rose—using their own inherent energy—inside his sealed glovebox. The dry anthrax had exhibited a static energy, and Stanley suspected the Leahy envelope contents would act the same. He speculated that the powder had built up static charge during the Leahy letter's constant contact and rubbing against mail during its travels from Trenton to Capitol Hill, and the charge transferred to the letter's fine powder. The contact and abrading resulted in a transfer and loss of electrons from the powder, resulting in an unbalance of electrical charge in the powder. Upon opening the envelope, the light powder would seek to neutralize the unbalance and fly off in search of positive charges. Stanley needed to preserve every bit of the powder for the battery of genetic, microbiological, chemical, and physical testing already under discussion with scientists around the country.

Conferring with experts in chemistry and physical science, Stanley decided that polonium would be his best option. The highly radioactive element has few practical uses, but one is neutralizing static electricity.[1] Dr. Marie Curie, with the help of her physicist husband, Pierre, discovered the rare metalloid in 1898. Already having established that uranium caused the air surrounding it to conduct electricity, Curie found a material that was several-fold more active than uranium.[2] Sometimes referred to as "Radium F," Curie named polonium after her native Poland in an effort to highlight that country's lack of unified independence.[3] The first woman to be awarded a doctoral degree in France, Curie would later die of complications from her years of unprotected exposure to radiation; amounts so high that her scientific papers and even her personal cookbook are stored in lead due to the high levels of contamination emanating from them.[4, 5]

More recently, polonium has become a topic of discussion in law enforcement circles. Russian operatives are suspected of using it to assassinate former Federal Security Service officer Alexander Litvinenko in London during 2006. Initially, the cause of Litvinenko's disabling illness confounded his attending physicians until a cancer surgeon passed by Litvinenko's hospital room and remarked, "How long has this guy been getting radiation treatment?" New Scotland Yard crime scene analysts found high levels of polonium contaminating areas of Litvinenko's apartment, and Litvinenko's autopsy results revealed organ and tissue damage consistent with radiation poisoning.[6] The United Kingdom's Atomic Weapons Establishment confirmed Litvinenko's blood and urine contained polonium, and in January 2016 the British government published its final report.[7]

Once Stanley had settled on polonium to neutralize the static charge expected in the Leahy powder, he asked John Ezzell to help. The letter would be opened in Ezzell's airtight, clear acrylic glovebox, the same one used to open the Daschle letter. First, Ezzell meticulously cleaned the inside of the glovebox; no trace of the friable powder could remain to contaminate the Leahy letter. Ezzell extended his arms through the glovebox's dual portholes and moved his fingers deliberately in the heavy white rubber gloves as he wiped over the clear surfaces. The inner layer of thin latex gloves kept his hands soaked in sweat, an occasional drop leaking out and rolling down his forearm to his elbow and onto the sleeve of his white lab coat.

After he was satisfied that he had completely cleaned the interior surface and corners, he wiped several areas with Dacron Q-tips that had been soaked in sterile water. He then rolled the Q-tips across the surfaces of blood agar plates and placed them in an incubator. After seventy-two hours the plates were free of growth, and Ezzell was confident the glovebox was again free of spores.

Ezzell prepared for a practice run. Inside the glovebox, he clamped two lead bars that had been coated with a thin layer of polonium onto small, gray metal tripods, and placed them to the right and left. The polonium continually released positively charged helium ions, known as alpha radiation, into the air of the plastic chamber. These alpha particles pulled electrons from the air's oxygen and nitrogen molecules, resulting in a mix of negatively and positively charged molecules that would neutralize any unbalanced charge contained in the spore powder.

Between the polonium rods, Ezzell placed a third tripod stand. To the rod, Ezzell clamped a clear glass vial labeled with a bar code. The vial, already tested for a long list of possible contaminating elements and certified clean by its manufacturer, was sealed with a black screw cap. Immediately under the vial, Ezzell clamped an opaque, flexible plastic dish. The small tray, about six inches square, would catch any powder that missed the glass vial. Under the vial and plastic tray, he carefully laid sterile scissors, scalpel, and tweezers on a piece of aluminum foil; the foil would catch any powder that might miss the tray. All of the items—the polonium and stands, the foil and the stainless steel instruments—had been wrapped in separate pieces of aluminum foil and sterilized in an autoclave the night before. Finally, Ezzell returned to the glass vial. He carefully unscrewed the cap and placed it on the aluminum foil beside the scalpel.

As Ezzell worked, Stanley stood out in the hallway outside the containment lab and watched through a two-foot-square window. Ezzell began cutting open a blank unused envelope, doubling his concentration as he held the scissors, his gloved fingers barely fitting into the scissors's finger holes. After slicing across the envelope's top edge and struggling to exchange the scissors for tweezers, he slowly pulled out a folded sheet of paper. Ezzell unfolded the paper and held it steady; Stanley could see a small pile of gray test powder lying in the creases. Holding the paper over the lip of the glass jar and pressing its folds into the shape of a funnel, Ezzell gently tapped the underside with his forefinger. The fine powder suddenly flowed down the paper and into the jar where it settled at the bottom. Finally, he continued opening the letter. As Ezzell straightened each crease, he looked across the paper's white surface to ensure that no powder remained. The letter now flat, he briefly held it up to the front of the glovebox. On the day Ezzell opened the actual Leahy letter, Stanley would take digital photographs of the wording.

Stanley pushed the button on his two-way radio. "Great work John! It looks like a go. Just a couple more dry runs and we should have it."

Ezzell, his face perspiring under the clear plastic hood completely enclosing his head, exhaled and managed a weak smile.

Once back at his desk in the Washington Field Office, Stanley typed up the plan that he and Ezzell would follow to open the Leahy letter. As he was getting ready to brief the front office, his telephone rang. "Scott, it's John. We may have found something you'd be interested in."

Stanley recognized Ezzell's North Carolina drawl. "Hi, John. What'd you find?"

"Terry has been doing some confirmation tests on the spores from the Daschle letter," Ezzell said, referring to his lab technician, Terry Abshire.

Abshire, a wispily built longtime Frederick resident with a penchant for turquoise and silver jewelry, had been culturing anthrax for the past twenty years, and Ezzell considered her one of the most experienced anthrax scientists in the country.

"She found some odd colonies growing out of the powder. We're not sure what they are, but they might be something that could be useful."

"Thanks, John, can I stop by tomorrow morning to meet with you and Terry?"

"Sure, we'll be here. The coffee and doughnuts will be waiting." Ezzell hung up his receiver.

Early the next morning, Stanley left his northern Virginia house and drove straight to Fort Detrick. He walked up to the front entrance of USAMRIID, through the double glass doors and around the walk-through metal detector. Following the narrow stairway to the second floor, he found Ezzell's small office and knocked.

"Hi, Scott, come in," Ezzell said. "Let me call Terry and she can tell you what she's been seeing. She let some of her culture plates sit in the incubator past seventy-two hours and started finding colonies with unusual shapes. We find that in older plates that have sat for a while. Sometimes it's contamination and not anthrax. Sometimes it's anthrax with spontaneous mutants beginning to appear. But maybe it's something useful. She's seeing the same thing in the powder from both Daschle and *New York Post* letters."

Terry Abshire joined them in Ezzell's cluttered office and found a seat.

"Yes, I really forgot the plates. I was doing some confirmation testing, just finishing up all the tests: ECL,[8] gamma-phage and looking at the morphology. The cultures were overgrown by the time I checked them. But on the plates that I diluted out for colony counting, I saw some different shapes. They looked like slow sporulators."

Stanley immediately recognized the significance of Abshire's observation. He knew the sporulation process that anthrax undergoes is a widespread phenomenon utilized by many bacteria species when nutrients become scarce. What makes the process so fascinating to microbiologists is the fact that at a time when the organism's food grows scarce, sporulation requires a great deal of energy. The bacteria cell switches on hundreds of otherwise dormant genes in its DNA, and an elaborate relay system comes into play. A cascade of phosphorylation, the exchange of phosphate molecules, begins. This transfer of phosphate groups, the currency of energy in living things, is costly for the bacteria cell. The *spoOA* gene is the final switch in this relay of phosphate exchange;[9] the end result is a heat- and weather-resistant spore in place of the metabolizing cell. The spores can exist for decades without nutrition. In the case of anthrax, it is these spores, once dried, that make such a deadly weapon.

"Scott, this is more than we can do in my lab, to really check out these mutants, if that's what they are," Ezzell said. "You might go see Pat Worsham in the Bact Division.[10] She just published a paper on anthrax sporulation mutants; she calls them *spo* mutants.[11] She describes different mutations in the sporulation genes. That's what you might have here. I'll let her know you'll be calling her, if you want."

"OK, but can you send isolates of these potential slow sporulators to Paul Keim? He'll be able to confirm if they're Ames strain or not. And can you give them a code? Don't label them Daschle or *Post*, okay?"[12] Stanley said as he stood up to leave.

Stanley realized if the odd colonies were part of the anthrax mailed to Daschle and the *New York Post*, and not contamination that had accidently found its way onto Abshire's culture plates, they could represent a unique signature for the mailed spores. The signature would serve as a morphological fingerprint and could be compared with the samples of Ames that I would be collecting. On the other hand, the oddly shaped colonies also might be the result of mutations occurring after Abshire placed the tiny bits of powder in water and spread them on blood-red agar. If that were the case, the aberrant colonies would be of little value to the investigation.

Stanley thanked Ezzell and Abshire and walked back down the narrow stairway to the first floor and through the silent hallways until he came to the Bacteriology Division offices. A nameplate on the light green cinderblock wall read, "P. L. Worsham, Ph.D." He knocked on the door adjacent to the name. Not hearing a response, he slid a card under the door and left for Washington.

Back at the Washington Field Office, I began looking for laboratories that kept stocks of Ames. The Miami FBI agents had started the search the day Robert Stevens had been diagnosed with inhalational anthrax. Working with the CDC, they identified laboratories in the United States that had requested authorization to transfer anthrax. The CDC's regulatory oversight came about when Congress enacted a new section of the Antiterrorism and Effective Death Penalty Act of 1996. Prior to their action, the United States had no requirement for individuals or institutions to be either licensed or registered in order to ship or receive pathogenic organisms such as anthrax. Congress passed the regulation in response to the country's growing concern over the threat of biological terrorism. The Act directed the US Department of Health and Human Services to establish a list of biological organisms and toxins deemed a threat to public safety and regulate their transfer. The Department handed this responsibility to the CDC.

As soon as Beecher announced the identification of the Stevens's anthrax strain, the Miami agents had sent subpoenas to the CDC-registered anthrax labs for any information about Ames. Upon designation of the Washington Field Office as Office of Origin, Miami sent copies of their investigative materials to Washington, including the incoming answers to their Ames subpoena. The results now lay in front of me; of the ninety-two laboratories located across the country that had shipped or received live anthrax since 1996, twenty-seven still had not responded. I began drafting a second subpoena to follow up. If an institution did have the Ames strain, I then asked, whom had they gotten it from, and when and where had they sent it?

My search did not stop with the CDC transfer records. I requested the FBI Laboratory's library conduct searches of scientific journals for mention of anthrax. The staff found anthrax mentioned in research projects as far away as France and Sweden. I contacted the US Patent Office across town and requested a search of patent applications. My list of anthrax laboratories grew to 103 institutions.

December began with the opening of the Leahy letter. The careful planning and dry runs had paid off. Ezzell, with Stanley and several FBI agents and scientists pressing against the small window, cut open the envelope and poured out a small bit of fine powder—powder appearing identical to that from Daschle's letter—into the clear glass vial. Using tweezers, he worked the letter from its envelope. The mailer had folded the note in an odd configuration so that most of the powder was contained.[13] Ezzell partially unfolded the letter and began pouring its tan contents into the vial when suddenly the letter slipped, nearly sliding through Ezzell's gloved fingers. A collective "Owwww!" sounded from the FBI crowd.

"I heard that!" answered a southern drawl from Stanley's two-way radio. Ezzell's jaw tightened as he strained to hide the slight smile beginning to cross his face. Without looking up, he continued following the typed protocol taped to the side of the glovebox. The polonium did its job and neutralized any static charges present—none of the powder escaped.[14]

As soon as Ezzell finished pouring, he held up the flattened letter and turned the writing toward his audience. Through the small glass window Stanley photographed the letter as he read, "09-11-01 YOU CAN NOT STOP US. WE HAVE THIS ANTHRAX. YOU DIE NOW. ARE YOU AFRAID? DEATH TO AMERICA. DEATH TO ISRAEL. ALLAH IS GREAT." This was an exact copy of Senator Daschle's letter; the wording was identical.[15]

As December passed, 91 of the 103 laboratories had responded to the question of possessing Ames; 29 answered in the affirmative. Our next step would be to begin collecting exemplars of the Ames and establish a repository for the collected specimens. After consulting with Doug Beecher and Paul Keim, and discussing with Ezzell the best way to sample and ship live cultures of anthrax, I started drafting a protocol. I also began a search for a secure storage location. The FBI Laboratory on the third floor of the Hoover Building would have been my first choice, but it had no microbiology or containment facilities for anthrax.[16]

Within days after receiving the strangely shaped isolates that Abshire had grown from several of the odd colonies, Keim telephoned me to confirm that they were anthrax and not contamination by another species of bacteria. Then, using his eight-gene MLVA test, he verified they were also the Ames strain. In a way, this was bad news. Had the odd bacteria colonies been a nonanthrax species, it might have provided the mailed powder with a unique signature to look for once we began to collect Ames exemplars. Even so, if Keim could show that the odd-shaped Ames were due to changes in DNA, they might still be a useful signature—if we could design a test for screening the future Ames collection. I relayed the news to Stanley.

The following day, Stanley drove back to USAMRIID to meet with Pat Worsham and follow up on Ezzell's and Abshire's observations. Stanley introduced himself and explained that he was part of the FBI team tracing the production of the recent anthrax attack spores. Worsham began by reviewing her work on anthrax sporulation mutants. She designed her research to decipher the genes responsible for controlling the phosphorylation cascade that triggered spore formation. Recent work had been slowed due to a recent trip to Boca Raton where she played a consulting role in the anthrax sampling at the AMI building.

Stanley told Worsham about the discovery of possible sporulation mutants in the mailed powders. He described the unusual colonies and how they differed from the majority of the colonies referred to as *wild-type* colonies—how their appearance varied in size, shape, and color. Together, they began to plan experiments. Stanley then asked Ezzell to transfer minute amounts of powder from the *New York Post*, Daschle, and Leahy letters to Worsham, and as he had done with the latest Keim shipment, replace the sample's origin with a code.

Worsham would first look at whether the late-appearing colonies arose from mutations occurring spontaneously during growth on culture plates. Only if the odd colonies were present in the mailed powder might they serve as a signature for tracing back to the sender.

Worsham and her laboratory technician diluted miniscule amounts of the highly concentrated Daschle material in sterile water. They made a series of dilutions, each successive dilution one-tenth the concentration of its parent. They labeled culture plates in triplicate and according to which titration would be spread across the agar. They designated times to periodically check the cultures until seventy-two hours had passed.

The time course study convinced Worsham that the variants were present in the powder and not the result of spontaneous mutations. Each of the three plates at the same dilution, from the same letter, contained equivalent numbers and shapes of the variant colonies; the differences in morphology appeared to be about 3 to 5 percent of the total colonies.

Worsham and Stanley then turned to the question of stability and asked if the morphology variant colonies would revert back to the wild-type Ames morphology. If the variants reverted as the culture plates incubated, it would suggest environmental conditions, such as nutrition levels, caused their odd growth patterns.

Worsham began the stability experiment by selecting several of the variant colonies at the end of the seventy-two-hour growth study. Looking closely at the variants, she noticed differences between them—one had a slight yellowish tint, and another grew flat, gray, and spread out with smooth edges, rather than the wild type's tightly growing white colony with rough edges. Worsham wondered if several types of variants existed. She began to pick single odd-shaped colonies from agar plates of diluted samples derived from each of the letters: *New York Post*, Daschle, and Leahy. She selected a large, smooth-edged colony with a bull's-eye center and labeled it *A*; then a smaller colony—but still larger than the bright white, rough-edged wild-type colonies—with a double bull's-eye and called it *B*; then one equal in size to the wild type, but colored yellow. It would be known as *C*.

Worsham divided each variant sample; one portion would be archived in her freezer. She diluted the other portion and spread it across blood-red agar, again in triplicate, and placed the palm-sized plastic dishes in her incubator at a constant temperature of 37° centigrade. After seventy-two hours, she found plates of pure, A, B, and C colonies. She repeated the subculturing, setting up new dilution plates of now pure variant colonies and again checking after three days at 37° C, and found that none of the variants had reverted to wild type.

I was particularly interested in the experiments Stanley coordinated with Pat Worsham. From Keim's work, we already knew the odd-shaped colonies were variants of the Ames strain. Worsham's experiments proved the variants existed in the mailed powder, and they represented a signature to use for attribution—identifying the mailer. The stability studies showed the variants cultured true from generation to generation, which indicate changes—mutations—had taken place in their DNA at some point prior to the mailings. But if Keim confirmed TIGR's finding of seventeen mutations in the Steven's isolate versus wild-type Ames, we might already have a signature to build a screening test around. After hearing Stanley's news, I placed a call to Keim and left a voice message.

When Keim called back, he had disappointing news. While comparing notes with the TIGR scientists, they had revised the original seventeen genetic differences between the Stevens's isolate and the Porton Down wild-type Ames down to four, maybe five. And more frustrating, each of the four to five was a single base pair change in the DNA, rather than a larger insertion or deletion of DNA sequence. Building a screening test around single base pairs would be challenging. The entire anthrax DNA sequence contained over five million base pairs, each doublet a combination of four chemical compounds: adenine, cytosine, guanine, and thymine. Adenine paired itself with a thymine and guanine aligned with a cytosine. The five million pairs stacked on top of each other, twisting thirty-six degrees with the addition of each pair, formed the iconic DNA double helix.[17] A change in one base pair of five million was a signature, but not one easy to build upon.

And then, during a second call to Keim, he told me he had abandoned comparing the Stevens isolate with the one from Porton Down. Originally thought to represent a wild-type Ames, he had learned Porton scientists had mutated its Ames in an effort to remove one of its two DNA satellite molecules. Removing one or both of these molecules, known as plasmids,[18] from wild-type anthrax undid its lethality. But in curing their Ames isolate of lethality in order to study how its toxicity came about, the scientists had also introduced mutations into its large central DNA genome molecule. The Porton Down Ames was an outlier. It did not represent an original wild-type Ames, and further comparison with the mailed Ames or Stevens's would be wasted effort.

Soon after getting the disappointing news from Keim, Stanley telephoned me from USAMRIID. Darin Steele, a microbiologist in the Hazardous Materials Response Unit at Quantico, had been assigned to work at USAMRIID as the crisis grew on Capitol Hill. USAMRIID had become inundated with test samples. For the next several months Steele served as the FBI's on-site representative, helping John Ezzell organize and track samples while reporting results to our task force.

Before joining the FBI, Steele, a native Alabaman, had earned a doctorate degree in protein chemistry at the Crimson Tide's Birmingham campus. From there he had gone to work in northern New Jersey's pharmaceutical industry.

In the late 1990s, he applied to the FBI Laboratory, and human resources assigned him to the Hazardous Materials Response Unit, where he quickly learned the biology of anthrax.

Naturally friendly with a slight and disarming southern drawl, he started up discussions in USAMRIID's hallways and break rooms, where the topic of Ames and anthrax frequently came up. In one instance, Bruce Ivins started to relate how he might know the whereabouts of the original Ames isolate; a sample sent to USAMRIID in the early 1980s. Steele followed Ivins into one of the biosafety laboratory suites. On a refrigerator shelf lay a cardboard mailing tube labeled, "Department of the Army" and "Attn: Gregory B. Knudson, Ph.D." and postmarked: "FEB 18 '81." The tube bore a label with prepaid postage and a return address of the US Department of Agriculture laboratories in Ames, Iowa, but the note inside was signed TVMDL, an acronym for Texas A&M Veterinary Medical Diagnostic Laboratory. The tube had been mailed from TVMDL's second largest facility in Amarillo, Texas.[19] Inside the tube, Steele found a small glass vial partially filled with dry yellow agar. Faint gray streaks stretched across the agar's surface—anthrax spores in their chilled dormant state.

I relayed the news to Paul Keim, and we made plans to approach TIGR about replacing the controversial Porton Down Ames with the rediscovered 1981 parent.

While we worked on developing a plan for genetic and microbiology analysis, Headquarters and our front office advanced the administrative side of the investigation. They approved formation of two separate squads, Amerithrax-1 and Amerithrax-2 (AMX-1, AMX-2), together forming an Amerithrax Task Force. We would be FBI special agents, postal inspectors, intelligence analysts, and a scientist on loan from the CDC. AMX-1 would be responsible for investigating leads not science related. They put Steve Hatfill at the top of their list. Special Agent in Charge Art Eberhart assigned Stanley and me to AMX-2. We would be responsible for coordinating forensic projects, most still new and untested. We moved our desks, files, and computers to the seventh floor of the Washington Field Office and contacted scientists we knew at Quantico, members of the Forensic Science Research Unit. They would be able to guide us in designing forensic tests for carbon-14 dating, attribution through stable isotope analysis, and trace analysis of agar and nutrients used in bacterial cultures.

11

Collecting Ames

February 2002

By midwinter, I had narrowed the original list of 103 laboratories working with anthrax in the United States to seventeen that possessed Ames before the mailings. But my dilemma was where to house our repository. I knew storing potential evidence would fall within the spirit of the memorandum of agreement the FBI had signed with USAMRIID when I was in the Hazmat Response Unit, and I decided to drive to Frederick to meet with John Ezzell.

I found Ezzell in his second-floor office. He had been helping me draft the sampling and shipping protocol we would send the Ames laboratories, but I had yet to mention needing a place for intake processing and storage.

"John, where could we keep the Ames? I don't know how many we'll get, maybe a hundred, little more."

"It's pretty tight around here, Scott. You've seen the size of my office. Since September 11 and then the letter on Capitol Hill, we've been at it twenty-four hours a day, every day. Even the little break room down the hall got taken over as a command center."

"I know, John, but this is priority. You know we wouldn't ask if we didn't have to. If we can get the commander to agree to give up a lab room, do you think we need to renovate completely?"

"We should strip it down to the paint, bleach all surfaces. We'll QC[1] the decontamination by swabbing and culturing. We can't afford even the perception that any of the samples got cross-contaminated. And we should buy all new equipment: a laminar flow safety hood, refrigerator and -70 freezer. Used equipment is too risky, even if we decontaminated it."

"Sounds good, John. Can you place the orders and we'll see about getting money MIPR'd over?[2] Can we make it priority?"

We went on to plan a protocol for the samples once they arrived. Ezzell agreed to assign Terry Abshire to process the arriving Ames samples, and I made a request to the Hazmat Unit for Darin Steele to assist. I found out that he had been accepted for a slot in new agent class at the FBI Academy. I knew he had been applying and training to decrease his running times and increase his pushups, pullups, and situps. I also found out the Academy would hold the slot for him until work at USAMRIID slowed; this was the first time I had heard of that—a reflection on the respect the Training Division held for him and the work being done by Amerithrax.

The live samples would arrive as duplicates growing on commercially available agar glass vial slants—named for the agar solidified at an angle to increase surface area. Abshire and Steele would photograph each shipment that came in and store the overnight shipping labels, and then take one of the duplicate slants and prepare ten small vials containing liquid agar and 10 percent glycerol. It had been learned long ago by microbiologists that as little as 10 percent glycerol will prevent complete freezing of bacteria at temperatures as cold as -70 degrees centigrade. The bacteria cells take up the glycerol, which in turn will displace the water in the cell and its protein enzymes. Without glycerol, ice crystals would form and tear apart the bacterial cell's internal structure.

"What about the second slant?" Ezzell said.

"Darin will send the second one to Northern Arizona. We've arranged with Keim to check and make sure each sample submitted is Ames. He'll check them using three mutations he has found unique to Ames.[3] His lab will also serve as a backup to store the repository, just in case something happens to your lab, John. You know, power goes out to your freezer, fire, water line break in the ceiling, something like that."

"OK, I'll let you know when the culture hood and freezer are here," Ezzell said.

The results of the traditional forensic analysis by the FBI Laboratory had been finalized as 2002 began. Just as the mailbox surveillance, canvasing veterinary clinics, university research laboratories, and milling equipment companies turned up few leads, the standard battery of forensic tests had developed little of value.

Getting to the point of being able to perform classical analysis for fibers, latent prints, composition of writing ink, and watermarks had been challenging. Once all visible powder was removed from the letter and envelope, any remaining traces had to be neutralized. The single caveat was the ionizing radiation's effect on DNA. Using the Armed Forces Radiobiology Research Institute's cobalt-60 gamma source risked damage to human DNA that might lie in the envelopes or on the surface of the letters. Both breaking chemical bonds of the double helix and crosslinking might occur. The damage would likely render the envelopes and letters untenable for future human DNA forensics.[4] We weighed the options. The possibility of finding unique or unusual fibers, a telling watermark in the paper, indented writing mistakenly left behind, trash marks from the photocopier,[5] identification of an odd and rare ink, and the biggest bonus of all—a latent print with a match in our Automated Fingerprint Identification System—were too much to ignore. We gave the go ahead.

But none of the envelopes and letters contained even a partial latent print.[6] The ink used to write the addresses and return addresses was common and of no value for tracing its origin. The document examiners could find no indented writing—impressions in the surface of the envelope and letter paper from previous writing on overlying pieces of paper. A microscopic examination did find fibers: black in the Brokaw envelope and brown in Daschle's, and black, blue, yellow, purple, and red in the Leahy envelope; these might serve as a basis for search warrants in the future, but they were not unique enough to lead us anywhere on their own.[7]

I walked into the main room of the third-floor Command and Tactical Operations Center—CTOC—as a meeting was beginning in the rear corner. In times of crisis, CTOC served as the FBI's base of field operations in Washington, DC. During the execution of search and arrest warrants at multiple locations, its rows of desks, telephones, and computers would be manned by agents and analysts serving as points of contact for the Evidence Response Team, Hazardous Materials Response Team, Special Weapons and Tactics Team, legal counsel, a media representative, and general investigation. A large display screen stretched across the front wall, displaying a timeline of events as they occurred. Now, the only noise outside our meeting was a voice on CNN in the adjoining switchboard room announcing up-to-the-minute news.

"Hello, gentlemen." I walked to the rear of the room and took a seat beside Scott Stanley, facing a small group of scientists. I knew everyone at the meeting from my four years in the Hazmat Unit. Scientists from the Forensic Science Research Unit were present, including Dr. Dean Fetterolf, and its former chief, Dr. Bruce Budowle. Fetterolf, with a doctorate in chemistry from the University of Florida, was well known for developing novel methods for detecting smuggled cocaine and explosive vapors and had assisted in the O. J. Simpson murder investigation. He had been the one to demonstrate pores in envelope paper, which helped explain the widespread contamination at the Trenton and Brentwood facilities. I had known of Budowle since my graduate school days in the Department of Human Genetics at the University of Michigan. I had read his early papers describing the beginnings of human DNA forensics. A pioneer in the field, holding a PhD in genetics from Virginia Tech, he had received the US Attorney General's Award for Exceptional Service in 1991, and he now held the position of FBI senior scientist.

Standing in front of a white dry-erase board, Budowle picked up a black marker and began to draw.

"We could use the plasmids to look for genetic signatures. Keim's work suggests the plasmids in anthrax mutate ten times faster than the genomic DNA,"[8] Budowle said as he drew two small circles followed by a much larger circle. "We're not sure why the plasmids evolve faster, but that's the thought coming out of Paul's lab now. Since the plasmids are almost thirty and fifty times smaller than the genome, the DNA sequencing will be a lot faster and cheaper. We could look at a dozen Ames samples in far less time than we could sequence a single genome."

"Can we get TIGR[9] to do the sequencing? Bruce, can you check into it?" Stanley said. "Scott, would Paul be willing to start purifying the plasmids, since TIGR doesn't have a biosafety lab or access to one, correct? Bruce, can you find out how much of each plasmid TIGR would need?"

"Sure," I replied. "His lab is starting to transfer the MLVA test to a company certified to work with select agents down in Richmond, Virginia, so Keim should have some time freed up. We've been keeping him pretty busy testing samples from all the crime scenes and trying to confirm the point mutations TIGR has been reporting."

Locating Senator Leahy's letter opened doors for us. Not only could Stanley and Worsham begin to experiment and characterize the variants—a tiny speck of powder would serve Worsham for a range of experiments—the chemists could now do their work.

Fetterolf made a suggestion to the group. "We could try carbon dating the spores." At first the idea seemed implausible. I thought carbon dating only worked for items thousands of years old, but Dean persisted.

"The bomb spike in 1963 gave us a new signal of carbon-14, so now we can date items that are modern. And atomic mass spec has reduced the amount we need to milligrams," Fetterolf explained.

He went on to give us a little background on his proposal. A small percentage of carbon in the atmosphere is one of its radioactive isotopes: carbon-14. While an organism is living, it is consuming organic material, a combination of nonradioactive carbon-12 and traces of radioactive 14. As carbon-14 decays with time, it does not replenish. When an organism dies, it ceases to consume, but the ^{14}C in its system continues to decay. A University of Chicago scientist, Willard Libby, measured this decay and in 1946 published it as a way to date organic matter. The method is complicated by small fluctuations in the ^{12}C, ^{14}C ratio over time; these fluctuations can make the range of error in carbon dating significant.

But one large fluctuation between 1955 and 1963 made the technique useful for dating modern samples to within a couple of years. In late 1963 all nuclear weapon testing in the atmosphere or ocean came to an end as a result of President Kennedy signing the Nuclear Test Ban Treaty in the fall of 1963. For the decade prior to that, nuclear weapon testing had created a "Bomb Spike," measurable as a dramatic rise of radioactive carbon in the atmosphere. The banning of all open-air and underwater testing halted this steep rise in carbon-14 levels, and it begin a sharp and predictable decline. Coupled with this phenomenon, the application of accelerator mass spectrometry, known as AMS, replaced the original method of measuring radioactive carbon. AMS requires one thousand to two thousand times less material to measure carbon-14 levels than past methods.

"So, Dean, how much would we need?" Stanley said.

"Maybe a few milligrams."

"We have almost a gram—nine hundred milligrams from the Leahy letter. We have enough," Stanley confirmed.

We spent the afternoon brainstorming, throwing out ideas of chemical and physical measurements, techniques that might give us a lead. I remembered a procedure I had helped with when I spent a year working in the Geology Department at Brown University, before beginning graduate school. We studied foraminifera fossils. Rather than using radioactive isotopes of carbon to date specimens, we used stable, nonradioactive isotopes to estimate changes in ocean temperatures. Foraminifera, "forams" for short, are tiny sea organisms, and many form plankton in the seas. They live in tiny shells of calcium carbonate. For climate study purposes, the carbonate is composed of two stable carbon isotopes—^{12}C and a lessor amount of ^{13}C. Studies over the years demonstrate that the ratio of ^{12}C to ^{13}C varies with water temperature. Research ships have drilled cores from the oceans' floors, and geologists take samples along the length of the cores. The cores can be dozens of feet in length. Measuring stable isotopes in the foram shells along the length of the core is indicative of changing ocean climates through history. As ocean salinity and temperature shifted, so did the stable isotope ratios in the forams' carbonate shells.[10]

We discussed how stable isotope measurement could be applied to anthrax. I convinced Fetterolf and Budowle the technique would be valuable in matching water content to where bacteria are grown. Stable isotopes of oxygen and hydrogen, the components of water, have also been used in climatic research. We could measure the isotope ratio in the Leahy spores and possibly match it with a water sample. If the oxygen-16 to -18 isotope ratios varied with geographic area, we might produce a lead to the origin of the mailed spores. Fetterolf nodded in agreement and said he would begin a pilot project detecting stable isotopes in nonlethal spores.

Near the end of the meeting, Stanley brought up a concern that had been bothering him. We had begun to collaborate with a number of scientific experts, and now we were proposing to add more. Stanley broached what we had hoped would be an unnecessary concern: the mailer might be one of our research partners.

"What about polygraphing?" Stanley said with a slight smile. Everyone in the room was aware of the controversies surrounding lie detectors. In the past, scientists in the FBI Laboratory had argued the machines' failings. But when Director Freeh took the helm in 1993, he mandated its use across the board for hiring. Police agencies around the country also used it to screen potential officers. Most of us in the room had been subjected to its vagaries, including those investigating terrorism or weapons of mass destruction. We visited the polygraph examiner every five years.

Stanley continued, "Anyone who has or had access to the original evidence would be our guideline. It will be voluntary of course."

He pressed on, "And nondisclosures?"

Stanley relayed how he had heard that Bruce Ivins already was aware of the morphology variants in the mailed spores and had pictures of Abshire's culture work. We all agreed we needed to maintain a strict need-to-know for information sharing. Having each person on our growing forensic team sign an Agreement Not to Disclose Information form seemed prudent.

"And I suggest everything leaving Ezzell's lab be coded, all evidence. Everything sent to Arizona and then to TIGR. Even given to Pat Worsham. We need to anticipate they might be called to testify at some point. We can't have the appearance of preconceived ideas about expected results," Stanley concluded.

"Agreed. Makes perfect sense," the group answered one by one. We ended the meeting by suggesting that we present our work to an outside panel of experts, approximately every six months, with the first to be convened here at the field office in June.

The meeting began a formal expansion of our forensic projects, in particular on the chemistry side. It also ramped up the genetic work. As Keim began devising a protocol to purify the anthrax DNA plasmids so they could be sequenced at TIGR in Maryland, the FBI's Laboratory Division looked to the future. With Keim's help, they began to transfer the procedure for anthrax strain determination—the Multiple Loci Variable Analysis, MLVA test—to a small company located seventy miles south of Quantico in Richmond, Virginia. The company called itself Commonwealth Biotechnologies Incorporated, commonly known as CBI.

Collaborating with Doug Beecher, Commonwealth Biotechnologies had begun working on ways to distinguish substrains of anthrax a year before October's attacks. Beecher and Tom Reynolds, one of CBI's founders, had been looking at the five-million-base-long anthrax genome for areas containing multiple changes in its DNA. They began by comparing strains of anthrax that Keim's MLVA test easily distinguished, such as Ames and Zimbabwe, a strain that had also been named for the location of its discovery. Beecher and Reynolds reasoned that if they could identify DNA sequences where two strains differed in multiple places, these regions might represent "hot spots" in the anthrax genome—stretches of DNA prone to higher than usual rates of mutation. Hotspots from individual isolates of a single strain could then be compared with the goal of finding differences between isolates of a single strain.

By the spring of 2002, I was directing large amounts of work to Paul Keim's lab. Transferring the MLVA protocol to CBI would give us a backup facility for strain confirmation when we began receiving Ames exemplars from laboratories around the country. CBI also had experience with courtroom testimony; they provided human DNA typing services and understood forensic validation. CBI would be the ideal place to authenticate the MLVA-8 and MLVA-15 tests invented by Keim, in anticipation of future legal proceedings.

As 2002's spring arrived, the hoaxes and white powder emergencies finally subsided. This freed up Hazmat-trained agents and personnel for two ambitious projects. The first, locating the one or more mailboxes that had been used to get the anthrax letters into the postal system, would be a big step forward for what was feeling like a stalled investigation. The work had originally started in October, after the Brokaw and Daschle letters identified the area around Trenton as the likely mailing point. Postal inspectors had identified 625 blue collection boxes that supplied the Trenton Processing and Distribution Center. Each required testing.

Doug Beecher recommended sampling based on the theory of secondary aerosolization—dropping an anthrax letter through the top, swing-down drawer of a mailbox—would be expected to result in a slight release of spores. Subsequent dropped mail would put pressure on the powder-laden envelope; more spores would escape. After a postal carrier removed the letter, the lost spores would remain—rising and resettling with time as more mail dropped through the upper trap door. Over time the tiny spores would accumulate in the corners and edges of the boxes' interior. HMRU's protocol would take advantage of these aerosolization cycles.

The Philadelphia FBI's Hazardous Materials Response Team led the way. Hazmat-trained agents from Boston and as far away as San Francisco joined them. They divided themselves into two-person teams, each accompanied by a New Jersey state trooper. The teams sampled each blue collection box that fed mail to the Trenton Processing and Distribution Center, visiting locations in thirty-two towns spread across the counties of Hunterdon, Burlington, Mercer, Middlesex, Ocean, Monmouth, and Somerset. Working at night in full Hazmat gear—white Tyvek suits, purple nitrile gloves, yellow or green rubber boots, and black respirators—they hoped to draw as little attention as possible.

One by one, the group moved down the list. The first member of a sampling team unlocked a box while the second readied Q-tips and sterile collection tubes. They carefully opened the lower access door in the front of the box using keys supplied by postal inspectors. Inside, they photographed and then removed the plastic box, or "flats tub," containing the day's mail and recorded the box's identification number, the time, place, and names of team members, and assigned an evidence number and barcode label. The first team member removed a sterile, white Dacron Q-tip from its package, moistened it with a mild salt solution, and handed the swab to the second teammate. Following Beecher's protocol, the second teammate rubbed the Dacron slowly across the lower half of the back wall, repeating a zigzag pattern four times before handing the ash-colored swab back to the first team member. Then they wiped a second dampened Q-tip through the corners and around the outer edges of the floor. Satisfied they had done a thorough job and recorded all the necessary identifying information, they replaced the mail, relocked the access door, and wrote down the time.[11] By the beginning of the summer of 2002, they had tested several hundred collection boxes—all without finding anthrax.

Doubly ambitious was our second sampling project. A circle was drawn around Hamilton, New Jersey, and its radius approximating a reasonable driving time. We then began to search the circle for any facility that might use a laminar flow safety cabinet, glovebox, or milling machine. Finally, we sent a request to the Hazmat Response Unit in Quantico—would it be possible to sample every biological containment device within driving range of Trenton?

The Hazmat Unit assigned the project to their newly promoted supervisory special agent from the Phoenix FBI office, Terry L. Kerns. Prior to joining the FBI, she had been an organ transplant nurse and coordinator in Akron.

In the Phoenix Division, her first FBI assignment, Kerns had been the overall coordinator for the Evidence Response Team. During the fall of 2001, she spent most of her days answering white powder letter calls, delivering the suspicious packages to the Arizona Public Health lab, and ensuring test reports—always negative for anthrax—got to the victims. Occasionally, she would take her Evidence Team to a nearby Indian reservation and process a crime scene. In January 2002, the Laboratory Division awarded Kerns a Team Leader spot in the Hazmat Unit and transferred her to Quantico.

At the FBI Academy, she began to develop a sampling protocol while we searched for places to test. Manufacturers and distributers of safety cabinets and gloveboxes were contacted for customer and client lists. Likewise were contacted laboratory service companies that tested and recertified the boxes and cabinets. Using the CDC's list we added the laboratories certified to work with dangerous pathogens. Finally, we reviewed customer databases from milling machine companies.

In parallel, a six-page interview protocol was developed and sent to FBI field offices. Each company, laboratory, and institution possessing a glovebox, biosafety cabinet, or milling machine was asked the same questions: Did they work with anthrax; did they grow bacteria cultures, and if so, how large; could they freeze dry; did they have centrifuges, and if so, bench-top or floor models and what capacity; if they milled, how small a particle could they produce; what was their staff's level of experience in freeze drying and milling; how did they rate the security of their laboratory rooms, overall facility, and personnel; who had access to the labs; was the staff required to vaccinate in order to work with cultures; how long ago and often did they decontaminate their safety cabinets and gloveboxes?

As the interview responses came in to the AMX-2 squad, we passed them to Kerns. With a team of FBI microbiologists and a Hazmat officer, she traveled the Northeast, visiting laboratories in New York, Pennsylvania, and beyond. Working at night to conceal the presence of their Hazmat suits, they sampled gloveboxes and laminar flow safety cabinets, using small swabs for the inner corners, larger swabs for surface areas, and occasionally, long-handled Dacron Q-tips for areas difficult to reach. Worksheets recorded the work, often reaching nine, twelve, twenty pages in length. The data included start time, ending time, who did which sampling, who sketched and photographed, and finally, who acted as recorder. A single location could require several hours, a small glovebox generating a dozen samples and nearly as many negative, blank controls. The blanks—unused swabs, water, and Q-tips, packaged and stored in parallel with the wiped samples—would also be examined for anthrax and guard against contamination of sampling supplies or the testing laboratory producing a false positive test result.

While we planned the expansion of the science projects, agents on the AMX-1 side of the task force continued to look at Steven Hatfill. They learned that he had been a postdoctoral research fellow in the Virology Division of US-AMRIID from 1997 through 1999.[12] There, he had conducted research under the most stringent conditions of biological containment, biosafety level-4. He worked with the deadly hemorrhagic viruses of Africa, including Ebola and Marburg. Hatfill gained a high level of expertise, and he began training other scientists in level-4 operations.[13] Publications of his work prior to joining USAMRIID detailed studies of human cell culture and tissue malignancies. But while his list of academic experiences did not reveal hands-on work with anthrax or bacteria, his resume did list William (Bill) C. Patrick as a personal reference. I was very familiar with Patrick and had attended monthly training classes that he helped teach in biological weapons of mass destruction during 1998. Originally from South Carolina, he had been chief of product development for the United States' former offensive biological weapons program in the 1960s and had overseen the production of hundreds of pounds of dry anthrax powder. He still lived a short drive from the gates of Fort Detrick and USAMRIID.

In addition to Hatfill, the task force continued to investigate other potential suspects. On several occasions, Bruce Ivins relayed doubts he had about former coworkers and provided evidence to support his suspicions. In confidence, he gave agents at the small FBI office[14] in Frederick additional details about Joe Farchaus. Farchaus once threatened an army supervisor, telling a coworker, "someone should shoot that SOB." Ivins also recalled that "Farchaus's mother lived just down the road from where the lady in Connecticut died of anthrax," and that "Farchaus is a fermentation and purification specialist," possessing "great technical expertise." Ivins had seen the spores from the Daschle letter, and he felt they were fermentation quality, better than could be produced at USAMRIID. He added that the pharmaceutical company where Farchaus now worked was a short drive from Trenton and had the equipment to make weaponized anthrax.[15]

Ivins also had suspicions about Gregory Knudson, the scientist that had requested the original isolate of Ames in 1981. Ivins had once been to Knudson's house. Knudson had many firearms and seemed to be "obsessed with bioterrorism." He had even wrote a paper once in which he advocated the United States abandon the biological weapons convention (treaty) and reinstate its defunct offensive bioweapons program. The USAMRIID command staff told Knudson to tear it up and "forget he ever wrote it." Ivins provided the agents with the location of Knudson's current workplace, the Armed Forces Radiobiology Research Institute where he performed radiation experiments. AFRRI had been teetering on the verge of closing until the recent attacks. Now the institution had additional research funding.

Ivins offered the agents evidence of his suspicions. When Knudson worked at USAMRIID, he had taken a small sample of spores from the slant of Ames that had been mailed to him in 1981. He spread the anthrax on a culture plate and incubated it, so the spores grew as bacterial colonies. Over time, Knudson transferred the growing anthrax from one agar plate to the next, rather than going back to the original slant as Ivins did when bacteria were needed to begin a new experiment. Knudson's serial passing—the continual transferring of the same anthrax culture—allowed DNA mutations to accumulate. Ivins produced two photographs of growing anthrax colonies; both labeled "42 hours." One photograph showed every colony looking the same—homogenous in morphology. In the second photograph the colonies appeared similar to the first, but were now intermingled with an assortment of odd-looking colonies. Ivins identified the origins of the anthrax in his two images; the first culture belonged to Ivins—clean, homogenous colonies. The second culture Ivins had grown from a stock of Ames that had belonged to Knudson.

Ivins then showed the agents a picture on the computer monitor in his office. The photo showed the variants grown from the mailed attack spores. Next to it, Ivins displayed a photograph of his Ames stock, variant-free. The Frederick agents relayed this latest information to us on the task force at Washington Field, making note of Ivins's curious passion to assist in the investigation. We added Bruce Edwards Ivins to the Persons of Interest list.[16, 17]

As the year pressed on, the AMX-1 agents and postal inspectors worked down the Persons of Interest list. Ten names stood out, including Farchaus and Knudson and now Ivins. But Steven Jay Hatfill remained at the top. Records obtained from the Special Immunization Program at USAMRIID showed Hatfill receiving anthrax vaccinations even though his research did not involve anthrax. Between 1997 and 1999, he had received four injections.

They learned that his personal security clearance, which he needed for employment with the government contractor Science Applications International Corporation (SAIC), had been permanently removed, and in March, the company terminated his employment. He had been with the large beltway contractor since late 1999; it was the highest paying job he had ever had. At SAIC he earned three times what he had as a research fellow at USAMRIID. The work was exciting and rewarding. When terminated, he had been developing training scenarios with biological weapons for Special Forces at Fort Bragg.

The AMX-1 squad decided the time had come to ask Hatfill some questions. In early spring they sat down with him. They reviewed his activities during the summer and fall of 2001, including travel and use of medication. He told them, yes, he had taken ciprofloxacin antibiotic earlier in the year, but not in the fall. He gave them the address of a pharmacy not far from the gates of USAMRIID and his apartment. The pharmacy's records disagreed. Contrary to his statement, Hatfill had filled prescriptions for Cipro in September, two days before the New York letters were mailed and again in October, two days before the Capitol Hill letters were sent. With this latest evidence, we contacted the office's Special Operations Group and requested Hatfill be placed under surveillance.

12

Many Directions
Winter–Summer 2002

As the investigation approached the half-year mark, we began another large collection project. The document examiners in the FBI Laboratory had found tiny spots of ink they called trash marks. The letters sent to senators Daschle and Leahy had been produced by either a photocopier or a computer laser printer and contained three small marks in their lower left corners—printing defects. A search of the exemplars maintained in the FBI's Photocopier File, established nearly thirty years earlier and maintained by the Questioned Documents Unit, failed to find a match. Likewise, a search of the Anonymous Letter File, established in 1934 and computerized in 1987 and the Bank Robbery Note File, begun in 1950, came up negative. In light of these results, we began to collect photocopier exemplars from machines in copier stores, such as Kinko's, as well as public libraries located near each laboratory I identified as having Ames.[1]

While Scott Stanley worked with Pat Worsham cataloging colony variants, I prepared the subpoena for obtaining the Ames exemplars. John Ezzell and I finalized the protocol for preparing the agar slants, and I sent it to Paul Keim for a final review. Ezzell's renovated laboratory room was filled with new equipment. The biosafety cabinet had had its laminar airflow certified, and the freezer and refrigerator both maintained a constant temperature. Multiple wipe samples from the surfaces of the walls, floor, and inner surface of the safety hood showed no presence of anthrax.

USAMRIID's records indicated that in addition to Ezzell, at least a half dozen of the institution's principal scientists managed laboratories actively growing anthrax. In addition to USAMRIID, I had identified fifteen laboratories around the United States possessing Ames.[2] I contacted the US Attorney's Office and requested they begin the subpoena distribution.

My telephone rang twice. Darin Steele was calling to tell me word had circulated through USAMRIID that our Ames subpoena was being distributed. Bruce Ivins had approached him asking questions about the subpoena and how he should prepare his samples, but Steele suggested that I talk to him instead. I took the number from Steele, dialed, and left a message. In a few minutes, Ivins called back. He had not gotten a copy of my subpoena yet, but wanted to begin getting his samples prepared. Could I send a copy by fax? He would prepare slants of four samples: the original 1981 sample of Ames; his own sample of Ames that he had taken from the original in 1985; a sample of Greg Knudson's Ames—the same one he had shown pictures of containing variant colonies; and a fourth sample from a large and highly concentrated batch of spores. Ivins called the spores a gold standard; a stock produced by fermentation at the US Army's Dugway Proving Grounds. Ivins had sent them a sample of his 1985 Ames as seed stock. The Dugway spores had arrived at Ivins's lab in several shipments, and he combined them into one batch, originally a liter in size. Critical for testing the efficacy of anthrax vaccine in monkeys, about two-thirds of the spore stock had been used, and Ivins kept track of when and how much in a detailed log sheet.

The next day Ivins called again. He had prepared four slants, and he was now checking to make sure all four would grow before handing them over to Darin Steele. Ivins reported in again the next day; all the slants showed growth. Ivins went on to say Steele could now have them—in duplicate as the protocol requested—the first entries in our new repository. Steele immediately relabeled the duplicate set and sent them to Northern Arizona.

Two days later Steele was on the telephone again. There was a problem with the slants that Ivins had brought to him; the protocol had not been followed. Ivins had made his own slants rather than use commercially available ones that came with quality assurance guarantees, and further, he had used the wrong agar. The prescribed culture conditions, time, and possibly temperature had also been ignored. I agreed; Ivins should resubmit, following the protocol this time. Five days later Paul Keim called to report he had identified the most recent four samples he had received as Ames.

Talking with Ivins about concentrated spores and fermentation told me that the science of vaccine testing and biological defense had facets few people understood. Ivins seemed to be among those few; he should be able to fill in the technical gaps still existing in my knowledge of anthrax. I left a message on his voice mail that I wanted to talk.

I walked down USAMRIID's main hallway toward the Bacteriology Division. Months ago Scott Stanley and I had been given unescorted access. We could also bypass the metal detectors installed after 9/11. Staying armed and not being searched, we felt a measure of trust from USAMRIID's Command. I walked down the laboratory's main hall and stopped before wide double doors. I placed the white plastic magnet card I had been given against a small box mounted on the wall. The doors swung slowly outward. Passing through and down the hall I turned left to face a single gray door labeled, "Bruce E. Ivins, Ph.D." and knocked. A thin man slightly taller than me opened it, and then moved back and leaned against a desk as he held out his hand. Behind him stacks of papers covered the tops of gray filing cabinets. Three gray metal desks completed the decor. The cabinets and stacks of paper obliterated any view of the office's back and side walls. A dusty computer monitor took up most of the desk nearest the back wall. Colorful pictures of cats adorned the rear of the desk.

As we shook, he introduced himself with a deep voice, "Hi, I'm Bruce Ivins. This is Pat Fellows, my assistant and coworker. I asked her to join us. She's the expert on growing anthrax spores. This is her office, too. Our technician uses that desk near the door, but she's not here today. What can we do for you?"

"I just wanted to learn a little about making spores. How you do it. How hard it would be for a novice, like me. Things like that. I was just looking for some help to try to learn the process."

"OK, the spores we use are for vaccine challenges. When I first got here in the early eighties, they were using spores that kept clogging up the aerosolizers. The preps they sprayed during the vaccine testing had impurities. I started using density gradient purification to clean up the spores. It's a technique I used at Chapel Hill,[3] before I came to RIID.[4] That's what Pat uses now to make spore preps."

Fellows took a seat beside her desk and began to explain their process for making anthrax spores. She first explained that the clogging problem is also alleviated by growing the bacteria in liquid broth instead of on plates of solid agar. The agar left behind contaminating debris that was difficult to remove. Also, growing in broth seemed to cause an increase in the spores' virulence. As the culture grows, the broth is slowly shaken and begins to swirl. Swirling aerates the culture and stimulates bacteria cell division. Fellows noted that the amount of aeration also influences spore production. Several other factors affect spore formation; for instance, the amount of light the cultures receive. Failure can result from what seem like insignificant changes in the protocol.

I asked how much information about spore production they included in their articles on vaccine research. Fellows nodded, "Yes, we do publish our spore methods."

"Do you include all the details of how to produce spores?"

"No. We leave out some of the critical points. If someone wants to learn the process, I will visit the lab and teach them how."

Fellows noted that she and Ivins had found that the strain of anthrax impacted sporulation efficiency, and they found Ames was well suited for spore production. Ivins noted that high-quality spores created a fine wet mist when discharged from the aerosolizers. The goal was a vapor—a gas and air mixture—floating and hanging in the air—efficiently infecting their immobilized test monkeys.

I stopped taking notes. "So biodefense research uses the same techniques as biowarfare? It's the same philosophy, you use the same science?"

"No! It is not!" Ivins looked straight at me, his face now taut as his eyes stared into mine. Almost imperceptibly, I shifted my weight back and made a slight adjustment in my stance. I didn't know what was coming next. His reaction had taken me by surprise. We had only just met, and until this moment I had detected nothing to suggest a quick temper. The reputation relayed to me the day before when I inquired around the task force was a quiet demeanor, a nerd. I immediately apologized, blaming the comparison on my naivety and insensitivity to their dedication. I realized our talk was over, shook hands goodbye, and made my way out of the cramped office.

As I walked out of USAMRIID, I made a mental note to record Ivins's reaction when I wrote up the interview report.

By the end of March, samples were being submitted to our Ames repository on a regular basis. They came from laboratories around the country, but scientists at USAMRIID still had not complied. Stanley and I decided to have a meeting, and we called USAMRIID's commander—he agreed to arrange a meeting for the next day.

Stanley and I walked into the commander's large office. John Ezzell greeted us as we took seats around the conference table. Pat Worsham, Ivins, and other members of USAMRIID's anthrax community soon joined. Stanley began by saying that any more delays in getting Ames samples would be unacceptable. Worsham supported Stanley and explained to the group the simplicity of our protocol and that she understood we only wanted to compare the collected Ames with the mailed attack Ames using a genetic approach. The commander ended the meeting with an order to comply as soon as possible. I gave Steele a heads up to expect more anthrax.

Ten days later, after more urging by Ezzell, Ivins resubmitted his four samples. His reason for delaying we found out later—indignation that his homemade slants were not up to par with those commercially available.

On the AMX-1 squad, suspicion continued to mount about Hatfill. Leads they had sent to the Legal Attaché in Pretoria failed to turn up proof of the doctorate degree from Rhodes University cited in his resume. It also cited service at the US Army Institute for Military Assistance, forerunner of Fort Bragg's prestigious John F. Kennedy Special Warfare Center and School. Military records did confirm Hatfill served at Bragg, but also contained instances of misconduct and a demotion.

After finding that Hatfill had received anthrax vaccinations, AMX-1 dug deeper. Hatfill had received four injections while at USAMRIID. USAMRIID's Special Immunization Program required blood for evaluation from those requesting access to the vaccinations and archived the samples. Hatfill had given blood three times before vaccination and seven times once he began injections; then ceased two-and-a-half years before the mailings. Presence of anthrax antigens in his blood in 2002 would suggest a recent exposure to anthrax or unauthorized access to the vaccine.[5] AMX-1 sent to a request to USAMRIID's commander for samples of Hatfill's stored blood.

As summer approached, the task force decided to increase the attention on Hatfill. They drew up search warrants for his apartment, car, and a storage unit they had found in Florida. But first they would ask for his consent; he had been cooperative during the spring.

One of the AMX-1 agents, Bob Roth, invited Hatfill to meet at the FBI office in Frederick. Hatfill accepted. Roth and his partner, an agent with a strong reputation for behavioral analysis, began with subpoenaed pharmacy records. Hatfill agreed that it looked bad for him, filling prescriptions for Cipro two days before each mailing, but he could offer no explanation for why he did not mention it back in March. Then Roth turned to a novel he had heard Hatfill was writing. Hatfill described his book, *Emergence*. He had started it when he was a research fellow at the National Institutes of Health, before he began the two-year stint at USAMRIID. He had applied for registration with the Library of Congress' Copyright Office, but was still revising.[6] His main character planned to attack the White House with plague, the same scourge that decimated the populace of London in 1665. Black Death struck in April of that year and killed 20 percent of London's residents in two months. Forty percent of the inhabitants fled the city, but half of them would perish also. Throughout the summer—the disease had still not peaked—death carts rolled down silent streets and alleys, collecting for mass burials. The carts were filled with grossly distended bodies bearing huge swollen lymph nodes—telltale "buboes" characteristic of the disease.[7] Officials marked the door of each victim's residence with a red cross below the inscription, "Lord have mercy upon us," a warning to stay out.[8, 9, 10]

The interview concluded with one more request: Would Hatfill allow them to search his apartment, car, and a storage locker? He agreed, and signed his name to the single typewritten Consent to Search form Roth placed on the desk.

Roth and Hatfill left the office and together drove toward Hatfill's apartment six blocks away. Chaos greeted them. Above, beside, and in front of a large white complex of brick buildings, television helicopters circled, satellite trucks blocked streets, and commentators talked into cameras. The Washington Field Office Hazmat Team—prestaged by Roth—went about their work as best as they could, documenting items in the apartment, car, and basement storage bin, focusing while ignoring the swirl of media.

The searches produced no clear evidence of the mailings, but the team did turn up some interesting items. They found a letter from Rhodes University informing Hatfill that his doctoral thesis had been rejected. The letter contained no further information, no reason for the rejection, but it was dated the summer of 2001. In Hatfill's black Camaro, agents found maps and sketches with drawings over Catoctin Mountain, Gambrill State Park, and a dirt road that leads to the Camp David presidential retreat.

By the beginning of July things were looking up for Steven Hatfill. While the government had terminated his security clearance and with it a lucrative capital beltway contractor job, Louisiana State University had offered him employment as director of their new National Center for Biomedical Research and Training, a program in counterterrorism with an emphasis on bioterrorism. By mid-July he left for Baton Rouge, with plans to return for his belongings at the end of the month.

With the start of the new millennium, the FBI Laboratory began exploring bloodhounds for identifying human scent at bombing scenes. Hazardous devices examiners from the lab's Explosives Unit conducted experiments with the Southern California Bloodhound Handlers Coalition. They detonated four pipe bombs and collected scent from the debris using sterile gauze. Twenty dogs were allowed to sniff the gauzes and then attempt to identify the person who had originally handled the ordnance before it was ignited. The results were promising; 78 percent of the time the canines identified the correct person.[11]

Human scent dogs, also called trailing dogs, are distinct from tracking dogs. Tracking dogs are trained to follow the odor of crushed vegetation, disturbed soil, and generic human smells. They will follow the freshest track and are best suited for rural natural environments. Trailing dogs take a canine's olfactory gifts to a higher level. Studies in Europe have demonstrated a properly trained dog can correctly identify individual human scents and that the scents will remain viable for days, months, and even years, if stored properly. The East German Ministry for State Security—Stasi, the Secret Police of East Germany—exploited the practice prior to the fall of the Berlin Wall. Beginning in 1973, Stasi collected scent from East German citizens during interviews, interrogations, and housebreaks and labeled, cataloged, and stored the samples in airtight glass jars.[12] By 1979, they began to use their collection to identify dissidents who had printed and distributed flyers protesting government oppression.[13] It is estimated that Stasi collected scent from thousands of their citizenry.

The East Germans began using a vacuum to collect human scent from evidence in the early 1980s.[14] A member of the Niagara County Sheriff's Department refined the technique and in 1998 patented a small battery-operated device, the Scent Transfer Unit, also known as the STU-100. While the STU efficiently collects human scent without disturbing watermarks, ink, human DNA, or latent impressions of fingerprints, what is being collected is not well understood. Flakes of skin, microbes, or volatile materials[15] are three suggestions. Scent is also suspected to be a combination of genetics, diet, and environment. Changing to a vegetarian life style, switching laundry detergents, or driving a different car may be influencing factors.

Once a trail of odor is left behind, variables are at work. The scent is subject to changing weather conditions. Individual handler experience and interpretation of a dog's actions—the canine is trained to signal, or alert, when identifying scent—is a factor, as well as fatigue. Forensic science requires protocols, and as the explosive examiners worked with the dogs, they implemented controls and standardized procedures for the number of times a location or person would be checked.

By late October, the Daschle and *New York Post* letters had been sterilized by radiation, and the Trace Evidence Unit had finished examining them for fibers. Normally, the envelopes and letters would then move on to a Latent Print Unit, the Documents Unit, and one of the DNA Units. But unknown to us on the Amerithrax Task Force, the assistant director of the FBI Laboratory authorized a new step in the forensic queue.

Back in the fall of 2001, the Explosive Unit collected scent from the envelopes and letters. They first scrubbed the suction end of a STU-100, a five-by-nine inch screen platen, with isopropyl alcohol before placing a piece of sterile gauze inside. Then holding the platen over the Daschle letter and envelope, the vacuum was turned on for sixty seconds. The examiner removed the gauze and placed it into a clear plastic bag, folded its top closed, and placed it into a second bag. After sealing the top of the second bag with heat, it was labeled, initialed, and dated. The operator repeated the process nine times before thoroughly wiping the platen face with rubbing alcohol and moving on to the Brokaw and *Post* letters. The process was repeated in early December with the Leahy letter.

By midsummer the genetic work was progressing, but it was still slow going. Several hundred samples of Ames had been submitted to the repository, but we still needed a way to distinguish the mailed Ames from the original isolate. We could not even venture a projected date when pressed by the director's office. Efforts with traditional forensics fared no better. The search of Hatfill's apartment, car, and storage units did not turn up any matches to the fibers from the envelopes or the scotch tape, no Federal Eagle envelopes, nor photocopies with trash marks, and no notes similar to the anthrax letters or matching handwriting.

Faced with the absence of viable leads, Amerithrax turned to the bloodhounds. The Laboratory Division stressed the reliability of the dogs and the validation studies conducted in southern California. The canines had provided investigative leads in the past and more validation was in the planning stages. Bob Roth knew that Hatfill would be flying to Baton Rouge in mid-July for a week of teaching. The Laboratory contacted the Southern California Bloodhound Handlers Coalition and at the end of July, bloodhounds Lucy, Knight and Tinkerbelle touched down at Dulles Airport.

The next day we met the dog teams and drove to the Detrick Plaza Apartments in Frederick, Maryland. One by one, the handlers presented the bloodhounds with scent gauzes from the anthrax letters. Tinkerbelle went first. She began trailing across the complex's black macadam parking lot, into the second building and up a set of stairs to a second-floor landing. Deliberately and slowly she continued. Suddenly, she stopped and faced an apartment door—the residence of Steven Jay Hatfill. Lucy and then Knight, separate and one at a time, repeated the walk. They each alerted in front of Hatfill's door.

The dog teams did not stop with the Detrick Plaza Apartments. We drove them from location to location, conducting a total of nineteen location checks in a single day. We checked known locations of Greg Knudson, John Ezzell, William "Bill" Patrick, and Hatfill's current girlfriend, visiting residences in Gaithersburg, Brooksville, Bethesda, Clinton, Sharpsburg and Frederick, Maryland, and Washington, DC, where Lucy, Knight, and Tinkerbelle showed no inclination to trail. During the day, the dogs alerted only once more—at the former residence of Steven Hatfill's past girlfriend.

Early the next morning, Lucy, Knight, and Tinkerbelle were in air, bound for the home of the Bayou Bengals. Once on the ground, the dog teams met with the New Orleans FBI surveillance team who had been keeping an eye on Hatfill. They gave the handlers a list of locations Hatfill had visited in Baton Rouge, as well as places Hatfill had not been near. The dogs trailed and alerted at the locations Hatfill had been and showed no interest in locations Hatfill had not been near.

As soon as the canine teams arrived back from Baton Rouge, we turned them toward Catoctin Mountain. Using the maps found in Hatfill's car, we drove through Gambrill Park and below three spring-fed mountain ponds that fed the Frederick reservoir system. One by one, the bloodhounds trailed around one pond and then another, alerting to points on the trails. We spread out to look for a campsite or small shelter.

Throughout the summer, FBI Hazmat agents in New Jersey had worked through the nights. Early in August, they pulled up to three blue mailboxes in front of 10 Nassau Street in Princeton, two blocks from the Ivy League University's historic Nassau Hall, once garrisoned by British troops as General Washington heroically crossed the Delaware River. The agents were nearing the end of their list of 625 mailboxes[16] and still had not detected anthrax. Dressed in encapsulating Hazmat suits, they pulled sampling equipment from the back of a black Suburban. There was little conversation. With practiced ease, they opened the front access doors, removed the flat tubs of mail, photographed, and took zigzag sampling swabs. Finished, they packed up as quietly as they had unpacked. Another set of samples would soon be on the way to the state public health laboratory north of Trenton. But this time a swab from one of the three mailboxes contained 350 colonies of live anthrax.

News of locating the mailbox spread quickly through the task force. Agents from the Trenton FBI's Resident Agency focused attention on 10 Nassau Street. They showed pictures of Steven Hatfill to store owners, looked for traffic violations and parking citations written during September and October, and searched the area for security cameras. But the excitement was short-lived. No one in the area recognized Hatfill. A review of citation records and camera films produced nothing.

After Labor Day we returned to the Detrick Plaza Apartments and met with the manager. We knew Hatfill had moved out of the apartment and in with his girlfriend in northwest Washington, DC. He did not return to Baton Rouge. In August, following the media attention surrounding the search of his apartment, Louisiana State University fired him. The apartment had not been rented yet, and the manager scheduled it to be painted later in the week. We asked if we could look around one last time.

The apartment was nearly cleaned out, but it still contained a few items—a glass laboratory flask and a small metal cylinder with an attached hose lay in a hall closet, along with a roll of clear vinyl tubing. As one member of our search team bagged and labeled what had been left behind, I took sterile Q-tips and plastic tubes out of the black nylon bag we had carried upstairs. In the kitchen, I pulled the refrigerator away from the wall and turned it around. Finding the generator in the refrigerator's rear, I wiped a Q-tip across an attached metal plate. After taking two more Q-tip wipes, I looked overhead. The apartment had two round plastic fire alarms mounted in the ceiling, one in the kitchen and one in the short hallway leading to the bathroom. Removing the faded tan covers, I wiped one Q-tip in the left side of the alarm and a second across the right side. I repeated the sampling at the base of the kitchen ceiling's light bulb and again on the single bathroom light. Finally, scraping through the layers of paint that covered the screws holding the light switch plates, I removed them and took Q-tip swipes from the sides of each plastic switch—anywhere a faint electric charge might attract a dry spore.

13

The Ponds

Fall 2002

The dearth of forensic leads continued through the summer. The Trace Evidence Unit finished its examination of the items taken from Hatfill's apartment. The examiners had compared more than seventy articles of clothing for a match to any of the nine fibers taken from the attack envelopes. They scrutinized pads of paper for a connection to the mailings—indented writing mentioning the victim addresses in New York City or on Capitol Hill, or a Greendale School, the town of Franklin, or the 08852 zip code of the return address. They inspected a roll of transparent tape for a match to the cut end of one of the pieces from the back of the envelopes, a dozen or so blue ink pens for chemical similarities to the ink in the addresses, and sheets of white paper for tiny trash marks. All negative—no matches. Likewise, results of my swab samples from Hatfill's vacant apartment came back negative for anthrax. Terry Kerns and her Hazmat team had traveled the Northeast, working down our list of laboratories having biosafety cabinets and gloveboxes. They wiped inside each containment cabinet they found, concealed the locations by labeling the samples in code, and sent them for testing. But after all the travel and all the work, often at night, not one sample showed even a trace of anthrax.

Scott Stanley and I continued to push the genetics forward. Working with Pat Worsham, Stanley selected individual A-, B-, C-, and D-variant colonies from the different attack letters, labeled them with disguising codes, and shipped the collection to Arizona. There Paul Keim and his staff worked to purify their DNA plasmids.

In addition to sending coded isolates to Keim for DNA purification, we also delivered them to Commonwealth Biotechnologies in Richmond, where Tom Reynolds and his director of laboratory services, Greg Meyers, also began to isolate plasmids in hopes of finding deviations in sequences of A, C, G, and T building blocks. But before the end of summer, our strategy had stalled. Comparing plasmids from multiple Ames isolates revealed no differences. Each DNA sequence from every plasmid preparation was identical. We consulted with Keim and the scientists at TIGR. I also began attending meetings chaired by Dr. Rita Colwell, the director of the National Science Foundation. Molecular biologists from the Washington-area intelligence agencies—the Department of Energy and the Defense Intelligence Agency— also attended. I laid out our genetic strategy. Colwell, a nationally recognized microbiologist and elected member of the National Academy of Sciences, encouraged us to keep trying and agreed that if the variants Pat Worsham had isolated were stable, they must be caused by DNA mutations. We just needed to advance the DNA sequencing past what it was capable of—perhaps the mutations were being missed. It was agreed that we would shift focus.[1] Instead of relying on the plasmid DNAs for a genetic signature, we would compare DNA sequences of the much larger DNA chromosome. The shift would not come cheaply or without risk. The time to sequence a plasmid was measured in weeks; sequencing the entire bacterial genome would add months, and a cost of close to half-a-million dollars. I telephoned Paul Keim, and he agreed with our strategy shift. He would begin purifying whole DNA genomes from Stanley's shipments.

By mid-fall of 2002, our efforts began to pay off. TIGR had determined the entire sequence of DNA from the original, the 1981 isolate of Ames. TIGR then turned its attention to sequencing DNAs from the A- and B-variants Worsham had cultured from the Leahy letter—the identity of these DNAs known only to Stanley and me.

As TIGR worked to sequence the variants, we turned to Commonwealth Biotechnologies for additional help. Now that we had a sequence for the ancestral, we hoped a comparison with the clinical isolate from the first anthrax fatality might reveal at least one difference between DNA genomes. Base by base Reynolds and Meyers compared the two sets of DNA. But after weeks of computer runs, scans, and crosschecks, not a single difference in sequence could be found.

Our hopes for a unique genetic signature in the attack Ames now rested solely with the work Pat Worsham continued on our behalf. A discriminating scientist, she cultured and characterized the odd-looking colonies. Consulting almost daily with Stanley, she changed the growth environment of her laboratory's incubator: temperature, percentage of carbon dioxide, even the type of agar in the petri dishes. Additional variants appeared, *D*, with a translucent appearance, then *E*, exhibiting an opaque quality. The closer Worsham examined the attack spores, the more apparent it became that an assortment of minor variations existed.[2]

While Stanley and Worsham worked to sort out the growing number of morphology types, my collection of Ames exemplars stored in our repository continued to expand. By mid-fall Steele catalogued more than 560 samples. Of those, scientists at USAMRIID had contributed 450. Answers to the questions I had listed in the subpoena about who and where the Ames had come from and been sent to now took the search abroad, to laboratories in England, Canada, and Sweden.

Scientists in the FBI's new Chemical Biological Sciences Unit expanded on our brainstorming earlier in the year. Dean Fetterolf had successfully estimated the age of the spores with his idea to use carbon-14 and nuclear fallout. The National Ocean Sciences Accelerator Mass Spectrometry Facility at the Woods Hole Oceanographic Institution on Cape Cod had done the measurements. The Falmouth scientists dated the spores in the Leahy envelope as modern, estimating that they had been grown within the past couple of years, most likely between 1998 and 2001. Lawrence Livermore National Laboratory's Center for Accelerator Mass Spectrometry made duplicate tests with the same conclusion. The results were consistent with the relatively recent 1981 isolation of the Ames strain.

In October 2002, Director Robert Mueller ordered a change of command. He promoted Richard "Rick" Lambert from assistant special agent in charge of the San Diego Field Office where he managed counterintelligence cases to inspector in charge and placed him over our investigation. An attorney before joining the Bureau as a special agent, Lambert spent three years as a street agent before being promoted to the FBI's Office of General Counsel. From there, he managed human resource litigations before supervising a field squad in the Norfolk office. His last stop before San Diego was conducting field office audits as a team leader in the Inspection Division. Lambert came to the director's attention after 9/11. Lambert had prepared detailed briefing materials that the director relied upon when appearing before Congress in the aftermath of al-Qaeda's attacks.

Inspector in Charge Lambert would report to the deputy director and the director. The appointment elevated the status of the still-unsolved case and sent a message. Lambert would have the clout to get whatever resources we required.

Arriving at our field office, Rick Lambert immediately introduced himself to the task force and got to work. He called the bloodhounds back from southern California. The handlers and their canine partners—Lucy, Knight, and Tinkerbelle—were dispatched to the suburbs surrounding the nation's capital.[3] I would take a break from science and provide security for Tinkerbelle. For five days we traveled in a rented black Suburban to Bethesda, then Frederick and on to Silver Spring. We checked locations of persons with an association to Hatfill or a connection with anthrax research. At each opportunity, Tinkerbelle's handler presented her with a scent pad containing odors of the Leahy letter. In Bethesda, she began to trail one block, and then a second before alerting at the apartment door of a Hatfill associate. We called in the senior canine, Knight. Lucy followed. One by one, as they had done outside Hatfill's apartment in the summer, each handler let his bloodhound sniff the scent of a sterilized anthrax letter and then was allowed to trail. On the first occasion Lucy ignored her opportunity, but given a second chance she trailed to the apartment door. As Knight and his handler and I watched, she jumped in an enthusiastic alert. Knight then followed suit, trailing and alerting, also on his second attempt.

For the better part of a week, the three canine teams traveled across two states conducting scent checks for almost twenty persons. In a small town northeast of Frederick the dogs alerted at the residence of Pat Fellows, Bruce's assistant. The teams noted the identification and made a note that negative controls would also need to be conducted at a future time, in accordance with Laboratory protocol.

When the task force learned of the Fellows's alert, it was immediately explained. There was no known association of Hatfill and Fellows, but we were aware that she had worked with the Daschle letter in the days following its recovery. Two days after Daschle's envelope was cut open, the letter and its contents had been mistakenly transferred to Ivins's lab, where he and Fellows attempted to determine the spore density before Ezzell was able to retrieve the evidence.[4] But an explanation for alerting to the Leahy letter did not follow; Ezzell had been careful not to let it out of his lab.

In November, just before Thanksgiving, Rick Lambert called the dogs back again. For two days, they combed Gambrill State Park and the Municipal Forest above Frederick for locations Hatfill might have traveled. A small pond elicited multiple alerts from the bloodhounds.

On the third day they returned to Frederick while there was still daylight. Continuing down the list the teams had started in October, the teams stopped at dozens of locations, presented the dogs with scent pads, and looked to the handlers for signs of trailing and alert. The inventory included the 600 block of Military Road and the residence of Bruce Ivins. Tinkerbelle trailed along the sidewalk to the front of the house and stopped, then continued on.[5] Realizing she would probably trail all the way to Hatfill's old apartment farther up the block, Tinkerbelle's handler folded his list, loaded the faithful canine in her Suburban, and moved to the next scent check. By the time three days had passed, three dozen individuals would be checked for an association with one of the five scents pads from one of the four letters. A positive association with one of the letters would prompt a call to a second team for confirmation. Occasionally, failure to trail and alert would also be confirmed. The dogs revisited the residence of Hatfill's old girlfriend, where they had alerted during the summer—this time implementing strict controls, both positive and negative. The results agreed almost 100 percent with the earlier results. When presented with an unused scent pad, the negative control, they remained motionless and uninterested. When asked to sniff gauze used to capture scent from either Hatfill or the girlfriend—positive controls—they enthusiastically alerted in front of the residence.

Back at the task force office, Bob Roth and AMX-1 studied results. What had Hatfill been doing in the Frederick Municipal Forest? Why the interest in ponds feeding the Frederick watershed? After a year we still had no direct evidence, and Headquarters wanted results. Perhaps Hatfill had thrown out makeshift laboratory equipment—the type he described in *Emergence*—into the pond the dogs had trailed to.

By December the ponds above Frederick had begun to freeze. The consensus was that we could not wait until the spring thaw. Waiting until after the holidays only increased the likelihood of harsh January and February storms and colder conditions bringing heavier ice to the ponds. But searching them would require divers with advanced training. They learn about how ice forms, how to recognize unsafe ice, dive site preparation, equipment requirements, and they conduct safety drills. Diving under ice brings hazards not faced in traditional, open water sport diving.[6] Margins of error narrowed. Ice divers require dry suits, thermal insulation, and buoyancy control, and they worked at the end of a tether. It required an experienced support team, a tender who guarded the line attached to the diver's harness, maintaining a constant tension and safeguarding against the diver becoming entangled in his lifeline. As the tender pays out and takes in line, he must be alert for a series of tugs, prearranged signals that help is needed. The team also includes a stand-by diver, also with his own tender, ready to descend should something go wrong. A third diver waits as backup should a rescue be needed. Divers risk hyperthermia and frostbite before and after a dive, the winter air often colder than the water below.

Bob Roth began to work the telephone. Again, as with the Leahy letter search, members of the Hostage Rescue Team raised their hand, offering members certified for ice diving. Roth also contacted agencies he had worked with in Northern Virginia, and they offered support. The Virginia State Police followed.

Roth set the operation for the third week in December. This time my role would be limited—sentry duty on the road leading north over Catoctin Mountain. In October, I had been diagnosed with an aggressive form of prostate cancer and elected for surgery as soon as I could arrange it. I returned to limited duty the second week of December anxious to pitch in.

The weather report for the night before we began predicted an ice storm before the morning, the first of the winter season. As I drove past Frederick and up the road to Gambrill State Park it became noticeably colder. I joined the line of Bureau cars winding along the mountain to Frederick Municipal Forest, as we suddenly came to a halt. Outside, chainsaws growled. Sudden crashes sounded as iced-over branches broke off from above. Ice covered everything: tree trunks, branches, shrubs. Slowly, we made our way up the mountain. At the top each blade of grass, every bush, shrub, and tree—none over six feet tall—reflected brilliant sunlight.

Along the edges of the ponds, we prepared for dive operations. Tents went up for warming between dives and checking and rechecking equipment. We brought out food for staying alert, maintaining energy and core body temperatures, and water supplemented with salts to maintain hydration and stave off cramping muscles. Heaters were brought in along with stools and cots and medical monitors to track vital signs.[7] Outside, the chainsaws began their alternating high and low whines as the dive teams sawed six-foot triangles through the ice.

The helicopters arrived shortly after the first divers went under the ice. The day became a repeat of the summer outside Steve Hatfill's apartment. Again, the media showed up in force; there had been another leak, and the threat to safety was imminent. The helicopters circled overhead, flying lower and lower to get the best look possible, the roar and chopping blades competing for the attention of support teams on the ice. The tenders redoubled efforts to maintain tautness in the anchoring lines, feeling for pulls and tugs signaling "Trouble, need help."

The helicopters continued circling above, and the teams rotated divers in and out of the water. They searched by feel. In the afternoon, clouds replaced the brilliance of the early morning. A muted December sun rose slightly above surrounding oak, maple, and pine trees, briefly illuminating the murky pond water. Cold crept in through neoprene gloves, stiffening hands and fingers.

Finally the skies quieted. The media crews in their helicopters had gone. The answer to why came over our two-way radios. Inspector Lambert had been on the telephone in our command center, a large recreational vehicle outfitted with encrypted communication equipment, computers and printers, generators, and lighting systems parked at the edge of the woods. He had convinced supervisors at the Federal Aviation Administration of the danger, and they issued a temporary flight restriction for the air overhead.

The radios broke the silence once more, the words cutting in and out, "We have a reporter . . . *Baltimore Sun* . . . name is . . . He . . . through the perimeter . . . got close to the dive."

The inspector answered from the command post, his voice clear and unmistakable, "Ask him to leave and follow him out."

"10-4."[8]

Then, the radio came alive again. A Red Cross worker handing out hot coffee[9] mentioned to a passing FBI agent that one of their volunteers was an anthrax expert. The agent relayed the information to the command post over the radio. The inspector answered, "Do you have a name?"

"They said his name is Bruce Ivins, he's an expert on anthrax, from US-AMRIID. He's a part-time volunteer. He's in the tent handing out food and coffee. I think he's on the POI list." Moments of silence followed. Then came the inspector's answer.

"Okay, tell them he has to leave. Thank him for his help and follow him out will you?"

Two hours before dusk, on the fourth and last full day of operations, just as the divers prepared for the final descent, a call came over the radio. The transmission again cut in and out, our hand-held radios not having the power to transmit as clearly as the hardwired units in the command post vehicle and government cars parked along the dirt roads. "We found a box . . . mud . . . holes . . . plastic."

A reply—Bob Roth's voice—responded, "Be right over," followed by a second transmission, "The Scotts, can you guys arrange to get this to USAM-RIID?" That was Roth's way of referring to Scott Stanley and me.

"10-4. I'll need a replacement at this post," and I started driving back to the dive operations.

Walking up the gravel trail to the uppermost pond, I approached the warming tent where a plastic box, approximately three feet by two feet in length and width, sat on a plastic sheet. Black mud—a combination of rotted leaves and silt—covered it, but from what I could see, it looked like a storage box that could be bought at homeware stores. It appeared to be made of clear opaque plastic and had a white plastic top. Two oblong holes four or five inches in diameter, cracked around their edges, had been broken through the plastic top. Inside, also covered in black mud, lay a dark bottle with a cord tied to the neck. The box was stamped *Sterilite*.

Within an hour the box and its contents rested on the bench in John Ezzell's cramped laboratory as Scott Stanley, Rick Lambert, members of the FBI's Chemical Biological Sciences Unit, and I sat with Ezzell in his small conference room and discussed the fastest way to test for anthrax.

As we entered January and the fifteenth month of the investigation, the task force called in the dogs again, this time to check more locations around the Frederick Municipal Forest ponds and to sort out the identification of Fellows's scent on the letters. I took another break from genetics, this time riding with Knight up to Catoctin Mountain. Maps and sketches from Hatfill's Camaro guided us through a cold mist that would turn to ice when the sun set.

We pulled the Suburbans over beside a wide jeep trail that wound uphill toward the ponds. Knight and his handler got out and looked at the jeep trail and the big dog sniffed a scent pad, but showed no inclination to move. We then noticed what looked like a deer trail thirty feet to the left, about three feet wide, with branches hanging four or five feet above the ground.[10] The handler brought Knight to the entrance of the trail, and Knight began to walk, following wet leaves and twigs with his nose. The handler looked at me and motioned that Knight had alerted; Hatfill had been up this trail that led to the spring-fed ponds. We recorded the alert on our log sheet and noted that we would need to return to conduct negative controls. I also made a mental note to discuss Knight's latest alert with the task force. Skepticism was building. Hatfill's scent on the deer trail—wet and then freezing at night—had to be at least months old. The deer trail was not easy to negotiate; there was a wide jeep trail thirty feet away. On occasion, I had seen the second and third handlers with their canine partners watch the lead dog alert before conducting confirmations—against protocol if I understood correctly. Was fatigue a factor? Did we run the dogs too long in a single outing?

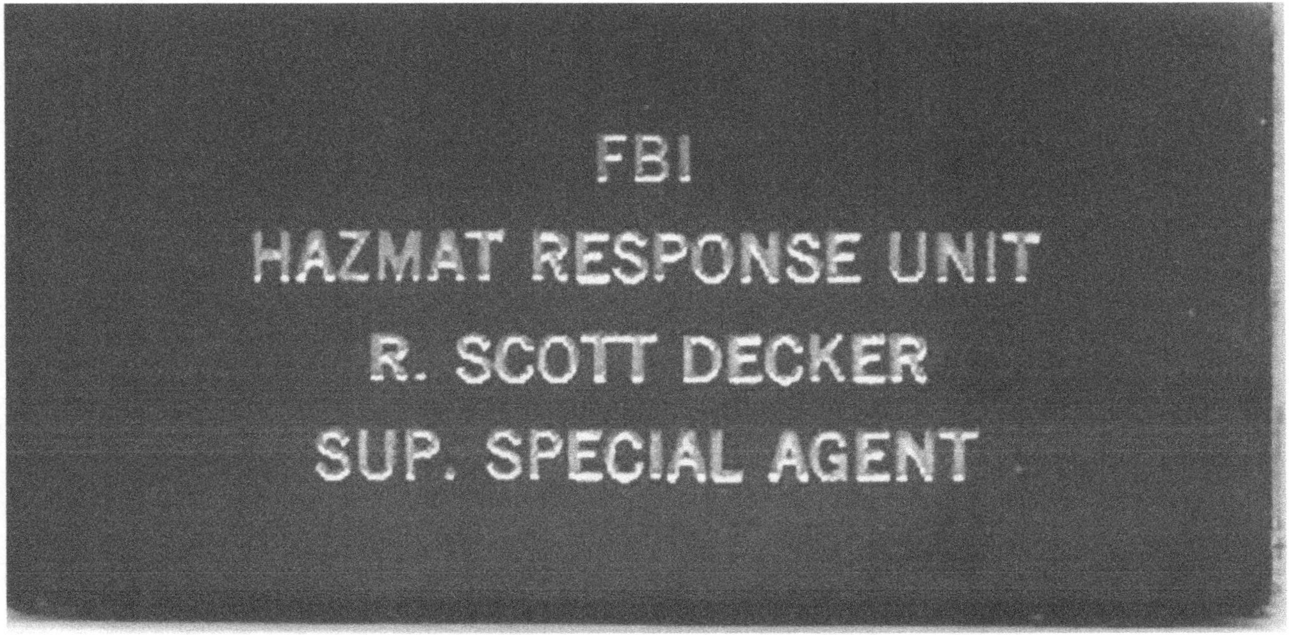

Figure 1. Author's name tag worn while at Ground Zero, September 2001. Photo by the author.

Figure 2.   Removing steel from World Trade Center towers at Ground Zero during the week following the September 11, 2001, attacks. Note the smoke and hot vapors rising from the crushed buildings. Photo by the author.

Figure 3. Urban Search and Rescue (USAR) markings on the first floor of a building at the perimeter of Ground Zero. Photo by the author.

Figure 4. St. Charlie's Bar on Albany Street, Manhattan, adjacent to Ground Zero. The photo was taken more than a week after September 11, 2001. The bar had been used as a rest area for exhausted rescue workers. Photo by the author.

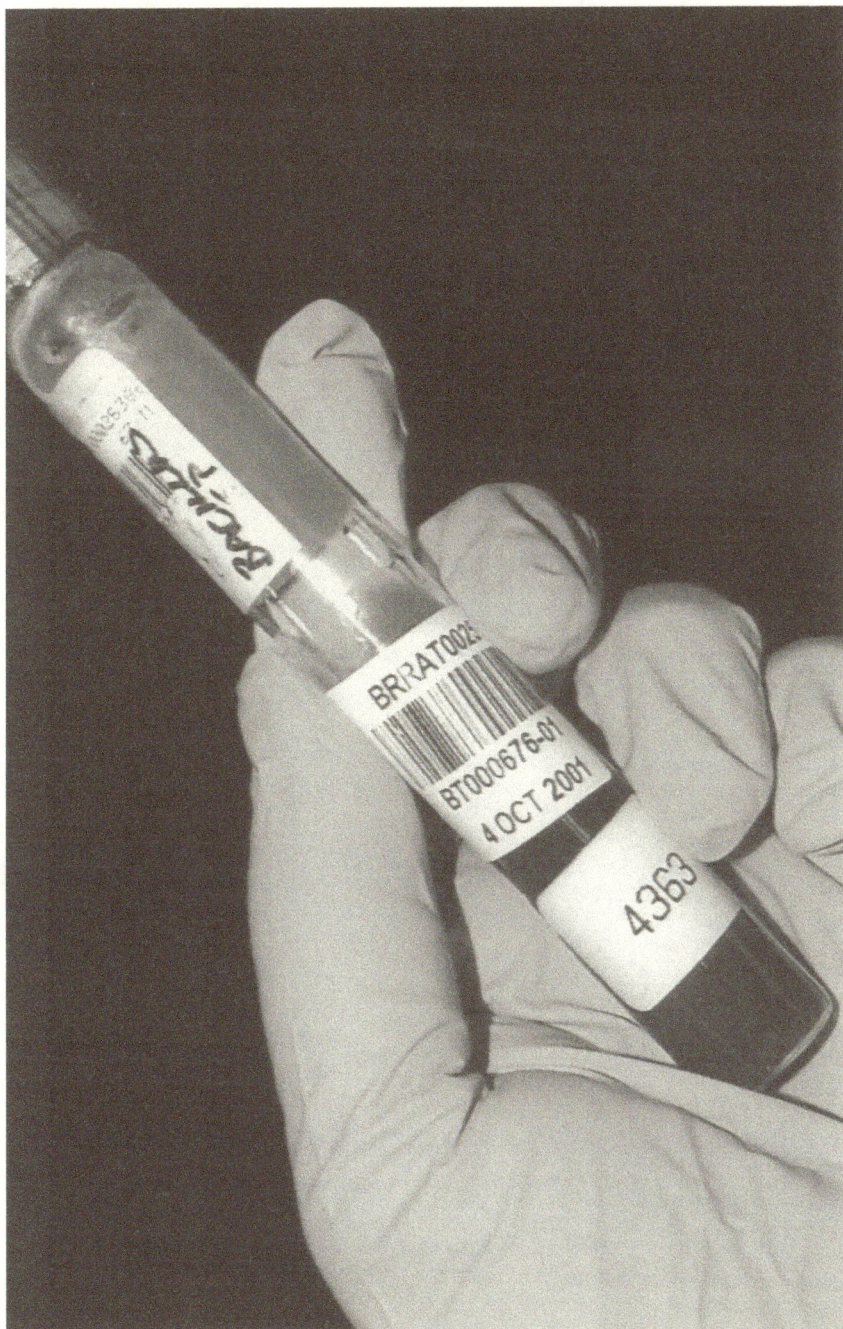

Figure 5. Isolate of *Bacillus anthracis* taken from Robert Stevens, the first fatality of the 2001 anthrax attacks. The test tube contains an agar slant with cultured bacteria growth. The *Bacillus* isolate was determined to be the Ames strain of *B. anthracis*. Courtesy of Dr. Paul Keim.

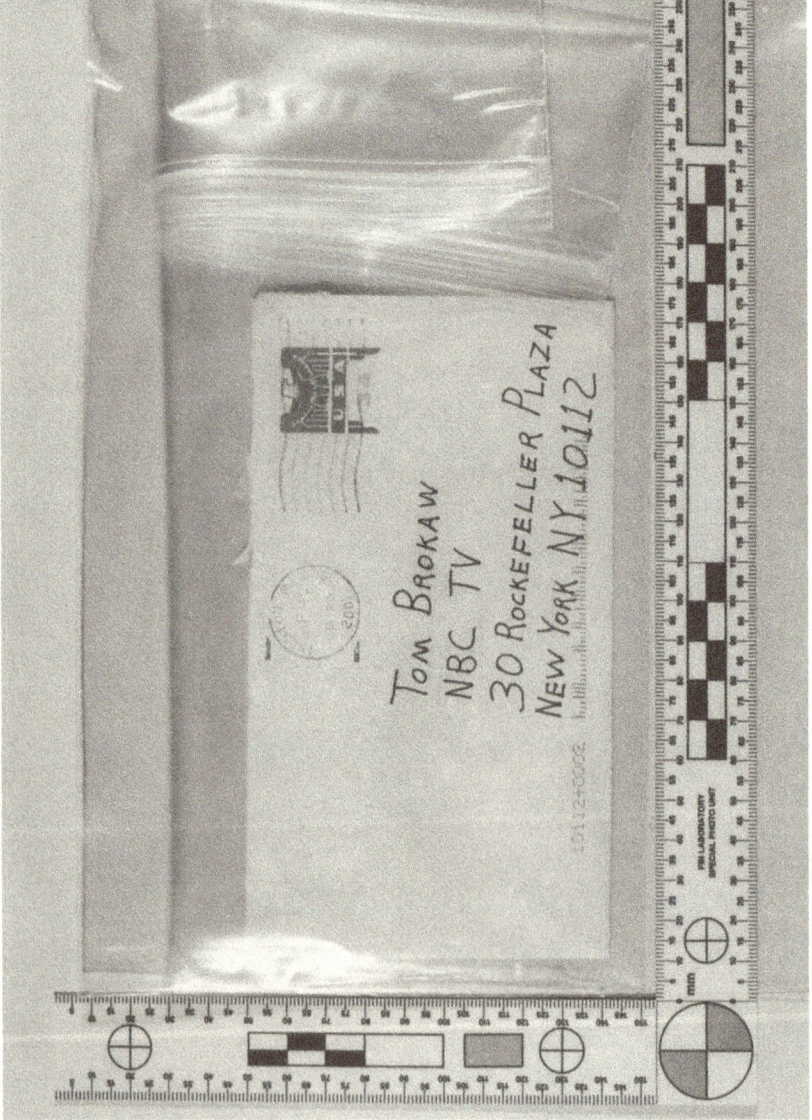

Figure 6. Photograph of envelope mailed to Tom Brokaw. FBI photo.

Figure 7. Envelope mailed to Senator Tom Daschle. FBI photo.

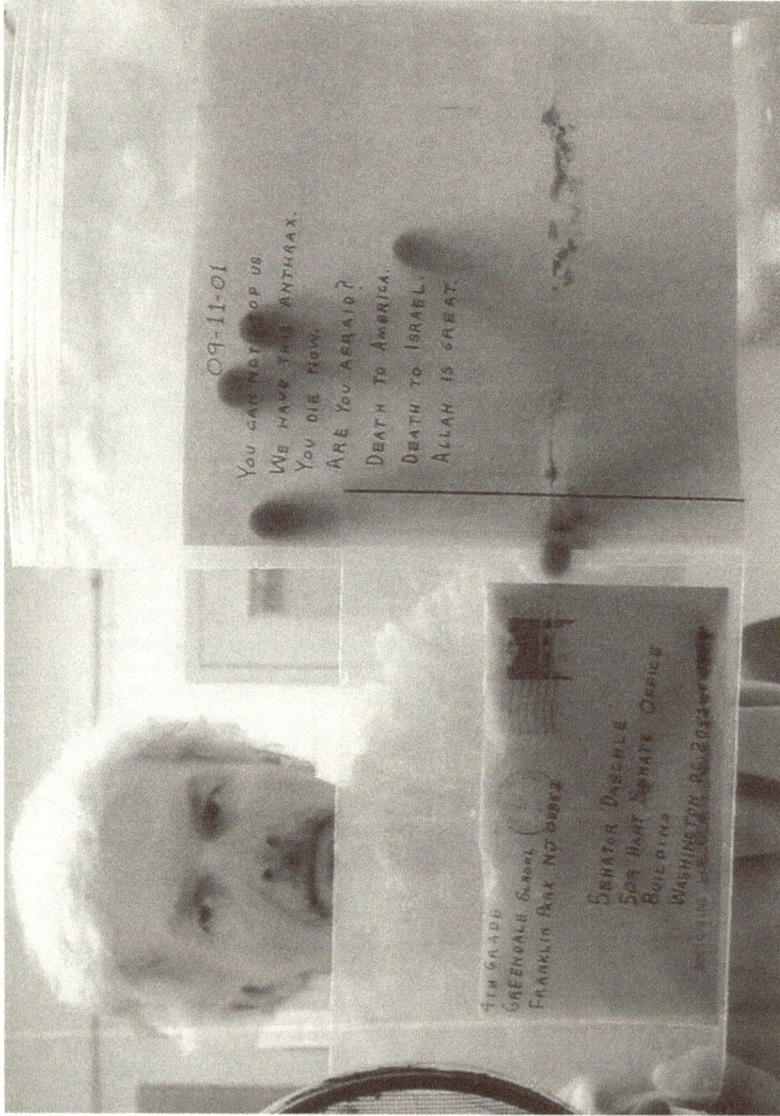

Figure 8. Dr. John Ezzell holding the envelope and letter mailed to Senator Tom Daschle. Note the distortion line at the lower edge of envelope caused by bleach disinfectant. FBI photo.

Figure 9. FBI and EPA personnel search for a fourth envelope filled with dry *Bacillus anthracis* spores. The facility is a biosafety level-3 containment laboratory. Note the biosafety laminar airflow containment cabinet in the background. FBI photo.

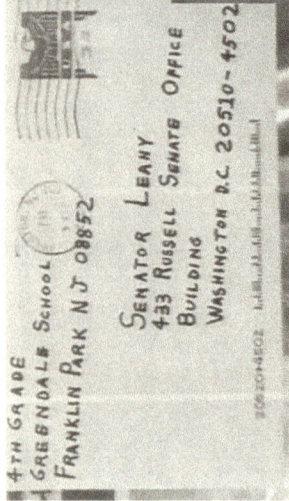

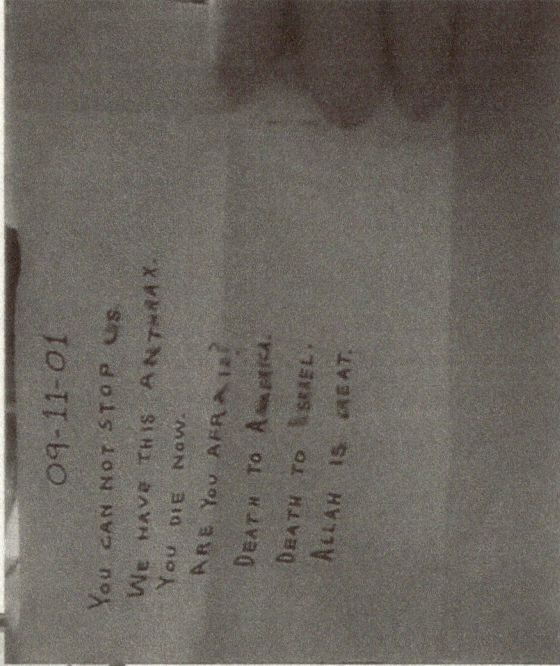

Figure 10. The envelope and letter mailed to Senator Patrick Leahy; found during the search of fifty-five-gallon sealed drums containing mail quarantined by the congressional Sergeant-at-Arms during October 2001. The envelope contained 0.9 grams of dried *Bacillus anthracis* spores and was located by Hazmat-trained FBI and EPA agents with support of the FBI's Hazardous Materials Response Unit. FBI photo.

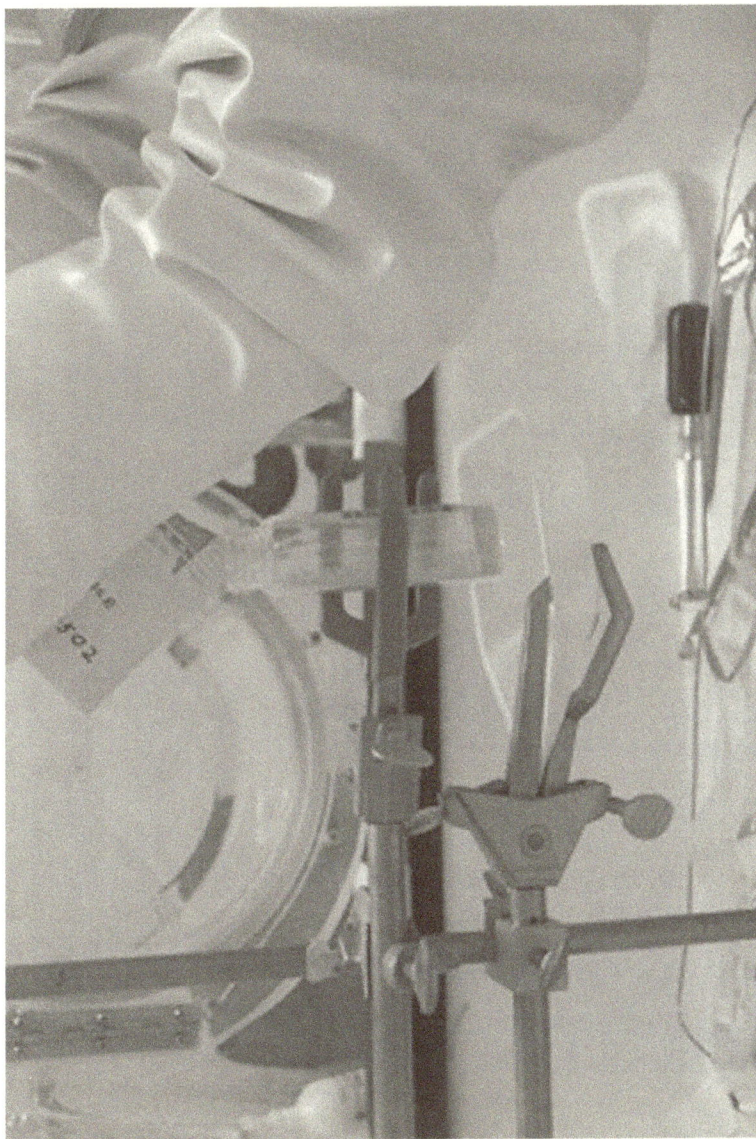

Figure 11. Pouring out the spore powder (0.9 grams) that was contained in the envelope and letter mailed to Senator Patrick Leahy. The work of opening the envelope and pouring the spore powder is being done in a sealed glovebox. FBI photo.

Figure 12. Hazmat-trained FBI agents, with the support of the New Jersey State Police, searching mail collection boxes in the Princeton, New Jersey, area. FBI photo.

Figure 13. Access badges used during search operations conducted by the Amerithrax Task Force. Photo by the author.

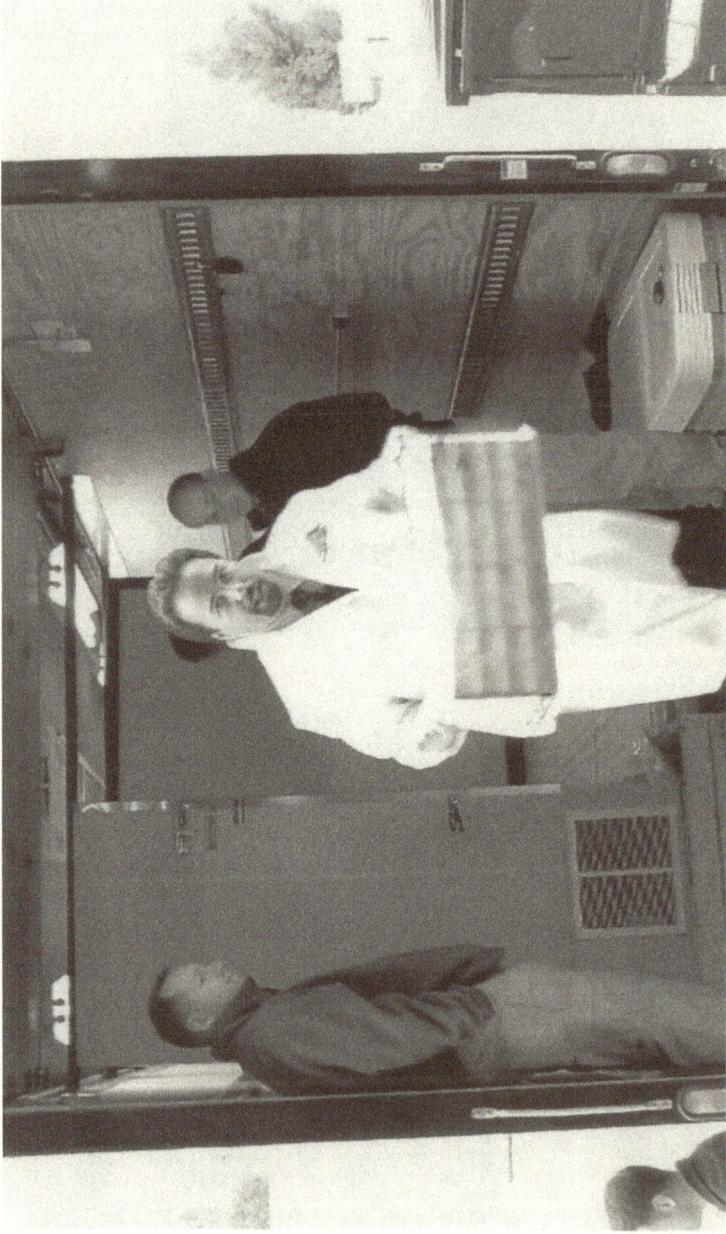

Figure 14. Repository of Ames exemplars arrives at Commonwealth Biotechnologies, Inc. (CBI) in Richmond, Virginia. The samples will be tested for one or more genetic mutations found in the mailed *Bacillus anthracis* spores. Pictured are (L to R) FBI Hazardous Materials Officer Tom Groel; CBI Vice President Tom Reynolds carrying frozen samples of Ames *B. anthracis* collected from North America and Europe; and FBI Special Agent Matt Feinberg. Note upright freezer in the background. Courtesy of Tom Reynolds.

14

Genetics

Winter–Summer 2003

Amerithrax-1 pressed on with the investigation of Steven Hatfill. They continued to sort through his life in Rhodesia and South Africa. Despite digging in the past and interviewing former special air service members, some of whom had immigrated to Northern Virginia, his claim of service could not be supported—at most a suggestion of one summer of mandatory service with a military clinic while in medical school. Any connection to the anthrax deaths of the late 1970s in the Rhodesian bush seemed remote.[1] Nor was there evidence of culturing bacteria—propagating deadly viruses, yes, but that required a different expertise than drying anthrax. Still, the task force kept up the surveillance, now assigning it to the office's Special Surveillance Group and hoping he would lead us to a hidden cache of evidence.

Meanwhile, the Sterilite box from the ice-covered pond became my immediate priority. Ezzell's staff began to take samples where the mud could be avoided. Scott Stanley and I had reservations; it seemed unlikely anthrax spores could avoid being washed away and DNA alone would not survive. Nuclease enzymes common in the environment, evolved long ago to destroy foreign DNA, would see to that. But the inspector and Bob Roth were insistent. Trace analysis in mud required expertise that Ezzell's staff had not yet developed, and I began searching among our anthrax testing contacts for a lab that could help.

In spring 2003, Inspector Lambert added a third squad, AMX-3, and stationed them in an off-site location five miles from the gates of USAMRIID. They picked up the pace investigating our various persons of interest, Bruce Ivins included. Ivins continued to raise suspicions—his proclivity to corner an FBI agent or postal inspector in the hallway and relay suspicions of current and former coworkers, appearing with the Red Cross during our ice dives, rushing to be the first to submit samples to the Ames repository but not following the protocol and then refusing to resubmit for another two months all contributing.

Over the course of 2003, during interviews and impromptu discussions, Ivins described his tenure at USAMRIID and the importance of his research. When he first arrived at USAMRIID in 1980, having finished postgraduate research at the University of North Carolina, followed by a short stint in Bethesda studying cholera, he began to research anthrax. At the time, the scientists in his Bacteriology Division worked on improving the anthrax vaccine using animal models.[2] Resistance of different strains of anthrax concerned the Division, and during the 1990s, Ivins and his colleagues experimented with ways of enhancing immune reactions by including additives they called "adjuvants." Including adjuvants in the vaccine can induce a stronger response than the vaccine alone.[3]

One adjuvant showing promise was monophosphyl lipid, or MPL.[4] MPL, produced by a species of *Salmonella* bacteria, significantly enhanced the anthrax vaccine's effectiveness, and in 1993 Ivins ordered a six-foot-tall freeze-drying instrument to aid in the production and purification of large amounts of the compound.[5] While there were smaller, more portable freeze dryers available in the rooms and hallways of USAMRIID, some on carts for ease in moving in and out of the laboratory suites,[6] Ivins's new machine, also called a lyophilizer, allowed for the rapid drying of large quantities.

Lyophilization is a relatively new development in biology. During World War II, life- saving serum shipped to Europe often spoiled before reaching aid stations and field hospitals and created a need for lyophilization. Once freeze dried, serum could be sent without refrigeration and remain stable for long periods. Adding sterile water reconstitutes the serum, making it ready for use. The technique soon found other uses in medicine, such as the preservation of equally important penicillin. The boom in gene cloning and biotechnology at universities and start-up companies during the 1980s saw a widespread use of freeze drying to stabilize purified DNA, proteins, and enzymes. The process is unlike drying with heat. It works on the basis of sublimation. During sublimation, a substance goes from a solid state to a gaseous phase without becoming liquid. In contrast to drying by heat and evaporation, water is completely removed without altering the material's structure. The process also allows material to be stored at room temperature without destruction by molds or bacteria. Materials chosen for freeze drying are first placed in a container, such as a round-bottomed glass bottle. The bottle is slowly rolled while slightly submerged in a mixture of alcohol and dry ice. Almost instantaneously, the material freezes, forming a thin layer coating the inside of the glass. Without allowing the thin layer to thaw, the bottle, in the case of portable freeze dryers, is attached to one of several black, thick-walled vacuum hoses extending from it, or in the case of Ivins's six-foot stationary machine, placed on one of several trays in its single vacuum chamber. As the freeze dryer's compressor pumps maintain a constant vacuum, the frozen water turns to vapor and disappears into the chamber of the machine. The remaining material—be it cloned DNA, a medically important protein such as insulin, expensive restriction enzymes, or Bt *israelensis* spores destined for insect control—will often be white or near-white and powdery when scraped out.

Testing the vaccines under the most realistic battlefield scenarios mandated challenging vaccinated animals with aerosols rather than injections of spores, and during the mid-1980s, the USAMRIID researchers moved from intramuscular inoculation to aerosol exposure. The switch to aerosolization required large amounts of spores. Whereas the injections realized very little waste, filling chambers with fine mists for sedated rabbits and monkeys to inhale was inefficient, and the majority of the aerosolized spores went unused.

Ivins produced spores by filling clear glass flasks with yellow broth, adding a drop of live Ames and clamping the flasks, up to eight at one time, inside a closed incubator preset to body temperature and fitted with a rotating metal floor. The flasks moved in slow circles, and the bacteria divided and multiplied as nutrients depleted. At the end of the third day—with skill, attention to detail, and an element of luck—more than 85 percent of the cells would convert to spores. Experience made the difference between lackluster or successful sporulation. The amount of light entering the flasks, the rate of rotation, and how much air mixed with the broth made the difference between success and failure. Ivins found that the Ames strain was a particularly strong sporulator, indicated by a ring of dried white froth above the broth's surface.

To clean the spores free of nonsporulated cells and debris, such as broken membranes, Ivins transferred the broth into plastic screw-top centrifuge bottles. Each bottle was placed in a heavy aluminum centrifuge rotor and spun for many minutes. Then he removed the bottles, poured off the yellow broth, and resuspended the spore pellet in cold, sterile water. He repeated the centrifuge spin and again resuspended the pellets. After a third centrifugation, Ivins combined the pellets, added a chemical preservative, and stored the spores in a refrigerator.

Throughout the 1990s, Ivins and his technicians produced batch after batch. Often the lots were Ames strain, which due to its high virulence[7] had become the gold standard for judging the efficacy of a change in vaccination protocol or addition of a new adjuvant. In an effort to standardize between different aerosol challenges, Ivins combined different production runs of his spores. He called the result Reference Material Research, RMR, assigned it number 1030, and shared it with his USAMRIID colleagues. Soon, only a small tube of RMR-1030 remained.

In 1997, Ivins calculated they would need ten trillion spores to complete the increase in vaccine challenges that were planned. It would take him two years to produce that amount, so Ivins contracted production to a laboratory noted for its past chemical and biological weapons testing, Dugway Proving Grounds in the isolated Great Salt Lake Desert, eighty-five miles southwest of Salt Lake City. As seed stock for Dugway's large production runs, Ivins took some of what was left of RMR-1030 and shipped it off. While the microbiologists in Utah worked to produce seven lots of concentrated Ames spores, Ivins and his technicians continued to make additional spores in their shaking incubator, which he planned to combine with the Dugway spores when they arrived. He designated his new mixture RMR-1029.[8]

During the spring of 2003, our search for a genetic signature in the mailed spores slowly gained momentum. Scott Stanley had set up a pipeline in which powder flowed to bacterial cultures, colonies grew out in variations of morphology, and noninfectious DNA entered a million-dollar-effort at TIGR. He expanded the coding system begun during the first meeting with John Ezzell and Terry Abshire. Ezzell, working in his sealed glovebox, wearing a double layer of thin and heavy gloves, placed minute amounts of powders in vials—one for Daschle, a second for Leahy, and the last for *New York Post*. He prepared a tube of agar and grew fresh colonies from the twenty-one-year spores of parental Ames. He made sure the vials bore only letters—a, b, c, d—and times and dates that would correspond to entries in his lab notebook, but no clues to the contents' true origin, and he transferred them to Pat Worsham.

Stanley asked Worsham to code the samples *GB*, standing for *Genome Bacillus*, to deflect attention from Ames and the ongoing investigation as the samples moved downstream for processing. Worsham herself did not know the exact origin of individual samples as she labeled variant A "GB8" and B "GB9," and the predominant morphology type—small, gray, and rough around its edges—the wild type—"GB10" before mailing them to Northern Arizona where Keim cultured them and harvested their DNAs and shipped them to TIGR for sequencing.

By May, TIGR had nearly completed the original isolate of Ames (GB6), the wild type in the mailed spores (GB10) and A- and B-variants (GB 8 and 9) from the Leahy letter. Even as TIGR sequenced, Worsham continued to select variants from the samples sent by Ezzell. She added Genome Bacillus numbers—GB11, 12, 13, and on—to Stanley's list. Comparing Ezzell's notes with Worsham's additions, Stanley requested more variants of Ames enter the pipeline: GB11, GB15, GB18.[9, 10]

Then, exciting news: TIGR had found a difference in sequence between the original 1981 Ames isolate and GB9. Word spread quickly, and the next day scientists from the Chemical Biological Sciences Unit called Stanley for the key to his coding system. The GB9 mutation was a single thymine that had switched to cytosine in an area adjacent to one of the genes controlling the cascade of phosphorylation during sporulation. Using the polymerase chain reaction test (described below), Keim quickly confirmed the mutation. Then, he confirmed the cytosine mutation in the B-variants from the *Post* and Daschle letters.[11]

Finally, we had a breakthrough. The B-mutation meant that the mailed Ames did have a unique DNA fingerprint, albeit faint, just one change in a genetic map of over five million. And the B-variant occurred only once in approximately one hundred bacterial colonies. But finding the mutation underlying the B-variant's odd morphology meant that we had been correct when I met with Rita Colwell and her National Science Foundation committee and we agreed to keep looking for DNA changes. Now, we could begin searching for a way to screen our collection of Ames for the cytosine mutation, as we asked TIGR to look harder at the A- and C-variants.

First, we would need an accredited biosafety containment laboratory, certified to work with live anthrax and with experience in forensics and courtrooms and the manpower to culture bacteria. Again, with the help of the FBI Laboratory, we turned to Commonwealth Biotechnologies and its vice president, Tom Reynolds. Reynolds had years of experience in research and applications of DNA diagnostics. Upon graduating Penn State University, he returned to his hometown of Pittsburgh and studied molecular biology at prestigious Carnegie Mellon before relocating to Richmond, Virginia, where he managed the Nucleic Acid Core Lab at Virginia Commonwealth University's Cancer Center. In 1992, he and two partners formed Commonwealth Biotechnologies and joined the ranks of biotech startups.

The modern-day biotechnology industry generally acknowledges its most successful progenitor as Genentech, a San Francisco company founded in 1976. In 1978, Genentech produced the first genetically engineered human drug, insulin protein, and called it Humulin. The scientists at Genentech made Humulin using newly discovered enzymes—restriction enzymes that cut DNA at precise locations. In nature, bacteria use them to restrict and to protect themselves against parasitic viruses, called bacteriophage, by cutting the invading DNA before the phage can usurp the bacteria's internal machinery. In modern-day technology, the enzymes—thousands have been discovered and hundreds marketed as tools for research—created a new business and fostered important advances in science and medicine. Genentech used restriction enzymes to cut the DNA of the bacterium *Escherichia coli* and inserted two genes that encoded human insulin. First grown on agar plates, then in liquid broth and culture flasks, and finally in forty-thousand-liter fermentation vats, the genetically engineered *E. coli* produced Humulin—synthetic human insulin. By the fall of 1982, the first human drug produced by recombinant DNA technology had received approval for use in the United States, United Kingdom, and Europe. By 1992, the drug giant Eli Lilly, partnering with Genentech, marketed Humulin worldwide in sixty-five countries.[12]

The first use of restriction enzymes also created controversy among America's scientific community. In 1974, the scientific community imposed a voluntary halt on recombinant DNA research. The field had advanced rapidly in the early 1970s, with DNA and its genes being cleaved and put back together, rearranged with novel insertions and deletions. Scientists experimented cutting the DNA of bacteria and simian monkey virus. Mixing gene fragments of one species with another worried some researchers, and debates swirled about new cancer-causing agents arising from overzealous experimentation. This was uncharted territory.

Leaders in the field organized an international meeting, held in early 1975 at the historic Asilomar Grounds on the Monterey Peninsula.[13] Attended by scientists, physicians, lawyers, and the press, the conference resulted in a list of recommendations for regulations, safety guidelines, and even experiments deemed too dangerous. The following year, the National Institutes of Health enacted guidelines based on the Asilomar recommendations.

The city of Cambridge, home to the country's most renowned institutes, leaders in biological research Harvard University and the Massachusetts Institute of Technology, went a step further. Within two weeks of the National Institutes of Health publishing their guidelines, the Cambridge City Council banned all recombinant DNA work for six months, buying time for a newly formed citizens' committee to review the matter.

But by the mid-1980s, laboratories across the country were using recombinant DNA to conduct routine experiments. The science community policed itself, gene cloning became the norm, and biotechnology advanced. The National Institutes of Health relaxed its guidelines. The fears of 1975 did not come to pass, and biotechnology start-ups have become multibillion-dollar corporations. Today, Genentech, now a Hoffmann-La Roche subsidiary—acquired in 2009 for $46.8 billion—employs over twelve thousand people worldwide.

Reynolds and his partners took Commonwealth Biotechnologies in a different direction. Rather than developing new pharmaceuticals for clinical trials, Commonwealth would devise new tests and diagnostic assays. Holding five patents for techniques that measure nucleic acids, he used his expertise and knowledge to run a state-of-the-art molecular biology laboratory. He also maintained a biosafety level-3 laboratory, had approval for access to CDC's National Laboratory Network protocols, and was certified to work with anthrax. Reynolds also performed the newest advances in polymerase chain reaction testing, a procedure that Reynolds thought would be useful for screening the Ames repository for the B-mutation.

Stanley, scientists from the Chemical Biological Sciences Unit, and I arrived at Reynolds's office early in the morning. Reynolds, assisted by his director of laboratory services, Greg Meyers, began by describing new tests that had been developed. They went by novel and creative names: Molecular Beacon, PNA-clamping, Snapshot.[14] All relied on the helical structure of the double-stranded DNA molecule and its ability to melt and become single strands when the temperature is raised, and then to rejoin—forming a helix exactly as before; each adenine, cytosine, guanine, and thymine pairing with its former partner—when the heat is removed. A change in the salt concentration of the liquid surrounding the DNA molecule induced a similar effect and could be used in combination with heat to fine-tune the melting and reannealing.

Two decades earlier, the Cetus Corporation, one of the original biotech companies, had patented a technique based on the ability of the dual strands of a DNA helix to melt and rejoin. They called the technology the polymerase chain reaction, now known as PCR, named after the polymerase enzyme that synthesizes long stretches of DNA as cells divide, grow, and multiply. The polymerase chain reaction came on the heels of restriction enzymes, and to-gether they revolutionized DNA research.[15] So much so that the 1993 Nobel Prize committee honored the inventors of PCR with a Prize in Chemistry, the first time a commercial company had been awarded a Nobel in science. A molecule of DNA can become two in less than five minutes, and soon, after twenty-nine more reactions, amplified to a billion. During PCR, double-stranded DNA is melted apart in the presence of short DNA fragments—ten or fifteen or twenty-five building blocks long—that serve to prime the synthesis of a new strand. A primer strand, matching in DNA sequence to one strand of the helix and a second primer strand, matching a sequence downstream on the opposite helix strand, bind to their complimentary sequences in the long, helical strands as the mixture is allowed to cool. A DNA polymerase enzyme is added that extends the short priming fragments. Completing one cycle of heating-cooling results in two new strands of DNA. Whereas one DNA molecule is undetectable with technologies available in either 1993 or 2003, when amplified to one billion copies, detection becomes routine. PCR changed the way infectious diseases are diagnosed, cancer genes detected, food contamination identified, and now, we hoped, would uncover an anthrax terrorist.

Reynolds described a recent variation of PCR. He called it TaqMan, a play on words with Pac-Man, the popular arcade game from Japan. In TaqMan, a third DNA fragment is added to a PCR reaction mix, complimentary to a DNA sequence within the target DNA to be amplified. Two chemical compounds are bound to the fragment, one at each end. The first compound is capable of fluorescing, but the second compound inhibits it, acting as quencher. The DNA polymerase also has an inherent second enzyme activity, a nuclease function. As the polymerase extends a primer fragment, its nuclease activity removes DNA fragments lying in its path. As the polymerase reaches the third chemically modified fragment, it cleaves off the fluorescent compound, which, now free from the quencher, begins fluorescing. As amplification proceeds, the fluorescence increases. But the change causing the B-variant was a single change, thymine to cytosine, and I knew from my own experience with PCR before joining the FBI that getting the third fragment to bind to B-variant DNA based on a single base change would be difficult.[16] A change of several building blocks was needed. But the B-variant was the only DNA fingerprint we had for the mailed anthrax, so we wished Reynolds and Meyers luck and gave them the go ahead.

As the summer of 2003 began, the scientists at TIGR continued sequencing. They had nearly finished GB8 (Leahy A-variant) without finding a difference from the original 1981 Ames. The only region remaining, impervious to their efforts, was a series of eleven duplicated genes encoding ribosomal RNA—part of the bacteria's internal machinery for the production of its thousands of diverse and essential proteins. Stanley requested more morphology variants be added to the pipeline. Worsham selected C-, D-, and E-variants, labeled them GB18, GB19, GB23, and GB24, and shipped them to Keim for DNA purification and transfer into TIGR's queue.[17]

Then, in June, TIGR called with great news. They had identified a mutation in GB8, a large duplication of over two thousand building blocks in the region of ribosomal genes, the area that so far had been resistant to their efforts. A close look and reassessment revealed the software that assembled the many fragments of DNA had erred, and once corrected, the missing sequence became apparent.[18] Stanley checked his code sheet and requested that GB11—the A-variant from the *Post* letter—be examined in the same region of DNA, and TIGR asked Keim to check GB15, the A-variant from Daschle's letter, using PCR. Again, TIGR found large rearrangements in the same area, similar but not identical to the change in GB8, and Keim found a similar rearrangement in GB15. Apparently the A-variant was a group of variation—A_1, A_2, A_3—in the ribosomal genes.

Stanley sent samples of GB8, GB11, and GB15 to Tom Reynolds and requested he confirm the results. If the rearrangements held up, the large changes in DNA sequence for the A-variants should be straightforward for detection by TaqMan.

15

Consent to Search

August 2003

The second anniversary of Robert Stevens's death approached, and we still had not uncovered any solid leads. I had flown the Sterilite box to a lab specializing in trace analysis of biological agents and spent four days watching scientists scrape mud and swab plastic, and as predicted, we found no anthrax DNA. But on the other hand, whole genome sequencing at TIGR picked up the pace. There, the scientists found that GB10's DNA (Leahy wild type) matched GB13's (*Post* wild type), and both matched the 1981 parental Ames's DNA. TIGR began using PCR to quickly examine the DNA samples arriving from Northern Arizona. They synthesized short DNA primer fragments matching DNA sequences on each side of the changes in the A_1, A_2, A_3, and B-morphologies. With PCR, TIGR could quickly determine the order of building blocks in a one-, two-, or three-thousand-length fragment in a matter of days, grouping variants as A or B or other, the latter then heading to the genome sequencing queue.

At CBI, Tom Reynolds confirmed the A-mutations using a PCR sequencing approach similar to that of Keim and TIGR, and he and Greg Meyers were confident that rapid screening tests could be designed. Using the TaqMan[1] assay, Reynolds believed that as little as ten DNA strands might be detectable if they designed the assay correctly.

The large duplicated regions of the A-mutants' DNA gave Reynolds options for choosing the sequence and length for both the priming and fluorescent fragments. Once the regions for fragment hybridizations had been decided, incubation conditions for the PCR—salt concentration and temperature, how long to melt, cool and reanneal—would be fine-tuned.

While CBI worked to develop A and B screening assays, I continued my search for Ames. I had compiled nearly 650 exemplars of Ames from sixteen laboratories[2] around the United States, but I had not yet collected any from outside the country. Interviews at USAMRIID revealed a shipment to the United Kingdom, and records in the institute's safety office verified Ames was sent to the laboratories of Porton Down, about one hundred miles southwest of London, equidistant from the ancient monuments of Stonehenge to the north and the city of Salisbury to the south.

The transfer made sense. Our two countries have cooperated on biological defense research since the onset of World War II. As early as 1934, information began appearing in the British press about Berlin's interest in spreading anthrax by aircraft. The British military took the news seriously and created Biology Department Porton—its mandate: study the feasibility of bacteriological warfare, defend against it, and develop a retaliatory capability.[3] The department found a home in the laboratories of the Chemical Defence Experimental Station at Porton, a small village at the edge of the Salisbury Plain chalk downlands. The British government had requisitioned seven thousand acres of rolling grassland in 1915 and established the Porton Laboratories and Porton Range following the start of the Great War, with the goal of preparing for chemical warfare with the Central Powers.[4] By the time World War II dawned, microbiology had advanced and weapons of bacteria could be added to England's arsenal. By 1942, the Biology Department at Porton developed aerobiology to the point that its microbiologists conducted bombing assault exercises using live anthrax spores. They targeted a herd of imported sheep on tiny Gruinard Island—rocky, covered with peat bogs, heather, and grasses—lying one-half mile off the coast of northwest Scotland. The scientists leading the assault on Gruinard traveled to the United States that same year and shared what they had learned with military personnel at Edgewood Arsenal on the Aberdeen Proving Grounds and Camp Detrick, the forerunner of modern-day Fort Detrick and USAMRIID. The Porton biologists began collaborating with the United States on experimental airborne infections. The alliance encompassed a diverse group—defense authorities in Canada, military officers from the Chemical Warfare Laboratories at the Massachusetts Institute of Technology, scientists in Columbia University and the University of Chicago, and leaders of the pharmaceutical industry.[5,6] Today, the Porton Down campus houses laboratories supporting both military and public health research in biological defense.

I contacted our legal attaché in London and requested that he initiate an inquiry of both military and public health components for samples of Ames. My request began a series of discussions followed by a trip to London and

Porton Down. Military officials agreed to transfer their samples, but the public health side was reluctant. A second meeting with officials in London was still unsuccessful. Finally, over coffee at the American Society of Microbiology's Biodefense Meetings in Baltimore I was able to convince a director in the Health Protection Agency that a genetic fingerprint had emerged and we were capable of distinguishing mailed Ames from the 1981 progenitor, and further, that a screening test was under development. He agreed, and I added over six dozen samples of Ames to our repository.[7, 8]

Between trips to England, Richmond, and Rockville an opportunity came up. Due to a promotion to Headquarters, a vacancy was created for supervisor of the AMX-2 squad. I had already been appointed its primary relief supervisor, which meant an acting role running the squad from time to time. Now, leading AMX-2 might become permanent. It would mean working more closely with the new Chemical Biological Sciences Unit at Quantico. I would also have a direct role in chemistry projects underway, such as detection of heme and agar[9] in spore samples and the stable isotope project I had proposed the year before. It would also mean handing off much of the genetic work and expansion of the Ames repository to the newer members of the squad—I had mixed feelings, but I decided to throw my hat in the ring—if I had the inspector's support.

As my search for Ames continued, I reread interview statements and subpoena returns and compared the information with the repository's holdings. My notes of Ivins's prior telephone calls and the interviews describing his submissions were vague. He never seemed to give the same answer twice. I decided to drive up to USAMRIID, where I located Ivins in his office and, undoubtedly annoying him, asked if he could tell me about the samples again. He replied that Pat Fellows had submitted the samples and could provide more information, but she had moved to another job. As far as he knew the four were: the original 1981 Ames; a culture he had taken from the original Ames in 1985; Dugway spores—thirty trillion in a single large glass flask that he now called *7737*; and Greg Knudson's culture of 1985.

Ivins went on to elaborate why one of the four samples would differ, patiently repeating what he had told agents last year. He explained that Knudson used a different method of subculturing anthrax. When Ivins had first arrived at USAMRIID, he was surprised to see that most researchers, including Knudson and John Ezzell, took a sample of anthrax by wiping a sterile swab through multiple colonies of anthrax growing on solid agar. They would use this group of colonies to inoculate broth or more agar plates to prepare spores for upcoming experiments. But during the early to mid-1980s, Ivins became aware that the newly discovered satellite DNAs—the two plasmids in anthrax—could disappear on occasion without affecting morphology. So, in a cluster of small bacterial colonies, one or more may contain a mutation, and over time mutations might accumulate. Ivins instead picked one, two, or at most three colonies from the hundreds growing in a culture plate. While the first, second, and third sample Fellows had submitted to the FBI would be homogenous in DNA sequence and morphology, in contrast the fourth sample, Knudson's, would likely contain variation. Ivins said that he had more samples that would prove his theory, specimens prepared by single colony picks that could be added to the FBI's collection. He called one RMR-1030, and there were three additional. All were leftovers of spore preps his group had grown between 1997 and 2001. He could also provide pages—almost twenty from his laboratory notebooks—that would show how carefully the preparations had been made following a single colony pick.

The pages detailed the density gradient that Ivins used to purify his spores. He began with the technique as a postdoctoral fellow at the University of North Carolina. After Ivins arrived at USAMRIID, the vaccine research group switched from agar plate to broth-grown spore preparation, but they still had trouble with nebulizer jets clogging during the aerosol challenges. Consistency from experiment to experiment proved frustrating. The water-washed pellet still contained an occasional broken cell wall, enough to block the fine tolerances machined into the jet's stainless steel. When Ivins learned of the clogging problem, he adapted his density gradient technique to preparing spores. After washing a pellet of spores in water, he carefully layered them on top of a dense solution, such as sucrose, or chemical compounds such as Ficoll or Renografin, and centrifuged the mixture. Spores themselves are extremely dense, while clinging debris, such as membranes from old, broken, or lysed bacteria cells, is lighter than the gradient material and remained on top. When the seven batches of concentrated spores arrived from Dugway in 1997, he had purified each of them over chemical gradients before combining them into RMR-1029 and adding another round of water washing. The dense chemicals should be easy to detect using standard biochemical tests.[10]

To prepare for a challenge experiment, Ivins took a small bit of RMR-1029 from its flask and diluted it to a predetermined amount depending on whether guinea pigs, mice, or monkeys would be tested. Ivins spread a tiny amount of the diluted spores across the surface of an agar culture dish. Twenty-four hours later he would count the tiny gray-white colonies, calculate the concentration of spores, and confirm his dilution correct. Ivins would also collect some of the aerosolized spores during a challenge and culture them on agar for one day to calculate the number of lethal doses the animals inhaled.[11] In each case, all the colonies appeared identical, proving RMR-1029 was a homogenous collection of spores.

Once back at my desk in Washington, I checked my notes but could find nothing called 7737, nor RMR-1030, and once again I telephoned Ivins for clarification. He answered on the first ring. He explained that the spores he called 7737 were the same as RMR-1029; USAMRIID used two different numbering systems to keep track of spore preparations. His 1985 culture of Ames was designated 7800a and Knudson's 1985 culture was 7800b. I told him that their system is confusing at best and made it difficult to keep track of each sample's origin. He again referred me to Pat Fellows, who prepared the submissions to the FBI. And then he continued, now claiming the submitted Knudson sample may not be from Knudson's stocks but from a collection that had belonged to a deceased scientist who had used Knudson's cultures. His freezer contained boxes of anthrax from both Knudson and the deceased scientist, in addition to Ivins's collection. Fellows may have provided the FBI repository with the wrong specimen. I thanked him and hung up the telephone, turning to my keyboard to write up this latest information and thinking how difficult it had become to believe anything he told us.

In the mid-1990s, the FBI switched from paper files and index cards to an electronic database called Automated Case Support, known in the office as simply ACS. Each document we wrote was uploaded into ACS, making it accessible to any FBI employee at Headquarters and all fifty-six field offices. Every agent, analyst, and postal inspector on the Amerithrax Task Force could rapidly search ACS for information on persons of interest, search warrants and their results, even laboratory reports. The downside was that we did not restrict access and ACS was a potential source for media leaks. At one point after reading details of our investigation in the newspaper, Bob Roth asked for a report of who accessed our virtual case file. The results showed that hundreds of people, many at Headquarters, routinely read Amerithrax files. But the good outweighed the bad.

Darin Steele joined my squad during 2003. While working in the Hazmat Response Unit as a postdoctoral fellow and then being brought on as a full-time microbiologist, he decided to try for the FBI Academy and become a special agent. His application moved along rapidly, and superiors at the FBI Laboratory gave him a stellar recommendation. Then 9/11 happened, and on its heels the anthrax attacks. Headquarters put his file on hold while he assumed duties at USAMRIID cataloging our anthrax samples. Once the flood of testing subsided, the Training Division reactivated his paperwork and assigned him a seat in new agent class. We immediately contacted the Transfer Unit and requested him for Amerithrax upon graduation. Now he studied the case and reviewed documents in ACS, including my interviews with Ivins.

He read about switching from agar to broth spore production, of multiple lots of culturing and harvesting, how Ivins and his assistants continued to produce additional batches while doling out small quantities of the trillions from Dugway. He reviewed the pages from Ivins's notebooks detailing multiple preparations of Ames spores made by fellow researchers at USAMRIID with assistance from Ivins. Steele wondered: *Was Ivins holding back?*

Steele approached Ivins and explained his concerns. Property sheets at US-AMRIID showed Ivins was assigned a stand-alone refrigerator and a freezer. That Ivins also had use of a cold room—similar to a butcher's walk-in meat locker—occasionally used to conduct experiments requiring constant refrigeration or to store large flasks, such as holding RMR-1029. *Would it be okay if Steele looked through them, just to be thorough, on the off chance that maybe Ivins's technician had overlooked or forgotten a spore sample or two?*

Ivins agreed, and the two walked to the Bacteriology Division's biocontainment suite, a collection of sixteen biosafety level-3 (BSL-3) laboratory rooms, each assigned to a researcher and their technicians. USAMRIID allowed access to its BSL-3 labs to only those who had received a battery of vaccinations and a schedule of Hazmat training. A former member of the FBI's Hazardous Materials Response Unit and new member of the Washington Field Office Hazmat Response Team, Steele had the training. As manager of FBI's Ames repository, he was part of USAMRIID Special Immunization Program and had received the requisite inoculations.

The two entered the suite and came to Ivins's lab room, B313. Ivins opened the door of his refrigerator and showed Steele racks of wide opaque plastic test tubes topped with blue screw caps. Steele recognized one from his reading: RMR-1030. It contained fluid, a small pellet at the bottom and a number designation not in the repository database. They left B313 and walked to the narrow hall running the length of the suite. Two doors down they entered the walk-in refrigerator. Stainless steel shelves ran along the walls. Flasks and racks of tubes sat on a bench, the shelves, and the floor. One clear glass flask, an Erlenmeyer flask, sat on the bench. It was named after its inventor, Dr. Emil Erlenmeyer, a German chemist, who created the original almost 150 years ago, in 1857. Designed to hold liquids of all kinds and manufactured in several sizes, they are extremely stable and heavy. This one, large enough to hold a quart, stood nine inches tall and was five inches wide at its base, narrowing to one-and-a-half inches at the top. Steele saw that it contained two, maybe three inches of turbid liquid, and someone had written *RMR-1029* on the glass in black marker and placed a long piece of yellow tape across the side, at an angle. It bore handwriting, also in black: *spores* and *7737*.

Steele followed Ivins out of the walk-in cold room and to the freezer used by Ivins. Opening it, Steele looked over the frozen tubes, boxes, and racks as frost vapors swirled in slow circles. He noted several boxes—seven after counting—labeled *Ames*. The boxes bore names of USAMRIID research scientists Steele recognized as having left army employment, including Knudson, along with dates of "1985," "Dec 89," "3/91," "9/92," "3/92," and "11/2000." One box bore Ivins's name. More boxes labeled *Ames* carried names of people unrecognizable to Steele. As he looked through the contents of the boxes, racks, and beakers he kept counting and reached forty-one— samples that had not been submitted to the repository he managed.[12]

During November, the Washington Field Office career board met and recommended me for promotion to supervisory special agent of the Amerithrax-2 squad. In December, the Middle Management Selection Board at Headquarters confirmed the recommendation, and Deputy Director Bruce Gebhardt signed off, making it official. I would begin meeting weekly with scientists in the Chemical Biological Sciences Unit, and I particularly looked forward to senior scientist Bruce Budowle's input. I would cease taking part in most interviews while turning my attention to conducting squad file reviews, assessing informant files for compliance to assorted Bureau requirements, and approving expense vouchers. I reassigned the genetics and repository collection initiatives to Rick Langham, a new agent on the squad with a doctorate in plant pathology, and I asked two agents on the squad with PhDs in chemistry to review the stable isotope project and the initiatives to detect heme and agar in spore preparations.

I also found there was considerable pressure from the inspector and Headquarters to analyze spores from the Leahy letter for these chemical compounds; evidently there was a feeling we were dragging our feet. But a preliminary look at the work contracted to the University of Utah's Stable Isotope Facility showed the situation to be more complicated than we had expected. The ratios of $^{18}O/^{16}O$ and $^{2}H/^{1}H$ in water did vary across the United States according to geography; this variation should be reflected in the composition of spores grown in different climates. But evaporation, temperature, and altitude also influenced the ratios of oxygen and hydrogen isotopes. Until the influence of these individual parameters could be understood, a test result might take us in the wrong direction. Scientists at the University of Maryland had contracted the heme detection work, and they could distinguish the

compound in spores grown on blood agar. But the assay detected a degrada-
tion product of heme that was not stable, making it difficult to standardize
the analysis between samples. I felt both assays needed additional validation
before committing to destructive analyses of precious Leahy evidence. The
agents on AMX-2 agreed, but we could feel the urgency coming down from
management to begin testing.

16

American Eagle

Winter 2004

Tom Reynolds and his Commonwealth Biotechnologies team worked through the fall and into the winter. They designed polymerase chain reaction primers and TaqMan probes of different compositions and lengths. They tested reaction conditions, altering melting temperatures and adjusting PCR phases: two, seven, or eight minutes to polymerize, one-half minute to denature, and another for annealing. An assay for the B-variant proved elusive; the single thymine to cytosine change in DNA sequence was not enough to allow stable binding of a mutant (C) primer fragment and no binding of a wild-type (T) primer during the annealing cycle of PCR. But as Reynolds had predicted, tests for the larger duplications of A_1 and A_2 and the triplicated region of A_3 showed promise.

Once conditions had been established for ultimate sensitivity and reproducibility, CBI's staff turned their attention to ensuring accuracy. They added control samples designed to generate positive and negative responses. The positive control guaranteed that if an Ames sample in our repository failed to give a TaqMan signal, it meant the sample did not contain an A-variant, rather than the result of a PCR malfunction. Failure could be due to a number of reasons: not maintaining correct temperatures, malfunction of the polymerase enzyme, using the incorrect salt solution. TaqMan probes could be made with dyes that emitted different wavelengths of colored light: blue, green, orange, pink. The positive control would be a different color than the probe for the A-variant. Polymerase chain reactions typically contained an added human gene not found in bacteria as the positive control. The negative control would have water substituted for a repository sample. If it generated a TaqMan signal then cross contamination would be indicated, a problem that plagued the polymerase chain reaction in its early days.

As the investigation entered its third winter, Reynolds contacted us to announce he had finalized development of screening tests for the A_1-, A_2-, and A_3-variants. I conferred with Scott Stanley, and we decided to send CBI blinded samples of wild-type Ames and the three A-variants. If Reynolds's team could tell us which samples contained the variants and which did not, with 100 percent accuracy, we would begin testing our repository. With Pat Worsham's help, Stanley prepared four dozen samples, coded, in duplicate, and drove them to CBI. There, Reynolds would test the duplicates on different days. His results would be a final assessment of accuracy, sensitivity, and reproducibility.[1]

On the task force, the news spread quickly. Darin Steele's finding samples of Ames that Bruce Ivins had not turned over after repeatedly being asked two years before raised suspicions dramatically. Authorization was requested for pen registers—dialed number recorders—on his house telephone and two cell phones. The electronic devices would record all numbers called from the three phones. Then we began surveillance at his residence and conducted periodic trash covers—a fancy term for sorting through the garbage he put out on the curb.

As supervisor of the Amerithrax Science Squad, I now delegated much of the daily genetic work and began to look at adding forensics projects. I sat down with Tom Dellafera, and we reviewed work done on the attack envelopes. A supervisory postal inspector with an office in the contaminated and now shuttered Brentwood facility, he had been our sole Postal Service representative on Amerithrax when we worked from folding tables and chairs in the cramped first-floor training classroom. He now supervised a dozen postal inspectors spread across our three AMX squads.

Originally from New England, Dellefera had moved to northern Virginia to become a US Postal Service auditor before joining the Inspection Service. The Federal Eagle envelopes were printed with a thirty-four-cents stamp, the equivalent of currency, and as a former auditor he knew the Postal Service kept detailed records of their manufacturing and shipping, storage location, and final destination for sale to the public. As we looked at what had been done, we realized that other than tracing the envelopes through the mail stream using postmarks and fluorescent printing on the reverse sides, nothing further had been attempted. I had spent summer breaks from college working in hometown paper mills[2] bordering the Delaware River in central New Jersey. Most of the time I drove forklifts and filled boxcars with one-ton rolls of specialty paper, such as dielectric paper for oil-filled transformers or fiber paper used in air, oil, and fuel filters. But I also spent time in the quality control department, closely monitoring paper chemistry as the huge rolls came off the line. I measured variation in nitrogen content, and we had saved the data in production files. Would similar information exist for Federal Eagle paper?

Dellafera and I decided to visit the mill that had made the envelopes and find out. The next day, with an AMX-2 agent-chemist in tow, we started out on a three-and-a-half-hour drive to Tyrone, Pennsylvania, home of the American Eagle Paper Mills. A small town, situated equidistant between Pittsburgh and Harrisburg, Tyrone is known as the Hub of the Highways. It is situated on the Little Juniata River, known as the Little J, where four railroads and three highways converge. The railroads once served the area's busy coalfields, but since the 1970s, coal mining in the area has grown quiet. One of Little J's tributaries is the Bald Eagle Creek. Beginning in the late 1800s, the creek served to power paper production for the West Virginia Pulp and Paper Company, later becoming Westvaco Corporation and most recently, American Eagle Paper Mills.

Arriving at American Eagle, we met with its president and discussed the paper used to make the attack envelopes. They had been produced from five-hundred-pound rolls of recycled paper. American Eagle specialized in the production of recycled paper known for high quality—customers have included *National Geographic* magazine. The process began with discarded paper, which is placed into a pulping container with water and gradually blended into a slurry of fibers. Soaps are added to clean the new pulp of ink and dirt. The slurry, quite dilute now, is pumped onto rolling mats, vibrated to help the water drain and to allow the individual fibers to interlock and form large sheets. The interlocked fibers are not continuous, but mixed with gaps and spaces forming the pores that had allowed spores to escape at the Brentwood and Trenton processing centers and along the mail delivery route. But when we asked about quality control records, the president shook his head. He agreed to show us around, but there were no files. We walked past pulp tanks, now quiet, down a smooth concrete floor, past red painted walls and into a dark, empty room. This was where records should be stored, but the file cabinets and banker boxes had vanished. The president explained that the Westvaco mill had closed its doors in October 2001 and he had only recently succeeded in purchasing it. He had reopened last year as American Eagle. Records may have existed, but no longer. We had come to a dead end.

Dellafera suggested we pay a visit to the company where the envelopes had been made. The rolls of recycled paper had been sent twenty miles south to Westvaco's packaging plant, which had reorganized into MeadWestvaco when the paper mill had been shuttered. Fortunately, MeadWestvaco's plant manager had kept Westvaco's production records. The contract to print envelopes had run from December 2000 through March 2002. Over fifteen months, forty-five million envelopes had been made. Studying the detailed records, we found that there had been fifty-seven separate production runs. Of the forty-five million, five-and-one-half million of the envelopes had been made after the first mailing in September 2001 and could be eliminated as being used in the attacks. We also discovered that in January 2001, after nine million envelopes had been made, the Postal Service had ordered a reformulation of the blue and gray inks used to print the Eagle stamp. With luck, we would be able to determine whether the mailed envelopes contained old or new ink using a nondestructive analysis. Old ink would mean that the mailed envelopes came from a pool of nine million; new ink enlarged the pool to thirty-one million. In either event, the Postal Service kept exacting records of where the envelopes had been sent, usually in lots of one hundred, five hundred, or one thousand.[3] MeadWestvaco shipped them in boxes of five hundred, either as individual envelopes wrapped in cellophane, or banded in packs of five destined for post office vending machines.[4]

After we had looked through the production records, the plant manager showed us a brightly lit room measuring approximately ten by fifteen feet— the heart of their flexographic printing process.

"Here is where we make the plates, in this room." He walked to the front edge of a long metal table. On the table lay a flat piece of plastic, twenty-four inches square, translucent with a yellowish tint.

"Is this one?" Dellafera said.

"Yes. What we do is place a stencil of the Eagle stamp on the flat photopolymer. Its acts like a film negative. Then we shine UV light on it. Exposure to the ultraviolet turns the polymer hard, so we can wash away the unexposed areas. The area on the polymer unprotected by the stencil stays hard and becomes the printing plate for the envelopes."

"How long does one plate last?"

"Normally for one production run, in your case, just under a million envelopes. So we make new plates for each run. One plate on each side of the print roller, two per run. Held on with self-adhesive tape on the back. Even the amount and type of adhesive in the tape we use can make a big difference on the quality of the printing. The polymer wears slightly during the production run. It can accumulate small bits of dust and specks of debris. Or, ink can build up."

"So, the first stamp printed during a run is slightly different than the last one printed?" I asked.

"Hopefully, not so the average person would notice," said the manager.

Leaving the polymer room, we moved to the center of the warehouse floor and stood in front of a twenty-foot-long printing machine, an assembly of metal cylinders, belts, and control boxes with red, green, and white lights and black switches. An eight-foot-long stainless steel roller at the right end, eight feet above the base, held the flexible printing plates. To the left, a six-foot roll of white paper hung on a round bar, horizontally, three feet from the floor. Against the plate roller followed three more steel rollers—the impression roller to hold the paper against the plate roller, the anilox roller covered with tiny inkwells, and the fountain roller that dipped into ink that was transferred to the anilox roller. Plastic jugs supplied the ink.

As we watched, the machine made white envelopes. The machine boss, or tender, a man in his thirties, medium height and slim, slid around the roller ends and control boxes. He moved quickly but not hastily, with practiced ease—confident, alert, and focused. He checked the ink levels in the jugs, the oil reservoir cups at the ends of each steel roller, and the speed. Too fast and the paper would break and tear across itself, jamming the machine. No oil and the hardened steel bearings keeping each roller's rotation smooth would overheat and seize. Run low on ink and an alarm would sound, but if the alarm malfunctioned the machine would produce blank envelopes, wasting money and time.

A two-person team at the left end of the printer gathered stacks of envelopes as they passed down a moving belt, picking them up in the order they appeared and stacking them in gray cardboard boxes. On one end of a box a team member wrote a series of numbers and letters in black marker—the date, time, and a number referring to the box's order in the manufacturing run.

Three years ago, the envelopes filling the boxes would have been printed with a small blue eagle standing upright over *USA*, head turned to the right and outstretched wings. Below, in gray: *34*. The back of the envelopes would also have black inscriptions: "This Envelope is Recyclable and Made with 100% Recycled Paper," and "©USPS 2000."[5]

Once back in Washington,[6] Dellafera and I relayed to the AMX-2 squad what we had learned at MeadWestvaco and debated the next step. The FBI laboratory had a Questioned Documents Unit, best known for handwriting comparisons. It also compared typewriting and maintained a watermark library and a collection of sneaker and shoe prints. But identifying minute printing defects that appeared during a production run of a million envelopes seemed more akin to detecting sophisticated forgeries, a mission of the US Secret Service. Its Forensic Services Division had years of experience detecting tiny differences in ink and print. One of my AMX-2 agents who had been a technician with the Secret Service laboratory before joining the FBI placed a telephone call to her former boss. Another went downstairs to check the attack letters out of evidence storage. It was the first time I had seen the Daschle, *Post*, and Brokaw envelopes in person. For a moment I studied them in silence, fragile pieces of deadly paper now a part of our country's annals.

At the same time, Dellefera directed his inspectors to begin collecting Federal Eagle envelopes. They located unopened boxes at a Postal Service warehouse in northern Virginia. Each box bore a marking code similar to what we had seen at MeadWestvaco. Then they found the records for envelopes that had been shipped around the country. The log sheets listed five hundred envelopes going to the main post office in Hagerstown, five thousand to a large postal facility in Baltimore, and two hundred destined for a postal retail store in Westminster, Maryland.[7] The logs included the day and time of shipment to dozens and hundreds of post offices. By the time we were finished, three hundred thousand Federal Eagles would be transferred to the Secret Service.

Spring brought the validation work at CBI to a close. Scott Stanley and I drove to Richmond for what we hoped would be a final review of test data and a kickoff for Ames repository screening. At CBI, the receptionist buzzed us into the front lobby and gestured toward the small conference room. There, Tom Reynolds and Greg Meyers greeted us with broad smiles, doughnuts, and coffee.

"The A_1 and A_3 assay are performing well. We have some false positive issues with A_2, but we should be able to get it fixed," Reynolds began. "Detection with the A_1 assay is down around five copies in one million. For A_3, it's one in a million."

"All the samples, Tom? Across the board? Do all the duplicates agree?" Stanley said.

"Yes, with the exception of A_2. The A_1 and A_3 duplicates all agree. Like I said, we have a few false positives with A_2 right now," Reynolds said.

I joined in. "Is the issue with A_2, that we need to pick new primers or probes? They don't hybridize with good fidelity and tend to mismatch when annealing?"

"Possibly, we haven't finished troubleshooting yet," Reynolds said.

"Is the difference in sensitivity between A_1 and A_3 because A_1 is a duplicate and A_3 a triple duplication?"

"We think so. A_3 has twice as many primers and probes binding, so we get a stronger signal. TaqMan lights up sooner with A_3," Meyers added.

"It looks good, Tom, let's go ahead with A_1 and A_3. Let's not worry about A_2 right now. We have to move forward. We could still get another mailing; whoever did it is still out there." Stanley glanced at me as I nodded in agreement.

"The sensitivity should be enough. You're detecting A_1 and A_3 in all three letters, *Post*, Leahy, and Daschle. That agrees with our estimates that the total A-variants are a little over 1 percent of the total, and if there are one hundred different A mutations—worse case—we think there are at least a dozen—that's one in ten thousand in the spore powder for either A_1 or A_3. So, your detection limits will do it."

"We can move the Ames repository down here at any time. When is good for you, Tom?" I said.

"We're ready now. We'll schedule around you, Scott. Just let us know when we can start."

Before adjourning, we reviewed how the repository would be transferred from USAMRIID to CBI. Duplicate samples of each submission would be transported in a -70 degree centigrade freezer by truck. A backup would be on standby. A waiver to bypass the commercial weigh scales would be requested from both Maryland and Virginia State Police. An FBI Hazmat officer would accompany the delivery as a safety precaution, along with an Amerithrax agent. An operations order would be written before the transfer and approved by the inspector, who would also notify Headquarters. The Command and Tactical Operations Center at the field office would monitor radio transmissions during the transport, and Jim Rice's Special Weapons and Tactics team would be on alert. Task force agents would drive in front and follow behind. All vehicles would be unmarked, and no one would wear identifying insignia—maintaining a low profile at all times.

Reynolds and Meyers reviewed the testing protocol. Both duplicates of each sample would be tested in triplicate—six TaqMan runs per submission by different technicians. All six results had to agree for a conclusion about the presence of A_1 and A_3. Following the TaqMan reactions, the DNA products of the PCR would be sequenced and compared to the A_1 duplication and A_3 triplication; again agreement was required for both strands of the DNA helix. Reynolds would also conduct weekly tests to gauge his scientists' proficiency. Samples would be prepared, coded, and analyzed for the presence of A_1 and A_3. All in accordance with accepted forensic practice. If Reynolds did find an A_1 and A_3 among the Ames exemplars, he could expect to testify about it in court.

Stanley and I recognized that the repository screening could not be perfect no matter what controls we included or how exhaustive our search for Ames. Screening for an A-variant was a negative experiment—not finding an A didn't mean the mutation had never been in a particular sample or held by a submitting laboratory. Mutations revert. Though rare, there was always a chance that A_1 or A_3 would mutate backward and return to the original wild-type gene each time the anthrax bacteria multiplied, every time its DNA replicated.

The submission protocol also had room for sampling errors.[8] Given the low percentage of each A-variant, a less-than-thorough swipe across the agar of a culture plate or incomplete mixing of a liquid culture might leave a variant behind. While carefully thought out with the help of both John Ezzell and Paul Keim, the protocol for submission was still subject to individual interpretation. And we recognized the flaws inherent with the subpoena process. It relied on the honesty, conscience, and accountability of recipients. But in early 2002, we did not have sufficient probable cause to shut down and search sixteen laboratories.[9]

As we joined the commuters and travelers and headed north on Interstate 95, we kept our fingers crossed. While not perfect, the repository screening just might point the way to the anthrax killer.

17

Discrepancy
May 2004

$\mathbf{I}$t was Monday morning as I walked into my office at Washington Field. I had spent the weekend hosing off gear in my driveway. Dirt and a fine tan silt dust covered everything. Four days ago, I had returned from Afghanistan and spent Friday afternoon unpacking and cleaning. The trip, temporary duty in support of the war on terror, luckily had been uneventful. Many FBI agents were making trips over to the Sandbox, as our military partners called the Afghan desert. We helped organize, sort, and catalog intelligence and collected evidence. The tours could last from weeks to months, and many agents volunteered multiple times.

I took a seat at my desk and turned on my computer and began to sort through three-and-a-half weeks of email messages when Scott Stanley knocked on the door. I had an inkling that there was good news but did not know any details yet.[1] He began to explain, more animated than usual:

By the middle of May, test results began to arrive from Commonwealth Biotechnologies. Tom Reynolds had tested a third of the Ames we had transferred to him, and the first two hundred had been negative, no sign of either an A_1 or A_3 mutation. Then, at the end of the first week of May, Reynolds had telephoned. A repository sample being tested for the A_1 mutation gave a TaqMan signal nearly one hundred times stronger than the negative water controls. The polymerase chain reaction products had been sequenced and matched the A_1 mutation. All the positive and negative controls had tested correctly.

As soon as he replaced the telephone receiver, Stanley rushed to locate his code sheet. The positive match came from Darin Steele's December search, the remains and dilutions of old spore preparations. Then Reynolds called back with bigger news. His team had found more samples containing the A_1

duplication and one sample containing both the A_1 and A_3 mutations. Stanley checked the codes. The A_1 matches were spore samples that belonged to Bruce Ivins and his coworkers, most from the boxes and racks Steele searched during December. But the A_1+A_3 double match interested Stanley the most. A notation on his code sheet indicated the sample was a dilution—designated 7738, adding further confusion—of 7737, the designation used for the flask of pure concentrated spores from Dugway. Interchangeably called Dugway spores or RMR-1029 or 7737, it was a combination of six fermentation lots produced at Dugway Proving Grounds and over three times as many small shaking broth culture lots added by Ivins in 1997.

When Reynolds reported the first double match, news had spread quickly. Knowing that Steven Hatfill had begun work at USAMRIID in 1997, AMX-1 agents pulled the laboratory access records and scanned them for Hatfill's name and access to Ivins's containment lab. The records, kept since mid-1998 when magnetic cards came into use, showed Hatfill entering his virus laboratory, but no activity around Ivins's B313 lab.

Before long, Reynolds called back to report a second A_1+A_3 double match. As Stanley scanned down the code sheet, its origin surprised him. A large government contract laboratory in the Midwest—Battelle Memorial Institute—had submitted the sample. The facility had been one of the first to comply with the subpoena. AMX-1 agents quickly reviewed Hatfill's travel records, credit card receipts, and telephone toll records for mention of the Midwest contract lab or a trip to Ohio and again came up empty.

As far as I was concerned, this was the first solid break in the case. At the same time, it became clear to Rick Lambert that we did not have every sample of Ames. Committed to a thorough, no-stone-unturned investigative approach, Inspector Lambert directed us to begin drafting search warrant affidavits. USAMRIID would be explored from top to bottom, each laboratory, freezer, refrigerator—every place a sample of anthrax could be stored. And USAMRIID would not be alone. The Battelle lab would be searched, and since Dugway Proving Grounds had supplied at least a portion of the spores matching the evidence, we would include them as well.

The underlying probable cause to believe more Ames samples would be found was abundant. The affidavits would cite noncompliance with the subpoena given to USAMRIID in 2002. It would describe how forty-one Ames samples had been found in Ivins's containment lab. And it would highlight the fact that one of those found samples matched the evidence. We would include our recent genetic test results and demonstrate to the court that we had a proven method for comparison. Looking back, we felt that we had come a long way in three years.

Supervisory Special Agent Terry Kerns arrived early on Saturday of July fourth weekend, well before 6:00 a.m. Within minutes, FBI Hazmat officers pulled up in black Chevrolet Suburbans and a white twenty-foot box truck containing a -70 degree freezer. They parked behind the main laboratory and administrative building of USAMRIID and backed the truck under the overhanging roof of the loading dock. Unmarked Impalas, Crown Victorias, and more Suburbans bearing license plates from Pennsylvania, New Jersey, and District of Columbia joined the Quantico team. One by one agents filed through the laboratory building's back door carrying large black nylon bags. They wore the ubiquitous tan cargo pants, a small green Royal Robbins label stitched to the top of the right bellows pocket.

The arrival of Kerns and her Hazmat teams followed tense negotiations earlier in the week when Lambert, Bob Roth, and I had met with USAMRIID's commander and his principal scientists. Behind closed doors, the commander began to describe our intentions, and the group immediately became hostile. They repeatedly questioned our need to search their labs. Heatedly overtalking each other, they cited ongoing experiments with animals to be fed, blood draws scheduled, bacterial cultures growing, and spores being produced that would need harvesting. They brought up a concern we had not anticipated—the monkey colony. USAMRIID housed an extensive collection of nonhuman primates. Living in cages, stacked two and three high, kept in the back corner of the laboratory building away from noise and interruptions were rhesus and cynomolgus macaques and green monkeys.

The primates were vital to USAMRIID's research. USAMRIID used the colony to test the efficacy of new vaccines against anthrax, botulism, tularemia, Q-fever, and plague. The monkeys also served to analyze the course of infection from deadly hemorrhagic viruses: Ebola, Cuevavirus, and Marburg.[2] It was important that the colony remain as calm as possible. A loud noise or perceived insult, even a sideways glance from one of us, could set off the entire group. One moment they would rest, lying in their cages, the next instant a screaming clamor, each one competing with their peers: standing, jumping, reaching, grabbing.

Lambert consented to several of the researchers' requests. If one of them would be willing to take an agent into the primate rooms so we could certify them free of freezers and refrigerators, there would be no reason to disturb the macaques and monkeys further. Researchers would also be allowed to check on experiments and ensure food and water was available for their rabbits, monkeys, mice, and rats, if willing to be accompanied by an agent. We would begin searching at the beginning of the weekend and make every effort to wrap up by Tuesday morning, the end of the holiday weekend. Finally, after more discussion, and learning we had obtained a search warrant they consented.

Kerns began by assembling the agents and reviewing her roster. The Philadelphia, Newark, Baltimore, and Chicago divisions had sent their Hazardous
Materials Response Teams. She had two more field offices on standby. She
grouped them into four-person teams, each with an Amerithrax agent who
would serve as team leader. The task force agents had institutional knowledge
of the investigation, and in addition to anthrax, they would also be on the
lookout for rolls of transparent tape, Federal Eagle envelopes, references to
the envelope's addresses, and language in the letters.

The operation began quietly and methodically. Each team member dressed
in level-C Hazmat gear, a fitted face mask, and two layers of thin, purple
nitrile gloves secured with gray duct tape around their wrists. They folded
the final inch of the tape over on itself and did the same around the tops of
the yellow rubber boots. Their equipment included several upgrades, added
since the early days of the investigation. The masks had been fitted with
microphones and receivers, synchronized with the encrypted radios hanging
on their belts. The microphone sets contained "bone mics"[3] for hands-free
communication. The transmitting microphone positioned itself against the
throat, touching the area of the Adams apple, and the receiver stayed against
the bone in front of the operator's ear.

The operation went through Saturday night and into Sunday. As Sunday
wore on, more and more calls came over the radio announcing additional
Ames.[4] We had made a promise to wrap up by Tuesday morning, but it looked
as if we might not make it. In the back of everyone's mind was the inevitable
arrival of the press and media. No one—not the inspector, the agents searching, nor USAMRIID's commander—wanted a repeat of the satellite trucks and
helicopters that we had at the American Media building and Hatfill's apartment. I asked Kerns to call in the field teams on standby.

The work dragged on. As the teams searched through shelves, freezers, and
refrigerators, they cross-checked the list of samples in the repository database
to avoid taking a sample we already had. The three hundred samples previously provided by USAMRIID numbered nearly half of those in the Ames
repository.

While Kerns and her teams searched the laboratories of USAMRIID, parallel
operations took place in Ohio and Utah. Tom Dellafera had taken a small team
to the Dugway Proving Grounds. Dugway, also a US Army base, consented to
the search as USAMRIID had. Meanwhile, a third team headed to Columbus
and the laboratories of Battelle Memorial Institute. By the end of the searches,
we added three hundred more samples to our repository of Ames.

Stanley drove through the checkpoint and entered Marine Corps Base Quantico. Hot, humid, and oppressive—another August day with the temperature

approaching three digits—he heard the thumping repetition of large-caliber machine guns in the distant woods. A thud of artillery interrupted the gunfire, followed by a slight jarring in the ground as he walked from the three-story parking garage toward the FBI's new laboratory building, its stacks of roof-top vents giving it the appearance of a modern-day *Titanic*. Blue-gray smoke carried the smell of burnt pine across the surrounding lawns. The Marines, always preparing to defend our country, had touched off the underbrush again.

Stanley took a seat at the end of the conference table and opened his spreadsheet identifying the hundreds of entries to the Ames repository. Tom Reynolds began the meeting by reviewing his confirmation of TIGR's sequencing of the mutated region in the A morphology variants and the development of the rapid assays for A_1 and A_3 testing.[5] He reviewed the controls—positive and negative—in place during the repository screening and how he had sequenced the DNA products produced during the TaqMan assay. Finally, he presented his last slide, a single page listing six samples by their coded identifiers: "FBIR[6] 049-004" and "FBIR 052-026" and so on.[7, 8] Since finding the first two matches to the attack spores, CBI had identified four more samples containing both A_1 and A_3 mutations. Stanley followed along, locating each identifier in his spreadsheet. Tracing his finger down the first column until he came to a sample listed by Reynolds as matching the evidence, he then traced to the right until he came to the column containing the descriptors that had been on each sample's original container. Three of the samples had been taken by Darin Steele last December, one marked "Dugway spores," another labeled "Ivins 3x10e10" and "7738." He came to another of the matching samples, this one designated "GLP[9] RMR 1029." The sample had only recently been added to the spreadsheet by Darin Steele and sent to CBI for the TaqMan queue. After CBI had reported 7738 as the first A_1+A_3 match, Steele had taken the flask of RMR-1029 as potential evidence and placed a sample into the repository. As Stanley looked up the samples matching the evidence, it was clear that each double match was related to RMR-1029—"Dugway spores," "7738," and "Ivins 3x10e10," which Stanley knew stood for $3x10^{10}$—the unusually high concentration of spores found in RMR-1029. Information had also arrived from the Midwest earlier that month. The contract lab possessing the double A_1+A_3 match had identified the submission's origin—it had been shipped from USAMRIID and labeled "RMR-1029."

Stanley moved his finger back up to the beginning of the log sheet, back to the samples added early on after the subpoena had been issued. He stopped at four samples submitted two-and-one-half years ago by Ivins in April 2002. He slid his forefinger again to the right, to the column containing the descriptions. The first of the four entries read "7737–Dugway Ames Spores–1997."

He glanced again at the handout on which Reynolds had listed the double-positive samples. The April 2002 submission appeared nowhere on Reynolds's slide of positive matches.

Reynolds also identified samples containing only an A_1 mutation. Stanley located them in his logs. Several had been sent from Defence Research and Development Canada in Alberta. The column to the right indicated their origin—"USAMRIID" and "Bacteriology Division, Dr. Bruce Ivins."[10]

The single and double matches began to tell a story. By the fall of 2004, after hearing CBI's results on the repository testing, we had little doubt that the attack spores originated from the flask of RMR-1029. We still continued looking for sources of Ames and the additional assays for the C, D, and E morphology variants that were being developed, but we now focused the bulk of our attention on the Dugway spores and who had access.

Notebooks Ivins had provided showed he had gone to lengths to characterize his stock. He had examined over one thousand spores in a series of fifty different examinations under a powerful microscope. He looked at individual spores using oil immersion, a technique that involved diluting the original slurry, placing a drop or two of the dilution on a clear, rectangular glass slide, covering the drop with a thinner square of glass, and finally overlaying the square with a drop of light oil. The oil allowed the polished glass microscope lens to rest on the thin, glass square, squeezing out air bubbles and eliminating light refraction. Ivins noted his gradient-purified preparation consisted of single spores greater than 99 percent pure. It contained no intact cells, no clumping, and debris he estimated at less than 1 percent.[11]

Ivins had RMR-1029 ready for use at the end of 1997, after he added twenty-two batches of Ames spores that he had made to the six large lots from Dugway.[12] The total mixture began as 164 liters of gray liquid, enough to fill forty-three-gallon jugs. Successive washing and centrifuging through opaque gradients had concentrated it to a one-quart slurry, which Ivins stored in two glass flasks.

The notebook also revealed the original donor for the Dugway production had been the earlier batch of Ames spores, RMR-1030.[13] When Reynolds tested it, he found it lacked both A mutations. Yet RMR-1030's descendant contained both A_1 and A_3. A_1 had been identified in quite a few samples, some predating the first shipment from Dugway and some from preparations made as late as 1999 and 2001, two and five years after RMR-1029's creation. Most were located in the B3 containment suite occupied by Ivins and coworkers. But A_3 was rare. It only existed in RMR-1029 and its derivatives and dilutions, and the evidence. The most likely explanation for its existence: a mutation during one of the six twenty-quart fermentations at Dugway. A small fermenter may have produced over one trillion spores, with as many as one hundred million containing a newly mutated A_3.[14]

While we focused our efforts on understanding the genealogy and distribution of RMR-1029 and who had access to the Dugway spores, CBI continued to screen samples. By fall, the additional Ames, nearly three hundred, collected at USAMRIID, the Dugway Proving Grounds, and the contract lab in Ohio had been inventoried, added to the repository, and shipped to CBI for testing.

The results so far were exciting, the biggest lead and most progress we had to date. But I also realized we had our work cut out. For some of us on the Science Squad, Steve Hatfill's lack of experience growing bacteria, coupled with the failure of the bloodhounds during the Ohio sniper manhunt (see chapter 16, note 6), put him low on the Persons of Interest list. But there was still a contingent of the task force that believed in him as a viable suspect. His access to RMR-1029 needed to be looked at thoroughly. RMR-1029 had been used in many vaccine challenge experiments, which took place in USAMRIID's second building, 1412. We would also have to look at every scientist that might have been in 1412, as well as in Ivins's B3 containment lab in Building 1425. And then examine Ohio's Battelle and Utah's Dugway employees for travel to Princeton during fall 2001. But at the top of our list of questions was why Ivins's submission of RMR-1029 in April 2002 did not contain the A mutants.

18

Midnight Access
January 2005

I drove through the light snow toward my new office on the Capital Belt-way. Most of our agents and postal inspectors had just returned from the end-of-the-year holiday break. New Year's Eve had passed without incident, although our Joint Terrorism Task Force had been on standby—standard procedure since the terror attacks of 9/11. Most of the Amerithrax members had young families and traveled home for a visit with parents and grandparents. Now they were returning from New Jersey, California, North Carolina, Alabama, upstate New York, and the Midwest. I remembered the first year of the investigation when all of us cancelled vacation plans and worked through the holidays, and the next year when many of us withdrew leave requests in order to begin analysis of the Sterilite box from under the ice. Over four years had passed since recovering the first anthrax letter. It did not seem possible.

I merged onto the five-lane highway and maneuvered left toward the sluggish fast lane. Our executive management had recently moved both AMX-1 and -2 squads from the seventh floor of the Washington Field Office, within walking distance of the US Capitol, to west of the city in an office building that towered over Route 495's inner loop. The Bureau of Alcohol, Tobacco, Firearms and Explosives had occupied the offices for ten years until their lease expired. The field office needed to make room for a new pornography task force, and we were moved to the suburbs, although Tysons Corner in Northern Virginia was anything but calming. It was its own small city, with a punishing commute. Fresh paint did little to help the line of drab two-person offices filled with used surplus government furniture and worn carpet. We even inherited a one-person holding cell, minus running water, which we quickly converted into an equipment storage locker.

But recent news made our new surroundings bearable. The Secret Service laboratory had made significant progress since we had given them the four attack envelopes along with three-hundred-thousand-plus unused exemplars. Using a low-powered dissecting microscope, Secret Service scientists examined inked Eagle stamps as well as the back of the envelopes advertising recycled paper and bearing a copyright registration. On the Brokaw and Leahy envelopes they identified a slight blue line along the bottom edge of the eagle's right wing, above the blue bar containing the white stenciling of *USA*. Microscopic imperfections also appeared on the envelopes' reverse side. A faint line could be seen between the *P* and *S* of *USPS* in the copyright print. They also found matching defects on the *New York Post* and Daschle envelopes, but different from those of Leahy's and Brokaw's.

The examiners turned to the exemplars. They found minute defects on some of the envelopes, first one error then another in the Eagle stamp, light lines of different lengths and widths. Each defect appeared, stayed, and then disappeared after one thousand to two thousand envelopes. The examiners noticed the errors alternated—from the first envelope in line to the third and then the fifth, probably the result of the print roller holding two polymer plates. It also provided an explanation for the two sets of defects on the Brokaw and Leahy envelopes, and the *New York Post* and Daschle envelopes.

The transient nature of the defects meant finding one would associate one thousand to two thousand envelopes as siblings from forty-five million cousins. The production and shipping records showed that the siblings would stay together and remain in the order of printing during delivery to the thousands of post offices across the country.

"Good morning, how is everyone doing? I'm Paul Keim. I want to welcome you to *Bacillus* ACT 2005. For this year's International Conference on Anthrax, we have joined with the International Workshop on the Molecular Biology of *Bacillus anthracis, cereus*, and *thuringiensis*. This is the first time combining the two meetings. Two years ago, at Nice, it was obvious that the work reported on *cereus* could be applied to anthrax and bioterrorism. So we thought for 2005, let's bring all the *bacillus* researchers together."

"We have quite a gathering, over 350 participants from twenty countries."

"I especially want to thank the organizers, all the volunteers who have taken of their time to make this a successful conference. And especially to single out one longtime volunteer who has helped with the anthrax meetings since Annapolis in 2001. Bruce Ivins. Bruce told me earlier this week that he is finally stepping down from the organizing panel. I want to thank him for his years of dedication."

"Finally, remember to take some time to see the sights. Santa Fe's beautiful this time of year. Enjoy the next four days."[1]

Keim helped organize an international anthrax conference every two years. The first and second had been in Winchester, England, outside Porton Down, then a third to the west in Plymouth along the Atlantic Coast. The last two had been in Annapolis, and finally, Nice, France. The next would be in Oslo. This year the FBI sent two participants from its laboratory, including Doug Beecher. I attended also. We felt there was a good chance the attendees would include the anthrax mailer, so Darin Steele and I flew out. We would listen for the attacks being discussed and be available if one of the scientists felt a need to confide. Pat Worsham would also present some of our forensic work during a scientific session—without giving specifics about evidence. It would begin the peer review and validation process for her work, steps we hoped the Laboratory Division would also soon start.

That evening, I found a seat at the bar of the hotel hosting the conference. As I rested, nursing a club soda, USAMRIID researchers gathered at a table behind me. At the head of the table Ivins spoke, "And we drove around and around. He kept drinking and we kept driving."

His voice became lost in the laughter, the life of the party, no more the unassuming scientist. "And then we found a place to pull over and got out to . . . "

More laughter and more drinking as the evening wore on and his voice grew louder and louder.

The next morning, the hotel hosted a breakfast for conference participants—cereal, bacon and eggs, coffee, orange juice, lots of pastry. I took a seat and waited to see if Steele would join me just as Ivins walked in. I could only stare. He wore a Zoot suit. Overly wide at the shoulders with exaggerated lapels and added length, high-waisted pants that flared out along the legs, narrowing at the bottoms—a black suit with wide vertical white stripes. The suits became popular in the 1940s. Wearing them is attributed as the root of street fighting across the country that began with the Los Angeles Zoot Suit Riot of 1943. The City of Angels banned Zoots because of the violence. In addition, they were deemed extravagant and unpatriotic—in conflict with the War Production Board's rationing act of 1942 due to the excessive amount of cloth and tailoring required.[2]

Ivins began to walk toward the pastry and juice table as he glanced around the room. The two of us momentarily locked stares before he abruptly turned around and headed toward the hotel's elevator bank. I watched as he disappeared; I never saw him again that day.

Records for access to the locations where RMR-1029 had been housed meant a fairly straight but laborious approach for the investigation. Well over one hundred employees had gone in and out of Building 1425, and more than two hundred were added to the RMR-1029 access list when we considered Building 1412.

Investigating employees at Battelle Institute in Ohio who had access to the sample of RMR-1029 proved to be easier than the nearly four hundred at US-AMRIID. A review of the contractor's records showed less than fifty people had access to the room where RMR-1029 was stored. Of these, less than two dozen had experience in growing bacteria. Travel time from Columbus to Princeton was sixteen hours round trip by car. Airline manifests would show any of the employees flying in or out of nearby airports during either of the windows for the mailings. Work in Battelle's anthrax labs took place during normal work hours, and at least two people were always present. On one occasion, a stretch of four nights in early summer of 2001, work had been done at night but by a different pair of researchers each night.[3]

In Frederick, the AMX-3 squad took a similar approach with USAMRIID employees. The squad went down the list of nearly four hundred people, ruling out those that had no experience or training in bacteriology or could provide sustainable alibis for one or both of the times the letters were mailed. On AMX-2, we continued to focus on the science, meeting every Monday morning with scientists of the Chemical Biological Sciences Unit in Quantico. There, we reviewed our forensic initiatives—stable isotope measurements, carbon-14 determinations, possible locations of more Ames, progress at Commonwealth Biotechnologies. The genetic screening was moving forward, and the carbon-14 tests had given us valuable information.[4] But stable isotopes, and heme and agar detection, seemed no further along than a year ago. The rest of the squad and I felt much more work was still needed, and we continued to argue against committing milligrams of valuable spores to any of the three tests.[5]

On AMX-1, they continued to scrutinize Steven Hatfill. For a third time, they reviewed the items collected from the three searches of his Frederick apartment. My AMX-2 squad pitched in, looking at everything from a scientific perspective. Hatfill's medical training in South Africa had centered on cancers of the blood and bone marrow transplantation.[6] At the National Institutes of Health, he had taken a Research Fellow position and cultured human and mammalian cells using technology originally designed by the National Aeronautics and Space Administration to simulate g-force stresses and weightlessness encountered during space travel.[7] Science has long been fascinated by what controls human cells and their growth. For many years researchers were unsuccessful in coaxing human cells to grow in culture dishes and incubators, in contrast to the success in propagating bacteria and molds. That changed with the discovery of HeLa cells in 1951. Their origin is a controversial subject and a topic of debate when medicine and human use and experimentation are discussed. The discovery is the subject of a 2010 *New York Times* best seller.[8] In 1962 researchers immortalized another cell line derived from African green monkey kidney, known as Vero cells. Growing mammalian cells in a laboratory is tedious and requires absolute sterility, but the skills are different than those necessary to culture bacteria and requires none of the artful experience and knowledge needed to generate concentrated spores.

At USAMRIID, Hatfill turned his earlier interest in hematopathology to the study of coagulopathy, the inability of blood to coagulate and form a clot. He researched dangerous hemorrhagic viruses—Marburg and the Ebola strains isolated in Reston, Virginia, and Zaire, Central Africa. He worked under stringent biosafety level-4 containment wearing cumbersome moon suits supplied with air pumped in through rubber hoses, as depicted in the Warner Bros.' movie *Contagion* and detailed in Richard Preston's third Dark Biology narrative, *The Demon in the Freezer*.[9] But as with his mammalian cell culturing, virology experiments under level-4 safety conditions required a completely different set of skills than those required to produce anthrax spores.

During Hatfill's tenure, USAMRIID expanded its use of an access control system. From August 1998 onward, computer discs captured the comings and goings of those entering the hallways and laboratory suites of buildings 1412 and 1425. The upgrade came in the year after Secretary of Defense William Cohen held aloft his five-pound bag of sugar on national television.[10]

Badge readers had been installed next to the entrance of the B3 suite and a numbered punch pad at a second inner door. Both a card containing a magnetic strip and a personal identification number were needed to access. Outside another door, this one at the rear of the suite, a second reader had been installed.

The AMX-1 and -3 squads returned to the entry and exit records. In the spring of the previous year, when the first A_1+A_3 double match had been identified, we had quickly looked for any indication that Hatfill had been in Ivins's B313 room where RMR-1029 was stored. There was none. Now, agents and postal inspectors scoured the logs for Hatfill's entry into rooms in Building 1412 where small amounts of the spore stock were used for vaccine challenges. Again, it appeared he had not. They mapped each location where RMR-1029 had been stored or carried: Ivins's B313 lab room, the B3 laboratory suite hallways, B3 walk-in cold room, the aerosol release and autoclave rooms of Building 1412. Nowhere did they find Steven Hatfill. They studied interviews of USAMRIID employees, clarified information, and double-checked to ensure anyone with knowledge of RMR-1029 had been talked to. They scrutinized the laboratory notebooks that described RMR-1029. The painstaking work still left open the question of September 1997, when Hatfill began work at USAMRIID, until August 1998, when the Institute started recording entries and exits. They returned to interviews of each person that had known or worked with Hatfill and asked the question: Had Hatfill been in the rooms known to contain RMR-1029? In each case, the answer was no.

As we reviewed the records for Hatfill's access to RMR-1029, we also noted the names of people who had accessed the B3 containment suite, in particular the rooms that had stored the spores. A pattern emerged. Rather, a change in pattern. Access to B3, specifically the B313 room, Bruce Ivins's anthrax lab, jumped in August, four weeks before 9/11. The increase in visits occurred during nighttime and weekends, and the records showed Ivins entering his lab alone. Between January through July of 2001, he averaged one-and-one-quarter hours per month at night in B313. In August the nighttime work jumped tenfold; in September the night hours leapt twenty-five-fold. His late visits continued into October, peaking the three nights before the Daschle and Leahy letters were mailed.[11]

The long late hours began on August 13. Ivins arrived at USAMRIID shortly after 7:00 a.m. and left at half past four in the afternoon. But that night he returned, entering through the same rear door he used earlier in the day. He first went to his office, then to the entrance of the B3 suite, where he placed his white magnet card on the reader, causing the main door to open with a loud click. He stayed in the front locker room for five minutes before punching in his personal code to open B313. He stayed inside for three hours. Ivins had not stayed in his lab for three hours at any period earlier that year. During March and May, he had not entered his lab at all during off hours. During one month, he worked only thirty minutes for an evening. In Ivins's notebooks, the January through July evening hours were reflected with notations of experimental protocols, and salts and growth media used and resulting data. But for the three evening hours of August 13, his notes were blank.

Ivins worked more than eleven evening hours during August. In September, he tripled that, working every night from September 1 through 11. He stayed one hour; sometimes two and on three occasions he did not emerge from B313 for three hours. Then, the weekend before the Brokaw and the *New York Post* letters were mailed he worked three nights in a row, each evening for more than two hours.[12]

In October, the pattern emerged again. For three nights in a row, immediately before the Capitol Hill letters were dropped in the blue Nassau Street collection box, Ivins worked an average of three hours each night alone in his anthrax laboratory.

We had suspicions about Ivins earlier in the investigation, but with the pattern of late nights in the lab, the same lab where the genetically matching stock of spores were stored—spores that he was the sole custodian for—I and a number of the agents and postal inspectors on AMX-1 and AMX-2 now wanted to open a full-blown investigation of him. We briefed Richard Lambert on this latest discovery; the inspector viewed it as interesting but still viewed Hatfill as heading up the Persons of Interest queue. During our occasional meetings with the director at Headquarters, we didn't mention Ivins. High-ranking FBI management and Department of Justice attorneys still attended the briefings, and we were always wary of media leaks—the ones about Hatfill were now the subject of a civil lawsuit against the director and attorney general. We wanted to give Dr. Ivins a very close look and establish concrete evidence before sharing our suspicions. On AMX-1, squad members, much on their own time during evening hours, began reviewing toll records and credit card expenditures. They contacted the National Crime Information Center in West Virginia for any license plate queries on his car by state and local police. AMX-3 requested copies of his travel vouchers and time and attendance sheets from USAMRIID, located copy machines in the Institution's library and studied its after-hours access records, and explored Ivins's past for a connection to Princeton. On AMX-2, we dug deeper through Ivins's notebooks and prepared a large wall chart of RMR-1029's genealogy, marking the spore concentration and quality of each of the six large batches from Dugway and the twenty-two smaller contributions produced by Ivins and his two assistants.

19

US Secret Service

December 2005

I took a seat in Tom Dellafera's small corner office ten stories over the 495 Capital Beltway. One by one, the rest of my AMX-2 squad filtered in as I stared out the room's single bank of windows, watching lines of cars waiting to park at the Tysons Corner shopping malls for last-minute holiday shopping. It had been months since we had delivered the envelopes to the Secret Service. Now, we would summarize what had been learned.

I had assigned two agents to coordinate with the Service, dividing up the work into chemistry and printing forensics. We began by reviewing the chemistry. It had been fairly straightforward to determine which formulation, old or new, MeadWestvaco had printed on the attack envelopes. They contained the new ink—a brighter blue in the eagle's folded wings and more vibrant gray in the denomination number, *34*. This meant the post offices receiving the nine million envelopes printed with the original, duller ink could be ruled out as potential points of purchase. Dellafera also reminded us that five and a half million had been produced after September 2001.

So that left thirty-one million. While the Secret Service had been interrogating ink chemistry and printing errors, Dellafera and his postal inspectors had studied the MeadWestvaco shipping records. They learned that once the envelopes left the MeadWestvaco plant in Williamsburg, they were shipped to eighteen postal bulk mail centers around the United States. From there, they traveled to stamp distribution offices—one hundred existed in the country—until they finally found a destination in one of nearly forty thousand large and small post offices.

"How many would a post office get?" I began.

"Not many, one box of five hundred. If it is large, maybe five boxes of five hundred," Dellafera answered. "We've collected from almost three hundred post offices so far. And have samples from two dozen production runs, about half of the total runs. We gave Secret Service nearly three hundred thousand exemplars to go through."

Then we came to the main reason for the meeting. The Secret Service had called not long ago to drop a bombshell. In what seemed like a search for a needle in a haystack, they had examined the envelopes we had collected for a match to the tiny printing imperfections on the attack envelopes—two sets of minute defects, occurring for a brief time during one of thirty-seven production runs that produced thirty-one million envelopes.[1] Among the three hundred thousand envelope exemplars turned over to the Forensic Service Division—only 1 percent of the total made by MeadWestvaco—the examiners had found a near match.

The US Secret Service has long been the country's recognized experts at detecting slight imperfections and subtle differences in inked impressions. In contrast to today's notoriety as leaders in executive protection, the Service was formed in 1865 with the sole mission of combating the spread of counterfeit money.

At the beginning of the War between the States, the federal government left the printing of folding currency to banks. Estimates are that some 1,600 state banks printed seven thousand styles of money. During the war, between one-third to one-half of the currency in circulation had been faked.[2] Counterfeiting was rampant. Noted nineteenth-century author Herman Melville devoted a scene to its description in his final novel, *The Confidence-Man*, published in 1857.[3] Bogus currency was not new; it has plagued civilizations for years. Producing money without authority in thirteenth-century China was a crime with a capital punishment. An innovation in thwarting the success of fake bills had been achieved almost twenty years before the start of the Civil War by papermaker Zenas Crane of central Massachusetts when he incorporated silk threads into the linen and rag stock used for a run of currency paper. Crane's descendant and future US Senator Winthrop Crane would, thirty-five years later, win the contract to produce paper for US currency, a contract the Crane family still retains in the new millennium.[4]

In 1862, the federal government mandated a single form of US currency, but it did little to halt the faking of money as the new bills themselves soon became the object of artful forgers. Finally, three years later, the Department of the Treasury formed a US Secret Service to halt the problem. Forty-three years later it would be Secret Service agents that President Roosevelt transferred to the Department of Justice to form a new Bureau of Investigation, renamed in 1935 as the current Federal Bureau of Investigation.

Over the years, even as it took on the dual mission of Executive Branch protection in 1901, the Secret Service has kept pace with technological advancements in paper production and print applications. Not limited to small-time criminal entrepreneurs, successful counterfeiting operations have the potential to undermine economies. Counterfeiting of continental currency by the British during the American Revolution rendered the infant country's money worthless.[5] Eighty years later, the North attempted to flood the Confederacy with forged notes, but their quality surpassed that of the South's real issue, making detection straightforward. The largest and nearly most successful effort took place between 1942 and 1945 in the Gestapo's Sachsenhausen Prison Camp north of Berlin. There, Operation Bernhard used prisoners with past experience in printing, engraving, and banking, supplied with a Dutch printing press, to produce notes in denominations of five, ten, twenty, and fifty pounds. The quality equaled that of the real thing and fooled examiners in the Bank of England. While only a handful of the nine million fake banknotes totaling 134 million pounds reached circulation, enough of it did to cause the British government to recall its currency and issue a new series of money. Before the war ended, Operation Bernhard had turned its attention to the United States' $100 bill and was on the road to an equal success when the world celebrated VE Day.[6]

Today, the US Secret Service's Forensics Services Division employs experts in microprinting, evaluating watermarkings, and analyzing microscopic lenses of colored plastic—akin to the iridescent and multifaceted dragonfly eye—making up part of the one-quarter flaxen, three-quarter cotton paper stock supplied by Crane and Company of Dalton, Massachusetts.[7]

Dellafera recounted the telephone call from Secret Service. Their examiners identified a single box of envelopes bearing defects strikingly similar to those on the attack letters. As expected from the earlier examinations of the collected exemplars, they also found that the envelopes in the box alternated. An envelope exhibited different defects than the envelope packed immediately next to it, and the third envelope in line matched the first—reflective of the Brokaw and Leahy matching each other, and the *Post* and Daschle being identical, but differing from the Brokaw and Leahy, as if the mailer had used the first for a Capitol Hill letter, mailed the second to New York, the third to Capitol Hill, and the fourth to New York.

But only Dellafera and my two agents knew where the matching box had been shipped. They had delivered the boxes of envelopes to the Secret Service but held back the shipping logs in order to eliminate any question of bias on the part of the forensic examiners, as Scott Stanley and I had done when shipping samples to Paul Keim, The Institute for Genomic Research, and Commonwealth Biotechnologies. Now, they scanned down MeadWestvaco's list for the production number on the box that contained the near matches.

The box of five hundred envelopes had been shipped to the main post office in Elkton, Maryland. They had first been sent to the Dulles Stamp Distribution Office in northern Virginia as part of a large batch of envelopes destined for sale in Virginia and nearby Maryland.

Dellafera's team then turned to the production records we had collected nearly two years ago from MeadWestvaco's plant manager. The Elkton post office's envelopes had been printed on February 14 and 15, 2001, during a production run that generated nearly one million envelopes over two shifts spanning twenty-four hours. On March 21, 2001, the Distribution Office shipped the production run's envelopes to twenty-one locations in lots of between one hundred to five thousand.

The Secret Service found more envelopes containing printing defects. Some of the microscopic blemishes differed little from those on the anthrax envelopes, while others differed slightly more. The examiners concluded that this variation resulted from continual changes in the polymer printing plates during production—changes not visible to an unaided eye but apparent under Secret Service microscopes.

The envelopes with defects most like the ones on the anthrax envelopes had been shipped from MeadWestvaco to the Dulles Distribution Office on March 2, 2001. The Dulles Office then sent them on March 21 to post offices in the city of Fairfax and tiny crossroads of Machipongo in Virginia, and Elkton, Severna Park, Cumberland, Galena, and Frederick, Maryland. The Frederick Post Office, less than three miles from Fort Detrick, had received one thousand Federal Eagles.[8]

A visit to the Frederick Post Office turned up no Federal Eagle envelopes, and the office manager had little information to share. When Dellafera's team examined the office records, they found that all one thousand envelopes received in March 2001 had been banded in packages, five to a pack. The post office began selling them in March, but in June 2002 the Postal Service had raised first-class postage from thirty-four cents to thirty-seven cents. While some locations continued to sell Federal Eagle envelopes along with an additional three-cent stamp, the manager of the Frederick facility returned his remaining Eagle envelopes to the Dulles office. There, disappointment greeted Dellafera's team. A destruction of obsolete stamps had been ordered, and it included the returned envelopes from Frederick. Back at Frederick, the team interviewed postal customers in an effort to locate unmailed Federal Eagles, but to no avail; none could be found.

But the five hundred envelopes sent to the post office in Elkton had been shipped immediately before the ones to Frederick, and of the envelopes shipped following the Frederick lot, two hundred had gone to Severna Park and then five hundred to Galena. The defects in the three shipments were almost identical to the attack envelopes, and Dellafera came to the conclusion that the anthrax envelopes had likely been purchased from the Frederick Post Office. The Frederick Post Office sold them from a lobby vending machine.

Still, we felt more proof was needed. Our work was charting new ground in forensic print science. Defects occurring during flexographic printing had not been widely reported in the peer-reviewed literature, either in forensic journals or during forensic science meetings.[9] The answer would be a controlled production run. MeadWestvaco would produce a full shift of envelopes under the same conditions that had existed at the company in February 2001. Dellafera contacted the production manager, who had introduced us to flexographic printing. Would they agree to it? Was it even possible, could they reproduce the same ink chemistries, the same production crew and teams, purchase similar recycled paper from American Eagle, was American Eagle still in business?

MeadWestvaco agreed and a cost was negotiated. They would use the same American Eagle paper and print it with the same Eagle stamp and words describing recycling percentage and USPS ownership, use the same formulations for the bright blue and light gray inks, and even schedule the same machine operator-tender.

Dellafera arrived at the MeadWestvaco plant the day before and met with the manager and production staff. Two polymer plates had been exposed to ultraviolet light and fixed to the eight-foot printing roller. Enough paper had been purchased and loaded onto the printing press to make more than one-half-million envelopes.

The next day, Dellafera monitored the fourteen-hour manufacturing process. The packaging team filled each box with five hundred envelopes and labeled each box according to its order of production. At the end of the run they had produced over one thousand boxes, numbered, initialed, and stacked neatly on two pallets for shipment to Washington, DC.

Over the next days, weeks, and months, scientists at the Secret Service Forensic Division studied the envelopes.[10] They found, at rare instances, minute defects in the printed ink. They documented and photographed the printed errors as they appeared, changed shape, and finally disappeared. Each time a new imperfection arose it differed from those seen before. They discovered that a printing defect would remain for as little as two thousand envelopes. As they scanned and sorted through the one-half million, a tiny blue crescent appeared and disappeared, just above "THIS ENVELOPE IS RECYCLABLE . . . " on the backside; four miniature dots came and went within the span of three thousand prestamped Eagles; another blue dot appeared for several thousand envelopes and then was gone; part of the *E* in *MADE* was missed for a run of five thousand, then reappeared.

Finally, the scientists returned to the inked defects of the anthrax envelopes and compared the printing errors with those on the collected envelopes from the Elkton, Severna Park, and Galena post offices. Given the high similarity of defects observed in the attack envelopes with those from the Elkton, Severna Park, and Galena post offices and comparing the rate of change observed in defects from the controlled run, the Secret Service concluded that the attack envelopes had been purchased, as a banded pack of five, at the main post office in Frederick, Maryland.

The anthrax mailer had planned carefully. Buying envelopes wrapped in cellophane allowed the mailer to carry them without wearing gloves and drawing suspicion on a hot summer day. Using prestamped envelopes removed the chance of transferring DNA while moistening the back of stamps, or leaving trace amounts of skin cells. But what we found most intriguing was the fact that Bruce Ivins leased a mailbox at the Frederick Post Office.

The memo, referred to as a "routing slip," the first of many, arrived before the weekend. Barring an emergency or an unexpected break in the case, the audit by the Inspection Division would be my priority for the next two weeks.

An assistant inspector in place, known as an AIIP, had authored the slip. The AIIP was normally a field supervisor, equivalent to me, overseeing a squad of street agents in one of our fifty-six field offices. Participating in the inspection process was a requirement for advancement in the FBI, a box to be checked off; Headquarters required at least six inspections to advance to assistant special Agent in charge. In my view, after having done several inspections, it was the most arduous step in the path to promotion.

The routing slip requested information needed to assess my effectiveness and efficiency as a supervisor and that of each agent on the AMX-2 squad. The usual metrics used to evaluate an FBI criminal squad, as I had been on in Boston, would include such things as the number of indictments, arrests, and convictions; amounts of stolen money recovered; and value of property forfeited to the government. But AMERITHRAX, Major Case 184, had not made a single arrest or supported an indictment in three years,[11] nor did we anticipate one in the near future. We had just finished drafting an interim prosecutive report, a document in excess of two thousand pages summarizing our progress in envelope forensics and genetics, the work of the bloodhounds and the progress in the investigation of Steven Hatfill. The tome, written at the direction of Rick Lambert, himself an inspector in charge and technically assigned to the Inspection Division, also reviewed our Persons of Interest list and people ruled out at USAMRIID and Battelle and Dugway.

Lambert had personally delivered the manuscript to the FBI director only a short time ago.

More routing slips soon followed. They asked where and how agents were recruited with science backgrounds, to what extent we had established an intelligence base of anthrax research, were other counterterrorism squads contributing to the investigation, the amount of oversight provided by executive management, number of documents authored by each agent, how confidential informants and witnesses contributed, which sophisticated techniques, such as pen registers and electronic surveillance, added value. And the answers were due—in writing by me—the next day. My two counterpart supervisors on AMX-1 and -3 received comparable requests.

Monday, Tuesday, and into Wednesday, morning and afternoon, routing slips appeared in my electronic mail, seeking more information and clarification of earlier answers: How did we retain experienced agents, analysts, and postal inspectors; how much assistance did Headquarters and the Laboratory Division provide? Did these divisions prioritize the investigation as one of the largest terrorism cases in FBI history, how did we supervisors address morale issues as the investigation ended its fifth year without resolution, did my AMX-2 agents share their newly acquired knowledge of anthrax with those outside the investigation, how many times did the task force meet with other government agencies and the value of those liaison efforts? When and how often did we meet with the US Attorney's Office?

While we had not made an arrest, we had certainly been productive, and our answers demonstrated that. Nearly four thousand documents had been drafted in the past three years: interview results, laboratory testing requests, updates and summaries of forensic progress, meeting and trip reports, records of interagency liaison and intelligence reporting. Amerithrax agents had been certified in collateral duties and in addition to adding institutional expertise during searches for anthrax evidence, they supported other large investigations. They had deployed with the field office Evidence Response Team, Hazardous Materials Response Team, and Underwater Search and Evidence Response Team during ricin scares in Washington, DC, and after a grenade assault on President George W. Bush to Tbilisi, Georgia, and searched Afghan riverbeds for a M16 rifle alleged to be used in an assault on civilians. One agent, Laro Tan, my primary relief supervisor[12] on AMX-2, had accompanied Director Mueller on a visit with law enforcement counterparts in Thailand, Phnom Penh, and Kuala Lumpur. Tan, still fluent in his native Cambodian, had fled the killing fields of the Khmer Rouge as a child, relocated in Chicago, and settled on a career as an FBI agent, becoming an expert in money laundering and terrorist financing before volunteering to investigate anthrax. More than once his gift for diplomacy, acumen for dangerous situations, and knowledge of Southeast Asian culture brought him to the attention of executive management and temporary assignments.

The AIIP asked further, in a follow-up routing slip, since the agents of the task force had developed a unique expertise in weapons of mass destruction and bioweaponry, did they share this? Had they assisted in training FBI personnel, local and state law enforcement officers, and other government agencies? Again, I answered yes. Amerithrax agents had traveled throughout Washington, DC, to Quantico, Virginia, and Columbus, Ohio, to provide anthrax collection and awareness training, canine tracking, and explosives detection. They had assisted in postblast evidence collection schools and evaluated underwater dive team candidates for safety and operational knowledge. The isolation and characterization of anthrax sporulation mutants and criteria underlying the DNA sequencing initiative had been presented before government and academic scientists at conferences in Santa Fe, Baltimore, and Orlando.

By the end of the week, each member of the Amerithrax Task Force had been interviewed. They described the criteria for inclusion as a person of interest—a prerequisite knowledge of science and microbiology, access to equipment, and the Ames strain. And as of a year ago, access to RMR-1029 spores. They described the amount of work that had gone into determining if Steven Hatfill had this access. And finding none, nearly every agent and postal inspector now believed him innocent of the mailing.

Then, as abruptly as it had begun, the deluge of routing slips and email ceased.

20

Change of Command
Summer 2006

A day ahead of schedule, the inspection team met behind closed doors to review their work, voice recommendations, and cite findings of deficiency—the worst would earn a squad or its supervisor an "I & I" rating—ineffective and inefficient. An I & I could result in remedial training, getting a derailed career back on track. In the most egregious situations, the remedy would be demotion in grade and rank and a transfer to another office due to "lack of effectiveness." Fortunately none of these applied to Amerithrax or me. In fact, the inspectors found much to applaud. They identified a "Best Practice" in the development of AMX-2, my Science Squad. It was the first instance the FBI had assembled an investigative squad dedicated to developing and managing forensic methods and development of leads. Rick Lambert received much of the credit. They recognized his efforts to recruit agents with science degrees and the energy he used to retain them as they gained specialized knowledge of anthrax and bioweapons. He had brought organization to the investigation and found additional resources, building not only AMX-2 but also establishing a third, AMX-3 squad, which he located in Frederick, five miles from the gates of USAMRIID.

They also said it was time for a change. The elimination of Hatfill as a suspect had taken an enormous amount of meticulous and detailed work. At the end of August, Director Mueller promoted Lambert to head up the Knoxville Division as special agent-in-charge. The search began for his replacement, but not to bring organization to a wide-ranging investigation with thousands of national and transcontinental leads as had existed in 2002. This time the director looked within the ranks of street investigators for someone to take the results of the genetics and RMR-1029 and follow it to the doorway of a killer. He found two, Ed Montooth and Vince Lisi.

Lisi, Montooth's junior by several years, had a reputation as a tenacious and astute agent, solving tough homicide cases around the nation's capital for years, known and respected by the city's top prosecutors. Growing up outside Pittsburgh, he earned a degree in accounting and become a certified public accountant before joining the ranks of the FBI as a special agent. He would head up AMX-1, taking Bob Roth's desk. Montooth likewise had a reputation as a solid street agent. Most recently he commanded the Washington Field Office's "Fly-Away" squad, where his agents traveled the world investigating acts of terrorism against citizens of the United States. Before that, he had personally traveled to the jungles of New Guinea and helped track down rebels for murdering two American teachers. Prior to that, he had worked in the Balkans solving war crimes. He and the director had a previous relationship. He had presented cases for prosecution when the director had headed up the Homicide Section in the District of Columbia's US Attorney's Office. Growing up in Illinois farm country, he had cleaned chicken coops and tossed hay bales into high-walled wagons. When not working the fields or studying for high school classes, he learned the art of combining focused concentration with practiced relaxation—projecting a demeanor of calm confidence while winning on Illinois trap fields and skeet ranges. At Western Illinois State, he majored in criminal justice and then investigated credit card fraud for a Fortune 500 company until offered a seat in new agent class during 1980. He would be our new inspector in charge.

My AMX-2 squad filled the small combination file and break room, sitting or standing where they could find room. Tom Dellafera and I followed and squeezed into the last empty chairs. Within minutes, Montooth and Lisi joined us. The two had been with Amerithrax in our cramped Tysons Corner office for three weeks. They had listened to how the polymerase chain reaction worked and stories of trips to MeadWestvaco and our collaboration with the Secret Service laboratory. How the tiny print defects in the inked-spread Eagle stamps had been identified and the controlled production run would validate the new forensics. They had looked over the list of laboratories around the world known to have possessed Ames strain anthrax before October 2001. Now we gathered to review the science pointing toward Dr. Bruce Ivins.

I began the meeting. "Ed, we have ten matches to the evidence, the mutation we call A_1, the A_3 mutation, and we just finished screening the repository for a third—the D mutation. Eight samples have all three. They all trace back to a single source, Ivins's spores. He calls them RMR-1029, the spores he contracted mostly from Dugway in 1997. Hatfill never had access to the Dugway spores, and Ivins always kept the flask in his walk-in cold room, inside the B3 hot lab. Not many people had access."

Dellafera took over. "Ivins spent a lot of time alone in his lab just before the mailings. He rarely worked at night, but then started at the end of August and three nights straight just before each mailing."

An AMX-2 agent added, "The first match we got when we started screening the repository was one of the samples Darin took from Ivins in December of '03. Ivins had almost three dozen Ames samples he never gave to us under the subpoena."

Steele continued, "And it looks like he obstructed justice when he submitted the four samples in April 2002."

"What do you mean?" Montooth said.

"The four samples he gave us for the repository in April; none of them matched the evidence. One of the samples was from the Dugway spores, RMR-1029. When I took RMR-1029 and submitted a sample to the repository, it matched all three markers when we tested it, A_1, A_3, and D."

"I thought I heard that Ivins gave samples earlier, but something was wrong with them?"

"He did, Ed. The same four as in April. It was in February, but he hurried and didn't follow the protocol, so we asked him to do it again."

"Too bad we can't test the February samples," Montooth said.

Steele jumped in. "We did. I had Keim send the duplicates back to us. He still had them stored with his duplicate set of repository samples in Flagstaff."

"And?"

"CBI just finished them. The Dugway spore sample from February '02 has all three mutations. Ivins's repeat submission in April has none."

Montooth and Lisi looked up and stared at each other, then back down at the notes and diagrams lying on the table, a photograph of the flask labeled *RMR-1029* in black marker, the list of eight matching samples of Ames, and the bar graph of late-night entries for Ivins into the B3 laboratory.

"So, what happened between February and April?"

Dellafera continued, "We think it was because of a meeting we had at the end of March, in the commander's office with Pat Worsham and a few other USAMRIID scientists. Ivins was there. The meeting was to get them moving and finish submitting samples they owed to the repository."

"Some of them were dragging their feet, Ivins one of them. Pat described the variants she was finding in the mailed spores and then the protocol to be used prepping samples for submission. We think that Ivins had one of his technicians submit the February samples. They didn't follow the protocol. He never resubmitted. Then we think Ivins prepared the submissions in April himself. Based on the handwriting on the tubes—I take pictures of each submission and store them with the FedEx shipping labels when they arrive. Ivins handed me the tubes himself, personally, in April," Steele added.

Montooth looked up and around the table, studying each face, one at a time. "So, is it Ivins?"

Silence. No one spoke, hesitating, knowing we still had no direct proof, no latent fingerprints matching Ivins, no human DNA linking him to the letters or envelopes, no fiber, ink, handwriting, or other commonly used forensics—no smoking gun. The lack of evidence against Hatfill stood fresh in our minds, and the fruitless investigation into his past and present that had consumed three years, and especially the trailing bloodhounds. The case of Richard Jewell, the falsely accused bomber of the 1996 Summer Olympics in Atlanta, went through my mind. Similar to Hatfill's situation, Jewell had been widely reported by news[1] media as a person of interest until being cleared three months later by the US Attorney for the Northern District of Georgia. The FBI placed the real bomber, Eric Robert Rudolph, on its Ten Most Wanted list in 1998. Rudolph had watched Jewell, a security guard at the time, inspect the backpack containing Rudolph's black powder pipe bomb coated with masonry nails.[2] Jewell then evacuated people from the area before the deadly explosion, saving dozens, maybe hundreds of lives.[3] Rudolph eventually admitted to the Olympic Park bombing and abortion clinic bombings, where he planted secondary explosive devices to injure first responders. He now serves consecutive life sentences in Colorado's federal Supermax prison. Jewell went on to become a sworn and respected law enforcement officer. The aggressiveness I developed while investigating bank and armored car robberies had tempered during the recent years. Being wrong in a major case and seeing it leaked in the press could be devastating to all involved.

Montooth asked one more time, looking straight at me, louder now—decibels higher, his frustration clear, "Well, Scott. Did Ivins do it!?"

Without looking around, I could feel the stares of Steele and the rest of my squad waiting for an answer. Finally I broke the tension, "Yes."

Late in the afternoon we began arriving at AMX-3's compact office in Frederick; Amerithrax agents with advanced training in evidence collection and certified in the preservation of hazardous materials. Terry Kerns, recently promoted to chief of the Hazardous Materials Response Unit, sent two of her Hazmat officers to take responsibility for the safety of the operation. An agent from the field office's Computer Analysis Response Team (CART) followed, an analytical investigator trained in recovering information, deleted or not, from any model or make of computer.[4]

While we waited for Ed Montooth to arrive, the AMX-3 postal inspectors told a story about being surprised as they returned to the office one day after running leads at USAMRIID. Next door a small delicatessen operated, serving the surrounding industrial park. In front, at an outdoor table, sat Bruce Ivins. He stared straight at them but made no acknowledgment, offered no greeting or sign of recognition. Apparently Dr. Ivins was conducting his own surveillance, however awkward.

We gathered in the office conference room as Montooth walked in. Darin Steele and Rick Langham passed out copies of a search warrant with its supporting affidavit. Langham, with an easygoing and amiable nature, had earned his doctorate at the University of California's Berkeley campus before joining the Bureau. Inspector Rick Lambert, always on the lookout for new agents with strong backgrounds in science, recruited Langham for the task force and specifically, my AMX-2 Science Squad.[5] Langham and Steele had the distinction of being the only agents in the task force to have received all the immunizations required for unrestricted access to USAMRIID's bacteriology laboratories. Langham had just finished writing the search warrant affidavit, his first. A magistrate judge read it earlier that day and signed without hesitation. Also that morning, the new commander of USAMRIID, Colonel George Korch, had given his consent for us to search Ivins's B3 biocontainment lab and the adjoining B4 lab suite—connected by a doorway in the rear and a mirror image of the B3 suite. He promised to keep the upcoming search to himself and pledged any and all cooperation. No one else under his command would know of our purpose that night; we wanted no repeat of the earlier media frenzy narrowly avoided at the ice pond dives.

Sitting in silence for a moment, we read over Langham's affidavit, refreshing ourselves with the list of evidence to look for: log books for a fermenter in the B4 suite and for a large freeze drier also in B4; scotch tape; any and all Federal Eagle envelopes; notes or written mention of addresses in New York City, on Capitol Hill, and for senators Daschle and Leahy. Ivins's computer would be mirrored under the direction of the CART agent. Lacking Hazmat training, she would direct the agents searching inside the B3 suite through a small soundproof glass window, using an encrypted two-way radio to communicate. Finally, we read about *Bacillus subtilis*.

Locating samples of *subtilis* would be key for the nighttime search. Unknown to most outside the investigation, additional progress in genetics had been achieved by the FBI's Chemical Biological Sciences Unit at Quantico and help from The Institute for Genomic Research in Rockville. Almost immediately after the CDC's Rich Meyer had begun analyzing the scant bit of powder he had recovered from the Brokaw letter, he also found contamination. Bacterial spores of another species were present, about one for every one hundred of anthrax. The CDC identified the foreign species as *Bacillus subtilis*. But they had no way of telling if the *subtilis* had been introduced after the envelope opened or had been in the powder before the envelope sealed.[6]

Pat Worsham had also found trace amounts of bacterial contamination in the powder from the *New York Post* letter. Colleagues at nearby University of Maryland tentatively identified the trace spores as being yet another related species, *Bacillus licheniformis*, and a private company in California specializing in *licheniformis* production tentatively concurred.

The genus of *Bacillus* includes many individual species. It is a very old genus, first described in 1872 by the German scientist Ferdinand Cohn. He renamed a bacteria, *Vibrio subtilis*, as *Bacillus subtilis*, a bacterium capable of forming endospores during times of starvation. Robert Koch followed with the identification of *Bacillus anthracis* four years later, and in 1884, Heinrich A. de Bary described a third cousin, *Bacillus megaterium*. In 1986, the first edition of the standard for bacteria speciation, *Bergey's Manual of Systemic Bacteriology*, named thirty-two species of *Bacillus* based on comparisons of morphology, metabolism, and limited DNA structure.[7, 8]

Bacillus bacteria have varying levels of medical, commercial, and scientific significance. Anthrax causes devastating disease.[9] *Cereus* is best known as a source of food poisoning. *Thuringiensis* has commercial value as an agricultural insecticide,[10] and *licheniformis* produces an enzyme added to laundry detergents and the commercial antibiotic bacitracin. *Subtilis* has become a standard in scientific research for elucidating the mechanisms, enzymes, and proteins controlling a cell's duplication of its helical DNA.[11] *Amyloliquefacieus* had prominence in early DNA cloning research. The bacterium produces the Bam H1 restriction enzyme that found wide application in cleaving and rejoining the DNA helix.[12] While each species has a specific niche and produces unique enzymes and proteins, a common thread binding the members of genus *Bacillus* is their ability to form spores. By 2009, based on the DNA sequence of genes encoding single-stranded nucleic acids, the second edition of *Bergey's Manual* named over 140 species of *Bacillus*, and the original genus now split between multiple genera.[13, 14]

The Chemical Biological Sciences Unit saw potential in the contamination. The Laboratory Division had established the unit, known by its acronym, CBSU, in the year following 9/11 and the anthrax attacks and gave it the mission of coordinating forensic analysis of evidence in cases of biological and chemical terrorism. It soon added nuclear and radiological weapons to the list.

With the assistance of The Institute for Genomic Research, CBSU scientists began sequencing DNA prepared from the *New York Post* contaminating *Bacillus*. They chose ribosomal ribonucleic acid genes, which hold the information for production of single-stranded nucleic acid components necessary for protein production in all metabolizing cells. In 1977, professor Carl Woese introduced the sequences of ribosomal ribonucleic acids as the new standard for bacterial speciation, and by the millennium, bacteriologists had accepted Woese's protocol as the standard. Methodically comparing the ribosomal RNA genes, CBSU determined the *New York Post* contaminant to be an isolate of the original member of the genus *Bacillus subtilis*.

The scientists then set out to locate collections of *subtilis* strains. The Agricultural Research Service of the US Department of Agriculture had a library of bacteria, molds, and yeasts and agreed to share their *subtilis*. CBSU then contacted the American Type Culture Collection with a similar request. While assembling a *subtilis* repository—finally obtaining over seventy-two distinct isolates—they also set about to answer a key question: Were the contaminating *subtilis* from the *New York Post* and Brokaw letters the same? Again with the help of the scientists at The Institute for Genomic Research they compared DNA, selecting a total of twenty-three different genes. Finding not a single difference, they concluded the contaminating *Bacillus* in the two New York letters to be identical, and therefore most likely present in the preparation of anthrax spores before being sealed in the envelopes.

The scientists then turned to their repository. Again, with the help of The Institute of Genomic Research staff, they found a single gene, *sboA*,[15] which contains the DNA information necessary to produce the protein antibiotic subtilosin A. *Subtilis* produces subtilosin immediately before spore formation; apparently one more protective measure as the bacteria brings vegetative growth to an end. They found the *sboA* gene to be highly conserved, unchanged in every seventy-two isolates, as well as in the *Post*/Brokaw isolate.

Turning to the polymerase chain reaction, they designed a test for the presence of *sboA* and then applied the new assay to each of the 1,056 samples in our Ames anthrax repository. They found 322—nearly one-third of the collected Ames—contained *subtilis* contamination.

They now began to answer the final question: Did one of the Ames exemplars also contain the *Post*/Brokaw *subtilis*? If so, would the exemplar's origin agree with our earlier results pointing to RMR-1029? Still working hand in hand with The Institute for Genomic Research, they identified three regions of DNA in the *Post*/Brokaw *subtilis* that differed in sequence from the analogous regions in each of the seventy-two isolates in their repository. Using the polymerase chain reaction, they again examined all 322 contaminated Ames exemplars. Not a single match.[16] But the *Post*/Brokaw contamination clearly represented trace evidence and provided a clue to the mailer's identity. Tonight, in Bruce Ivins's lab, we would look for it.

As we read, the affidavit listed more than adequate probable cause to believe we would find samples of *Bacillus subtilis* that night. Darin Steele recalled seeing tubes in the walk-in cold room when he had collected the forty-plus samples of Ames from Ivins back in December almost three years ago. AMX-2 had also done searches of the scientific literature as we had done when looking for Ames. We had found publications by USAMRIID bacteriologists citing multiple strains of *subtilis*. The notebooks that Ivins had given Steele noted work on several species of *Bacillus* and included a fermentation of *subtilis*. Scientists of the Bacteriology Division had once prepared a large batch in B4, the laboratory suite next door to Ivins's B3.

As our team of Hazmat-trained agents prepared to enter the B3 laboratory, a second team waited in silence, hidden in the shadows a few blocks away. They had followed Ivins home from the lab at the end of his workday, and now waited outside his house in case he resumed his fall 2001 habit of returning to his lab at night. In unmarked white Grand Prixes, black Explorers, and green Bonnevilles they stayed in touch, transmitting sporadic messages over encrypted two-way radios. When the lights finally went out at Ivins's residence, the team radioed those of us at USAMRIID to begin. We hoped the operation would remain a secret, known only to the commander, and avoid feeding the rumor mill of USAMRIID hallways in the coming week and anonymous tips to the media.

21

Increased Scrutiny
April 2007

Spring had finally arrived. The ice-covered roads and three-hour commutes through Northern Virginia were gone until next winter. I had decided on a change. For the past months, I had felt that we had exhausted our ideas for forensic initiatives with the technology available. Newer, rapid DNA sequencing techniques known as next generation sequencing were becoming available, but we already had our answer. I was also confident that we had identified and collected all the samples of Ames available. Last November, around the time we searched Ivins's lab, we had added one last shipment from Porton Downs, and it had tested negative for the A-mutations. I had requested that the Chemical Biological Sciences Unit put together a test to detect the density chemical that Bruce Ivins used in his spore purification centrifuge gradients, but I didn't give it much chance of success. He was smart enough to wash away all traces. I recalled him telling me back in 2003 that the chemical would be easy to detect with routine science. I began applying for jobs at Headquarters, in the Security Division with a step up in rank.

At Ed Montooth's urging, AMX-1 abandoned their remaining investigation of Steven Hatfill and directed all resources toward Ivins. They had just received another pen register[1] authorization, this time for email address goldenphoenix111@hotmail. Over the course of weeks and months, they read through pages of email traffic that the Computer Analysis Response Team had retrieved from Ivins's computers. Last fall's search of Ivins's containment lab had yielded little forensically—there were no matches to the *subtilis* contaminating the New York letters, no Eagle envelopes, no copies of anthrax letters. But his computer did provide information. Within a week of the laboratory search, AMX-1 had set up their first pen register on Ivins's personal address: Kingbadger7@aol. That led to more email accounts he accessed: goldenphoenix111@hotmail, jimmyflathead@yahoo, and bruce. ivins.@amedd.army. Registration information at Yahoo! listed Mr. Ed Irving of Frederick, Maryland, as jimmyflathead and having the alternative email address of Kingbadger7@aol. At America On Line, Kingbadger7 was assigned to Bruce Ivins of Frederick, Maryland 21702—the zip code for the main Frederick post office that had received and sold envelopes matching those from the attacks.[2]

Ivins's email messages now filled large notebooks in our office. They captivated us; we began to get glimpses of a different person than the public Ivins. Rather than a somewhat goofy eccentric career scientist who played keyboard at Sunday services, gave juggling lessons, and dressed as a clown to amuse children, a more sinister person emerged. We read about two personalities, his preoccupation with our investigation, and an emotional dependence on his former technician—nearly thirty years his junior—who had resigned from USAMRIID to attend medical school.

Mara Linscott worked for Ivins before leaving for upstate New York in mid-1999. He sent her repeated emails, cajoling and coaxing her to return, that her loss to his laboratory left him anxious and depressed.[3] He admitted returning to psychiatric care and counseling sessions, something he had not committed to since the late 1970s during graduate school in Cincinnati and then in Maryland as a fledgling microbiologist. He saw Linscott as a confidant, disclosing his feelings about his late mother, who he believed had been afflicted with paranoid schizophrenia.[4] She had become increasingly violent with age—manic one moment, raging mad the next until her death at age sixty-three.[5] Ivins was afraid he was becoming his mother.

In a July 2000 message to Linscott, Bruce Ivins admitted that the doctors diagnosed him first with depression, then upped it to paranoid personality disorder, which he understood as a possible precursor to schizophrenia. He went on to describe feeling like two people and watching himself as he worked at his desk.[6] He claimed the drugs Celexa and Zyprexa helped, but that his therapist thought he should be jailed, so he had changed counseling sessions.[7] The messages also described heavy drinking and hiding empty liquor bottles from his wife.[8]

An email from Pat Fellows to Linscott on October 16, the day after Daschle's deadly letter arrived at USAMRIID and eleven days after Bob Stevens died, described Ivins as a "manic basket case these last few days."[9]

Ivins's emails also complained about his professional life. His career since arriving at USAMRIID in 1980 centered around anthrax—testing the efficacy of its vaccine, developing a second-generation vaccine based on DNA engineering. USAMRIID listed Ivins as a coinventor on the synthetic vaccine's patent application. But controversy surrounded the one currently in use, the one mandated for members of our country's military. In 1999 and 2000, articles appeared, notably in *Vanity Fair* and *The Washington Post*, attributing Gulf War Syndrome to the immunizations. Congress took notice. In June 2001, Senator Tom Daschle sent a letter to the Pentagon that heightened safety concerns about the mandated inoculations. Two months later, the author of the *Vanity Fair* article, Gary Matsumoto, had filed a Freedom of Information Act request with the Department of Defense, to include information from Ivins's laboratory notes. Ivins responded by email to a ranking supervisor, "Tell Matsumoto to kiss my ass."[10] That same month, Ivins met with his former colleague and USAMRIID microbiologist Anna Johnson-Winegar, now deputy assistant secretary of defense for chemical and biological readiness at the Pentagon. Johnson-Winegar questioned the need for the next-generation anthrax vaccine and the unwieldy immunization program. She went so far as to draft a letter about it to the USAMRIID Command.[11]

USAMRIID responded. Before the end of the summer, the command suggested to Ivins that anthrax research funding would be disappearing, vaccine development was near an end, and it might be time, after twenty years, to switch directions. Why not take a look at Glanders disease until retirement?

Although not at the top of the CDC's Select Agent list, Glanders does rank as a potential biological weapon. The disease is caused by infection with the bacteria *Burkholderia mallei*. But Glanders is viewed as more of a danger to livestock than man, and unlike *Bacillus* bacteria, it is not given to sporulation and formation of aerosols.

Both anthrax and Glanders are zoonotic diseases, capable of passing between and infecting humans and animals. But for man to be infected, he must come in contact with an infected animal's body fluids through eyes, nose, mouth, or a break in the skin. The disease first appeared as a weapon in 1915 when German operatives brought *mallei* to Baltimore and inoculated horses being shipped to Allied Forces on the Western Front.

The email messaging about psychiatric problems and his changing diagnosis led us to request assistance from the US Attorney's Office. First, the assistant attorney assigned to the case issued a directive to Ivins's health insurance company commanding all billing records. The information dated to the late 1990s. It contained insurance claims from multiple doctors for a series of disorders, each defined by a specific numbered code. By year 2000, six months following Linscott's departure, a psychiatrist diagnosed Ivins with depression, anxiety, psychosis—a second doctor concurred. They wrote prescriptions for the antidepressant Celexa, then added Valium and two other drugs to lessen anxiety. The popular Ambien and Lunesta would be added during the month he provided his second and controversial submission to our Ames collection. By mid-2000, they prescribed Zyprexa and a second medication to ward off episodes of psychosis. Billing codes and notations of diagnoses cited affective psychosis, mania disorder, and depressive psychosis, hinting at complex and potentially serious emotional problems.[12, 13]

The indication of complex mental problems, both in the insurance codes and Ivins's own admissions in emails to Linscott, prompted a second request of the US Attorney's Office in Washington—access to records documenting his treatment. But the assistant attorney assigned to our case said no, citing the Health Insurance Portability and Accountability Act (HIPAA) enacted by Congress in 1996, Title II of which safeguards electronic, paper, and verbal medical data, "Individually Identifiable Health Information." Congress assigned its regulation to the Department of Health and Human Services and, in 1999, the department issued guidance in the form of its HIPAA Privacy Rule. The rule included a Law Enforcement Provision and allowed for subpoenas and court orders to secure insurance records. But it also singled out psychotherapy notes in a provision separate from the ones governing insurance records.[14] Our repeated pleas, encouragement, and argument would not prevail—psychiatrists' notes and therapists' observations would remain sealed.

By spring 2007, we had collected volumes of insurance records, and pages and pages of printed email messages. The email messages contained veiled threats, discussions of psychiatric visits, and a layman's understanding of Ivins's diagnosis, and what seemed to be alternating distrust and confidence. The billing records contained dozens of numerical codes and pharmaceutical names. It became clear that to understand it all, we needed expert help.

Montooth turned to the Behavioral Analysis Unit-1 (BAU-1) at Quantico and an Amerithrax alumnus. The FBI formed the original Behavioral Analysis Unit in the mid-1990s, more than a decade after eleven agents in the Behavioral Sciences Unit at Quantico began interviewing convicted violent criminals in an effort to identify common themes and psychological traits. Their goal: analyze a crime scene for clues to the suspect's personality traits and develop a behavioral profile to aid detectives and case agents around the country. By 2001, behavioral assessments came into such high demand that the single unit became three. Behavioral Analysis Unit-1 specialized in terrorists, arsonists, and bomb makers. Former AMX-2 member, Scott Stanley, had joined it.

The Behavioral Analysis Units recruited seasoned agents from field divisions. One-and-a-half years ago, Stanley stopped by my office and asked if I would support his leaving our task force for a job in BAU-1. I tried in vain to talk him out of it. I stressed that we needed him to finish additional genetic testing of the Ames repository and we were probably going to drop Hatfill as a suspect once testing was complete. But I knew it was a promotion for him and he would work out of pastoral Quantico instead of congested Northern Virginia. He countered that Rick Langham was up to speed and ready to coordinate the remaining genetic work. I also felt a little envy. I had applied to BAU back in my Hazardous Materials Response Unit days but never got the job. But I had put that in the past. Realizing his mind was made up, I wished him luck and guaranteed my recommendation and support. Now, in 2007, it proved to be a good move for Amerithrax. In his new position he would use his investigative knowledge of our case to provide valuable resources.

Montooth arranged to have copies of the emails and insurance records sent to Quantico. The amount of material surprised Stanley, as well as the complexity of the medical codes and the often confusing and incoherent email messages, especially those written late at night. Stanley placed a call to a long-time BAU consultant, a psychiatrist and associate professor at the University of Virginia School of Medicine.

"Hi, Greg, its Scott Stanley, BAU-1."

"Scott, how are you, what have you been up to?"

"Oh, a couple of new cases, and still working on the anthrax case."

"How's that going? Are you making any progress?"

"Yes, the genetic screening is working out well, much better than we originally had hoped. I think we're on to something," Stanley said.

"That's great, how can I help?"

"Can you look at some material for us? We have a box of Blue Cross insurance records going back ten years. They have medical diagnostic codes and lists of drug prescriptions for someone we're looking at," Stanley said.

"Sure, be glad to, send them to me."

Dr. Gregory Saathoff had been consulting for the FBI's Behavioral Analysis Units since 1996. He had graduated from the University of Missouri Medical School in the mid-1980s and gone on to a residency in psychiatry at the University of Virginia, and in 1987, he accepted a position on the medical school's faculty. In 1991, he had taken a break from academic life when, as a major in the Army's Reserve Psychiatric Medical Corps, the Pentagon activated him for Desert Storm.

As Saathoff looked at the box filled with bundles of insurance billings, he thought about how he would organize the information. A tenet of science teaches to graph the results; a picture makes things much clearer and brings out patterns and unique features. One by one he began to categorize the drugs that had been prescribed, those for depression, psychosis, and anxiety.

Then others for angina, infections, breathing, skin irritation, pain and stomach ailments—nearly three dozen prescription drugs in all. The ones for depression, psychosis, and anxiety interested him most, they signaled mental issues. Saathoff charted a timeline for the years 2000 through mid-2007. Ivins had taken Celexa since the beginning of the psychiatric consults for depression in 2000. The dosage doubled during mid-summer 2001, two to three months before the anthrax attacks. Antianxiety medications and powerful sleeping aids increased dramatically in 2006. Ivins also took Lunesta, Ambien, Valium, and Rozerem, and at times prescriptions overlapped and new ones written before existing ones ran out. As Saathoff reviewed the records from 2000 through mid-2007, he noted a steady use of Celexa for depression, and at the same time, alprazolam, Ambien, lorazepam, Lunesta, diazepam, Rozerem for anxiety, and occasionally, Seroquel and Zyprexa for psychosis.[15] The billing for antianxiety medication spiked in early 2002—at the time the Ames subpoena was given to USAMRIID microbiologists—and continued through 2006.

Saathoff also noted the antibiotic doxycycline had been prescribed in mid-October 2001, five days after Daschle's letter contaminated Capitol Hill. A second doctor prescribed a different antibiotic, cephalexin, ten days later.[16]

Within two weeks, Saathoff telephoned Stanley, and told him that he suspected Ivins suffered from a severe substance abuse problem, citing the years of Celexa and multiple antianxiety medications. Saathoff also mentioned the antibiotics. "Ivins also saw two different docs and was given two separate prescriptions for antibiotics in mid-October 2001. Insurance billing recorded a diagnosis of 'cellulitis' and 'open wound of hand.' But, there was no indication the attending physician biopsied the damage or attempted further diagnosis.[17] Do you know what that was about?"

"No, there's nothing listed in the annual medical report he's supposed to fill out each year at RIID. It's part of the Special Immunization Program set up for those receiving vaccines. He's required to list all illnesses and injuries," Stanley said.

Stanley ended the consultation with another request. "Would you be willing to look at some emails? We also have surveillance logs that record some bizarre behavior."

As Saathoff read through Ivins's typed messages, it quickly became clear why Stanley wanted a psychiatric opinion. In June 2000, Ivins had written Mara Linscott, "Even with the Celexa and the counseling, the depression episodes come and go. . . . What is REALLY scary is the paranoia. . . . It's when I get these 'paranoid' episodes. Of course I regret them thoroughly when they are over, but when I'm going through them, it's as if I am a passenger on a ride.

. . . I think the problems started in 1997, and by the time you left, things were very bad." Saathoff read on to July 4, "The thinking now by the psychiatrist and the counselor is that my symptoms may not be those of depression or bipolar disorder, they may be that of 'Paranoid Personality Disorder.'" Within days, Ivins wrote, "Right now, anti-anxiety medication such as diazepam (valium) is helpful. I've been told that eventually, depending on the course of things, anti-psychotic drugs may be included." In August, he described, "I get incredible paranoid, delusional thoughts at times, and there's nothing I can do until they go away, either by themselves or with drugs."[18]

One email to Linscott, in the spring of 2000, talked of hiding spent liquor bottles at home.[19] A review of surveillance logs mentioned trips to the liquor store. Interviews of coworkers discussed Ivins and tequila and vodka and whiskey after hours. At times, the agents and postal inspectors noted a disheveled and unkempt Ivins going out to the trashcan late at night. A habit of taking Ambien with large doses of liquor before ending his email sessions for the evening accounted for the bizarre late-night messages.

Experienced dealing with mentally ill criminals at the men's penitentiary in Stanton, Virginia, and seeing dozens of patients dependent on prescription medication and alcohol, Saathoff came to his conclusion: Ivins was physically and emotionally dependent on prescribed medicines and alcohol. He also suffered from severe mental disorders.

In July the career board at Headquarters met and awarded me a new job, assistant section chief over the Security Operations Section. I would oversee the daily business and budgets for five units totaling approximately 340 FBI employees. The uniformed FBI Police comprised one unit, and it maintained a force of 250 officers, with primary responsibility for FBI Headquarters and its employees. As I shook hands and wished Ed Montooth good luck, I had mixed feelings. The investigation was on track, and we were making progress toward a solution, maybe within the year. I promised to stay in touch and be available for questions about the early days of the case. I turned to my office overlooking the Capital Beltway and began to pack.

In October, Stanley telephoned Saathoff again. "Greg, we're going overt with Ivins, do you have any suggestions on how we should handle it? We'll be searching his residence, office, cars, and interviewing him, the wife, and two children. His Internet activity says he likes guns, so we expect to find some. Do you have any concerns?"

Saathoff expanded on his earlier assessment. Ivins was a middle-aged male with significant health concerns, a history of treatment for depression, anxiety, and paranoia, and access to dangerous pathogens. The email traffic included discussion of mental illness in his family history, and he was nearing retirement and had bought weapons recently. He had an unhappy marriage and abused alcohol and prescription medications. Saathoff countered this assessment with Ivins's support of a therapy group and years' long attention by the same psychiatrist. Saathoff's conclusion: Ivins presented a threat to both himself and others. The task force should take that into consideration.

Stanley relayed the information, layered with the Behavioral Analysis Unit's recommendations. Amerithrax should minimize any outside attention by the media, USAMRIID employees, or the public in general. During the interview of Ivins, be especially alert to odd behavior, any suggestion of deepening depression or heightened anxiety. Montooth appreciated the heads up and heartily agreed with the recommendations; he wanted no repeat of the media circus he had heard about in the case's early days. He invited Stanley to take part in the search, and to drive Ivins to a hotel room following an interview with the task force, perhaps get Ivins to talk during the trip across town—an unusual step for an FBI field office to allow a Headquarters supervisor to conduct an interview in an active investigation. But Stanley knew the case as well as anyone did—he had been involved since the day he responded to Daschle's office, he understood the science, and now he had been trained to assess deviant behavior. Stanley accepted; he would be paired with Postal Supervisor Tom Dellefera.

Montooth then contacted Unit Chief Terry Kerns at the Hazardous Materials Response Unit of the FBI Laboratory in Quantico. In a case of this magnitude, involving live anthrax spores, it had become protocol to conduct searches wearing level-C Hazmat gear: rubber boots, purple nitrile gloves, hooded white suits of paperlike Tyvek, and black masks with protruding filter cartridges. Standing by outside the residence would be blue tents and buckets of diluted bleach, brushes, and four-foot trays to catch diluted Hazmats—a scene that would attract attention within minutes.

Montooth requested her help, both in advice and sending a team to sample Ivins's home for residual *Bacillus*, both anthrax and *subtilis*. He also asked that, if at all possible, it could be done without Hazmat gear. He reasoned that of the three people living in the house, two had never been vaccinated against anthrax, nor had contracted the disease after years of Ivins's work. The sampling would be a precaution, proof that no live anthrax was in the house. After consulting with her Hazmat officers, she agreed. They would also plan on arriving well after midnight, further lessening their visibility. Montooth's application for the search warrants would include a request to search outside the normally approved hours of 6:00 a.m. through 10:00 p.m.

By October 31 Amerithrax was ready. They arranged hotel rooms for Ivins, his wife, and adult son and divided themselves into teams for searching his office and clothes lockers at USAMRIID, his house outside the gates of Fort Detrick, and five automobiles. The cars would be towed to a garage on Fort Detrick and sampled for traces of *subtilis*. Montooth assigned two-person teams to conduct interviews of Ivins, his wife, and son, and his daughter living in nearby Hagerstown. Montooth assigned Darin Steele to the Bruce Ivins interview, and Steele planned to approach Ivins the next day at USAMRIID. The search of his house would begin after dark at 7:00 p.m., starting with all windows being darkened to prevent eavesdropping. The Hazmat team would arrive four hours after midnight and finish sampling before daybreak.

Steele first approached USAMRIID's commander, Colonel George Korch, and explained that they wanted to talk to Bruce Ivins and in such a way to avoid attention. Korch fully agreed with a low-profile approach and called Ivins to the commander's office, leaving him alone with Steele and an AMX-1 agent. Ivins immediately asked if he should call his attorney. They replied that they only wanted Ivins to listen, not talk, and he could leave at any time. Ivins sat down at the conference table, and the two agents took seats across from him. They began with his submission of Ames samples in April 2002 and the fact that they did not contain genetic mutations found in the parent material, RMR-1029. They told Ivins that they had thoroughly investigated the events surrounding the April submission, and they knew it had been Ivins, not one of his technicians, that had prepared the samples—his handwriting was on the tube's labels—there was no doubt. Ivins looked at them and said, "Okay."[20]

The two then told Ivins they could not understand why his April submissions lacked RMR-1029's mutations. They reminded Ivins that he had first submitted samples in February of 2002 and that the duplicates had been archived at Northern Arizona University. Steele had recently retrieved them, and when tested, they matched parental RMR-1029 exactly. So, what could be the explanation for the difference in the February and April submissions?

Ivins offered that perhaps he had taken only a single colony of bacteria from a plate of solid agar. Impossible, they countered, and read aloud the FBI's protocol for preparing samples of Ames: "*If the stock (Ames sample) is a agar culture, do not use a single colony, rather an inoculum taken across multiple colonies.*"

Ivins then offered that the traces of the phenol chemical he had added to RMR-1029, a standard precaution to inhibit mold contamination, may have prevented the Ames sample from growing. Wrong again, they said; the protocol stated the samples should be incubated for twelve to eighteen hours before submitting to confirm viability—each submitted sample had showed growth.

Ivins offered that maybe he did not submit RMR-1029 in April and only in February. They countered again, asking why had he sent an email message to the task force on April 9 stating that he had included RMR-1029?

Ivins suggested a mistake on the part of the FBI's testing was to blame. No, the two replied, both April duplicate samples tested identically, and were tested at different times.

Without pausing, Ivins stated that he probably did not have the instructions for how to submit the samples. But the two corrected him; Ivins had the protocol in February. They told him that they had read my telephone notes from February 2002 when he had asked me for a copy of the protocol. Further, Ivins had attended a meeting in late March with Scott Stanley during which Pat Worsham had described how to prepare Ames submissions. During the meeting, Stanley quietly sketched a diagram showing where each attendee sat—*Ivins* was clearly printed at the edge of the conference table. The two agents looked at Ivins. It was time to be blunt. They told Ivins that, in their opinion, based on the investigation of the last three years, multiple rounds of genetic testing and after recovering the back-up samples at Keim's lab, that Ivins had tried to deceive them with his submissions. And by being deceptive, he had caused a two-year delay in their investigation—obstructed it—from April 2002 to April 2004, when Steele had seized the flask of RMR-1029 and tested it.[21]

The three had been talking for four hours, and both agents were prepared to continue for another four when a knock sounded on the office door. Commander Korch needed to retrieve a set of keys. As Korch stood in the doorway, Ivins abruptly stated that he did not want to continue listening to the agents. He wanted to leave. Steele asked if he would stay five more minutes; they needed to tell him something very important in private—his house, office, and vehicles were being searched as they spoke. Also, his wife and two children were being interviewed. The two stressed that the FBI had made every effort to keep the searches confidential, and as far as they knew, no one outside the anthrax task force knew what was taking place. Ivins could not go home at this time, but they had reserved hotel rooms for him and his family, and Scott Stanley waited outside to give him a lift.

Within a few minutes, Stanley and Tom Dellafera pulled up to USAM-RIID's glass entrance and the waiting Ivins. As Dellefera moved into the rear seat, the agents nodded to Stanley, indicating that Ivins had been searched for weapons. Ivins said hello and climbed into the front seat. Driving slowly out of Fort Detrick's main gate, Stanley mentioned that Ivins looked strained and preoccupied.[22]

"I don't want to be labeled a mass killer or terrorist."

"I've known you for several years, Bruce. I don't think of you like that," Stanley said.

"I can't believe you think I'm the anthrax mailer."

Stanley glanced into the upper rearview mirror and looked at Dellefera. At the same moment, Dellefera looked into the mirror and caught Stanley's glance. Neither had mentioned the anthrax murders.

22

Inconsistency and Contradiction

December 2007

Searching Ivins's house and vehicles had taken eleven hours. At the same time, teams at USAMRIID searched his office, his clothes locker in the B3 lab suite, the rooms and inner hallway of his hot suite, each freezer and refrigerator, and the desk and closet.

Immediately following the searches, Commander Korch took decisive action and ordered his security office to terminate Ivins's access to all biosafety level-3 laboratories. Ivins was now barred from working with all but a few harmless strains of anthrax.

For two weeks following the searches, the Amerithrax Task Force poured through boxes, listened to cassette tapes, and read documents. During the residence search, as expected, they found weapons: a pocket-sized 22-caliber Beretta, a nine millimeter five-inch-plus barreled Glock built for accuracy, and a smaller, three-inch Glock 40-caliber pistol for concealment. They found an extra pistol barrel and a basement firing range, and a beige lockbox containing a Taser, pepper spray, and stun guns.

In Ivins's bedroom, they had found documents and papers related to our anthrax investigation: a 2003 *Baltimore Sun* article, *Test Points to Domestic Source behind Anthrax Letter Attacks*[1] implicating Steven Hatfill, and a ten-point typewritten list of why Joseph Farchaus had mailed the anthrax letters. It also contained an email message he sent himself citing reasons why his former technicians, Mara Linscott—the object of his obsession—and Pat Fellows, were also behind the attacks, and a request of the USAMRIID security office for entry records to laboratory B3 for himself, Fellows, and a contract technician from February 15 through April 15, 2002. They discovered four articles on handwriting analysis along with lists of expert witnesses and telephone numbers, four articles on chemical analysis and advertisements for forensic services, and an article from a forensic conference on paper identification and one on the legalities of DNA evidence. Most curiously, they found a note written in Ivins's hand:[2]

Themes

1. That psychiatric problems "made me do it"
2. That political reasons (get Patriot Act + other legislation passed) "made me do it"
3. That financial reasons (make money off new vaccine) "made me do it"
4. That I deliberately submitted anthrax samples that were either contaminated, altered, adulterated, or otherwise different from what they were stated to be

But they did not find the smoking gun. No Federal Eagle envelopes, no addresses to the offices of senators Daschle or Leahy nor for Tom Brokaw, or the editor of the *New York Post* or the *Sun*. Not a mention of Greendale School or Franklin Park, New Jersey. No copies of an anthrax threat letter or maps of Princeton.

After finishing their review of seized items, the task force began interviewing coworkers. We already had a good understanding of where RMR-1029 had been stored and who had access to it, and we understood aerosol challenges and who had what role. Now, Ed Montooth and his team needed information about Ivins: his demeanor before the mailings, his reaction to November's searches, plans for retirement. They confirmed what he had told Linscott in his email: USAMRIID command had planned to shut down all but menial work on anthrax vaccines; the funding had dried up; there was more work and money in other organisms, such as Glanders. Ivins opposed the switch and let his feelings be known, more than once reminding those nearby, "I'm an anthrax researcher! That is what I do."[3]

After the anthrax attacks, the command switched its stance and predicted a need to provide spore preparations to researchers on a regular basis and asked Ivins to formally document his standard procedure. USAMRIID management considered him a pioneer in the field of anthrax spore production.[4]

Montooth knew it was time to speak with Ivins again. It had been three months since Darin Steele's four-hour interview followed by the drive with Scott Stanley and Tom Dellafera. Montooth was fairly confident he could get Ivins to agree to a meeting. Since 2004, we had suspected him of falsifying evidence, and in November 2007, he finally admitted that he had been the one to submit four samples, including the Dugway RMR-1029 spores, to the

FBI's Ames repository in April 2002. Ivins would see the proposed meeting as an opportunity to dissuade the FBI from believing he had anything to do with the anthrax letters. But Montooth thought Ivins might instead implicate himself, or at the least make admissions to lessen the veneer of all-around fun-loving eccentric—someone who shows up at an international conference in a Zoot suit, offers help with colleagues' research, puts on juggling shows for free.

Montooth and Vince Lisi prepared meticulously, reviewing and discussing what we had learned to date. In 2005, Ivins had admitted to Inspector Rick Lambert during a marathon interview—summarized in twenty-three single-spaced pages—of driving miles at night, for ten to eleven hours, to drop off anonymous gifts—a bottle of Kahlua, a second of wine—on Mara Linscott's doorstep. He had also admitted to mailing packages with false names and return addresses, at locations far from his home, disguising the gifts' true origin.[5] In the email messages of 1999, 2000, and 2001, AMX-1 had read of Ivins's depression and paranoia, the feeling of having a personality outside of his own, and family history of mental disease. From computer searches Montooth and Lisi knew about his keen interest in the Kappa Kappa Gamma sorority, and combined with the pen registers results, had identified his numerous email accounts, some registered under assumed names. Repeatedly, Ivins wrote messages to himself, sending and receiving them with one or more of his alternate email accounts.[6] During the search of Ivins's home, a printed copy of one of the emails had been recovered; Kingbadger7 explained to bruce.ivins[at]amedd.army that there were eleven reasons to believe Mara Linscott and Pat Fellows had attacked the Senate and New York media with anthrax. Montooth and Lisi suspected Ivins in the theft of a fellow graduate student's thesis notes—returned anonymously by dropping them in a mailbox. The graduate student,[7] a Kappa alumnus, also suspected Ivins had vandalized the fence and sidewalk outside her house along with her car by spray-painting the Greek letters KKΓ.

Montooth sent AMX-1 agents to see Kappa Kappa Gamma administrators and alumni.[8] They confirmed that a person identified as jimmyflathead—one of Ivins's pseudonyms—would consistently put derogatory information in the sorority's page on the public Internet encyclopedia, Wikipedia. Kappa administrators would remove the material, but jimmyflathead just added it back and more, threatening to reveal secret sorority information.[9] Investigators found one item particularly interesting; the Princeton University chapter of Kappa Kappa Gamma maintained an office at 20 Nassau Street. The mailbox where the attacker had mailed the letters was located at 10 Nassau Street.

The task force continued to monitor the bank of pen registers recording Ivins's email activity.[10] Trash covers—we had begun them sporadically in

2004 when pen registers had been placed on his house and cell telephones, and continued into 2005—now occurred weekly. In the evenings, once on Tuesday and again Friday, surveillance teams watched Ivins place his trash at the curb. Well after midnight, the task force collected it.

Two weeks into the New Year, Ivins and his attorney agreed to a meeting. Montooth and Lisi met with him and his two lawyers at the US Attorney's offices in northwest Washington, DC. This time government counsel would also join in, including Assistant United States Attorney Rachel Lieber. Fast talking and quicker thinking, she had joined the US Attorney's Office in 1997, after graduation from Georgetown University Law Center. Her office assigned her to the investigation only months before, and she brought a fresh perspective. Starting slowly, she absorbed concepts of genetics, polymerase chain reactions, and mutation rates. She turned to the evidence and what form a future prosecution memo should take. Many of the leads and information about Ivins came from his own email messages—the psychiatric problems, their multiple diagnosis, split personalities, fixation with a single sorority, use of aliases. She began issuing letters requiring preservation of the information stored in the multiple email accounts registered to Ivins and his aliases. Placed into law during 1986, the Electronic Communications Privacy Act provided for preservation requests and safe storage of all information—address books, email content of any age, subscriber information, alternate email accounts and addresses, usage logs, to/from and subject line content—for 90 days; additional letters would extend the period to 270 days.[11] She then followed up with new affidavits and search warrants for Ivins's personal email accounts—jimmyflathead, Kingbadger7, goldenphoenix111—at companies Yahoo!, America On Line, and MSN Hotmail.

Ivins walked into the US Attorney's office looking at the floor, not saying a word as Montooth and Lisi stood to shake hands. Ivins looked first at one and then the second of his attorneys before accepting the gesture. As the group took seats around a large table, Lisi began to talk, slowly with a practiced calmness.

Lisi first asked about Ivins's interest in the Kappa Kappa Gamma sorority. Immediately came Ivins's response, "Oh no, you don't understand. It's not an interest. It's an obsession. You can't understand."[12]

Montooth glanced up and wondered what would come next; he had not expected such candor. Ivins continued, sitting up slightly and moving his hands. It started in college, forty years ago, in the mid-1960s at the University of Cincinnati when he asked a member of Kappa Kappa Gamma for a date and she refused. Ivins soon became fixated with the sorority and set out to learn all that he could. Months later, he asked a second member out, and she also refused. He watched the newspaper for any mention of Kappa members. He often walked around the outside of their campus sorority house. Over time, he gathered the names and locations of dozens and dozens of Kappa chapters up and down the Eastern seaboard.

Ivins described visiting Kappa Kappa Gamma houses in Chapel Hill and Charlottesville, College Park, and Morgantown, and Knoxville, Durham, and Philadelphia. While a postgraduate researcher at the University of North Carolina, he broke into the Kappa house by climbing through a window when no one was home and stole decoding lists. Later, when he lived in Maryland, he drove to West Virginia University and broke into its Kappa house. There, he stole a ritual book and used the loot from his Chapel Hill burglary to decipher the recordings. At the University of Tennessee in Knoxville, he walked into a Kappa office when members were present and tried to talk with them. The women became nervous and called security. Apparently, the Tennessee chapter had alerted sister chapters because the University of Maryland Campus Police later contacted Ivins and accused him of breaking into College Park's Kappa house. The officer mentioned Ivins's Knoxville visit.

No one in Ivins's family knew of his obsession. He made the campus visits by driving at night when his wife was not home. He left their house and drove to a Kappa location, parked, walked around the house for short time, "maybe five minutes," Ivins said, before returning home.

Lisi asked him about the stolen laboratory notebook. Ivins admitted, yes, he had stolen a graduate student's research notes, but he returned them using a campus mailbox. He also confessed that when he learned the student had moved to nearby Gaithersburg, he occasionally drove to her apartment. On one trip, he sprayed Greek symbols for Kappa Kappa Gamma on the fence, sidewalk, and rear window of her fiancé's car.

Ivins continued to talk, apparently comfortable that his crimes of burglary and vandalism had occurred too long in the past to be charged. He told them yes, he had used several aliases—Carla Sander, Ed Ivings, Bruce Ivings. He maintained email accounts under different user names—Kingbadger7, jimmyflathead, Prunetacos, goldenphoenix111, bigsky, bruceivi, bruceiv—and used the same identities on multiple servers: MSN (Hotmail), America On Line, and Yahoo!. Ivins reserved the jimmyflathead account for communicating about Kappa Kappa Gamma.

After the interview, Montooth felt that he was beginning to understand Bruce Ivins as a person, but they had not probed into details of the attacks. They would need to meet for a second time. At the least it would provide another opportunity to lock Ivins into his statements during the first interview. Ivins had already described his habit of long midnight drives, which his wife knew nothing about. In doing so, he followed a routine, which Rachel Lieber felt rose to the legal standard of an established pattern and could be admitted into evidence at trial and also prevent his wife or children from providing him with an alibi.

The day before Valentine's Day, the group met again. They began with Kappa Kappa Gamma. Ivins took them thirty years back. He described burglarizing the sorority house in Chapel Hill, entering through a first-floor window hidden by shrubbery. Once inside he used a small flashlight to guide him upstairs and to a locked hallway closet that he opened with a coat hanger. Inside, he found documents about KKG rituals, a cipher decoder, and what looked like blindfolds torn from bed sheets. He stayed an hour.

Ivins did not limit his late-night drives to sorority houses. At times he headed to no specific location, just driving to think.

The discussion turned to items found during the search of Ivins's house, the many letters to members of Congress and *Newsweek* and the *Frederick News-Post*. Ivins told them he now writes letters to the editors of newspapers and magazines via the Internet, using a new system recently put in place. But for his congressional mailings, he still uses the postal service. Two years ago, he purchased monitoring software for his computer and discovered his computer activity was being watched. He then bought countersurveillance equipment and searched his house for electronic listening devices.

Montooth and Lisi asked Ivins to look at a drawing that he made for the FBI during the early days of the investigation: Would he explain it? The sketch showed different lineages of Ames; that of Ames original, of Greg Knudson and John Ezzell and Porton Down, and Ivins, Dugway, and Battelle. An arrow ran from Daschle's name in quotes to Knudson and Ezzell; an arrow crossed out with two lines pointed to Ivins's culture.[13] But instead of answering, Ivins questioned the agents, "Did I draw that?"

"Yes."

"When did I draw that?"

"That's not important. We just want to know what it means." Ivins asked again: What did he tell them at the time, what did they talk about, what was shown in the drawing?[14]

Neither Montooth nor Lisi responded, but only repeated their question. Looking down, staring into the table, Ivins did not answer.

The two pressed further, more insistent, wanting answers. They laid a color photograph on the table, dated "29/11/2001 17:07." It was a culture plate of blood red agar. Wide swaths of gray bacteria spread across its surface, tiny white dots speckled on top. The photograph had been labeled underneath with typed sentences, beginning with "Ames Strain—From Greg

Knudson's culture collection at USAMRIID."[15] They placed a second photograph in front of him, labeled "Ames strain" and "Bruce Ivins." He studied both. Yes, he had typed the labels, he understood what the captions meant, but he did not remember the interview when he handed them to the FBI. He also did not know if he believed the wording he had typed.

The agents returned to the diagram: Did Ivins remember now what he meant when he sketched it? Ivins looked up and down again at the diagram. He explained the series of short, curved arrows stretching from the original Ames culture meant "serial passage" of the bacteria. Knudson would take a sample from the 1981 stock of Ames and grow it, then take a sample from the new growth and repeat. Each time Knudson needed more Ames for experiments, he would propagate it by serial passing. With each passing, there would be new mutations in a few of the bacteria colonies—with time the number of mutants, seen as morphology variants in Knudson's Ames, would accumulate, and the growing Ames would now have mutant colonies scattered throughout. The single long arrow from the original Ames to the Ivins's culture meant that Ivins sampled the 1981 Ames a single time, grew a large amount of bacteria and then placed it, divided into many small vials, in the freezer. The frozen stocks would last, dormant, for years without accumulating mutations.

Ivins pointed to the colored photographs on the table and continued. Growing the spores on blood agar made it easier to spot variant colonies than the way Ivins grew anthrax. He used an agar called tryptic soy agar. It formed a clear, yellowish hard surface in the plates, and Ivins had not seen morphology variants in the mailed attack spores when he had grown them on clear tryptic agar in the fall of 2001. Someone from Ezzell's lab had grown the attack spores on dark red blood agar, however, and showed Ivins. That's when he saw the variants in the mailed spores and realized that they looked like Knudson's and Ezzell's Ames cultures.[16]

By the end of the interview, Montooth, Lisi, and Lieber made the same observation: Ivins's demeanor had changed over the course of the meeting, most notably when the topic switched from Kappa Kappa Gamma to anthrax and spores. He became cautious, wary, and vague. As they walked out of the conference room, Lieber also detected a change in his attorneys' attitudes. She suspected this signaled a change in their client's willingness to meet.[17]

Through the winter, the team continued its surveillance outside Ivins's house. At times they followed Ivins walking down a street, talking to himself, oblivious and seemingly incoherent. Twice a week they sorted through plastic bags of garbage, discovering forged prescriptions for atomoxetine, an attention deficit disorder and antidepression drug, and forms from more than one doctor,[18] mixed with empty liquor bottles. A confidential source at US-AMRIID reported that Ivins appeared at work with a black eye and the front office called him in. In mid-March, the USAMRIID command proposed Ivins for dismissal. He had spilled cultures of anthrax.[19] Rather than immediately reporting it as required, he simply cleaned it up and left for home. When he did fill out accident forms the next day, he blamed the accident on a technician and signed the document himself, without his supervisor's approval. But the command relinquished. He could keep his job and retire with a pension, but he would no longer step inside a laboratory of any kind.[20]

The following day, Montooth received a telephone call; medics had rushed Ivins to the Frederick Memorial Hospital—unconscious. A review of the Emergency Center 911 recording revealed Ivins's wife had found him at home in the afternoon, unresponsive but breathing. She believed he had taken too many Valium pills and mixed them with doses of alcohol.[21] Toxicology reports would later confirm her suspicions.

For a brief stint in April, Ivins checked into Bethesda's Suburban Hospital. He told the staff that he took seven times the recommended dosage of Ambien with twelve shots of vodka each day—but still found sleep difficult. They prescribed antipsychotic medications normally used to treat schizophrenia and bipolar disorder. On May 1, he again entered a detox center, this time as a patient in a four-week treatment program of the Joseph S. Massie Unit in western Maryland.

While Ivins embarked on his new bid for sobriety, Rachel Lieber and his attorneys agreed to one more meeting. When Ivins emerged from the Massie Unit, he would be free of alcohol, his drug use closely monitored; he would now be lucid. The attorneys hoped that by accepting the opportunity to proffer a statement to the US Attorney's Office, their client might convince the government not to seek a five-count indictment for murder using a weapon of mass destruction. Anything that Ivins said during the meeting would not be used against him, as long as he told the truth. It was a gamble usually reserved for a plea agreement process, but could also be used to persuade the government not to file charges, or to gauge a person's suitability as a witness. For the FBI and the US Attorney, the meeting would provide an assessment of how Ivins might present his defense.

For the June meeting, Montooth, Lisi, and Lieber met Ivins and his attorneys in Rockville. This time, Lisi immediately began by asking about anthrax. What was Ivins doing in his biosafety lab late at night in the summer of 2001, on several nights before each mailing?

"I just liked to go in there to get away from home, it was a bad situation there."

This time the two agents countered Ivins. They told him his answer was not true, emails he had written at the time stated things at home were better than ever.

"I went in to get away from the security guard. If I am in my office working, he stops in and talks, or asks for the newspaper."

They countered again. They had reviewed the access records. The guard worked only one of the nights when Ivins had been in the lab, and on that night the guard had not come near Ivins's office. Ivins looked down at the tabletop, arms folded in front, not answering. One of his attorneys spoke, "Bruce, just explain why you were there. That's got to be easy."

Silence continued, until finally, "I can't explain it."[22]

Lisi shifted to New York. Did Ivins have a particular dislike for the city, its people? Yes, Ivins did. In particular, he did not like the Yankees; they win too many games. And he had little use for the city's inhabitants. In the late 1960s, he had attended a microbiology conference in New York City. At lunch a waitress had thrown his food down on the table, a spinach salad, and walked away. Ivins had heard of another tourist being mugged and running to their hotel and reporting it. A hotel employee simply replied, "So what? That's New York. If you don't like it, you can leave."

Lisi brought up Ivins's use of aliases and post office mailboxes. Ivins confirmed that since the 1980s, he had subscribed to three mailboxes, using his name and also the name of a graduate student's husband, the same student he had stolen notebooks from. One mailbox had been located in Washington, DC, a second in Walkersville, Maryland, and a third on Seventh Street in Frederick.

Ivins still believed that Joe Farchaus was responsible for the anthrax mailings, and prior to the attacks he looked up where Farchaus lived in New Jersey. Farchaus had been part of the vaccine development team and would be entitled to royalties, so Ivins wanted to provide management with a mailing address. Ivins added that Farchaus's mother had a residence close to where the victim from Connecticut had died, and that could not be a coincidence.

Ivins also wrote email messages to himself at work from his personal Kingbadger7 account, outlining reasons why Mara Linscott and Pat Fellows were responsible for the mailings. But now Ivins did not think either one did it. He wrote the email at a time when he was frustrated. He had secretly gotten Fellows's email password and read some messages between Fellows and Linscott. The two women had discussed him in an unflattering way and Ivins wanted to strike back.

Montooth and Lisi returned to anthrax. When did Ivins learn his large batch of spores, the one produced under contract by Dugway Proving Grounds—RMR-1029—matched the mailed spores? Ivins believed that a fellow scientist and friend of his who owned a cabin in West Virginia told him early on, in 2002. Ivins had no memory of Special Agent Darin Steele telling him. When he told Inspector Lambert that Steele had told him, it was a mistake, although Ivins's technician may have heard it from Steele and then told people in the lab—Ivins could not be certain. But if the mailed spores had been grown from a sample of RMR-1029, then no one in his lab could have done it; they would only use a single colony to grow large batches of spores, although Ivins did not recall when, how often, or why his technicians grew spores. Ivins did remember Fellows growing spores for a project to examine anthrax of varying strains, but the project did not include Ames.

When the mail attacks did occur, Ivins and everyone he knew in the anthrax world believed Ames was widely available, in many laboratories, and it was not possible to know who possessed it. Ivins knew the FBI had established a collection of Ames, but he did not remember why. Ivins recalled attending many meetings about the anthrax investigation, but he had no memory of what was discussed. He also did not recollect a meeting in March 2002—the meeting presented by Pat Worsham on how to prepare samples for submission to the FBI—and he certainly was not given a protocol for submission until later, well into May. He did make the labels for his lab's second round of submissions, but he did not have a memory of who added anthrax to the agar.

At this point the interview drew to a close. After questioning the late-night lab visits, Montooth and Lisi stopped confronting Ivins with his inconsistencies. They did not bring up his receiving a protocol in February 2002, nor the drawing by Scott Stanley of the seating arrangements—including the seat occupied by Ivins—at the March meeting. Nor did they review his statements during the summer of 2003 when he detailed how, when, and why his technicians made spores with Ames. They did not bring up his admission to Darin Steele that Ivins had made the April 2002 Ames submissions and that access records showed him taking the samples to the FBI's collection. They would save his contradictions for later, when they asked a grand jury to indict.

23

Final Resolution
July 2008

The proffer interview did not pan out as Bruce Ivins's attorneys had hoped; in fact it had been a disaster. His lawyers told him to expect an indictment for capital murder—five counts—along with a recommendation for the death penalty.[1] By the end of June, Rachel Lieber had almost finished drafting a prosecution memo for the District's US attorney. With approval, she would then ask for a certification by the attorney general of the United States, a requirement in weapon of mass destruction cases.[2] A long process ensuring everyone in the chain of command—including the president's cabinet—concurred that sufficient evidence existed to indict the subject of the largest federal investigation in the country's history.

The surveillance teams kept up their Tuesday and Friday trash collections, recovering scribbled notes—barely legible—about strategies, forensics, and meeting dates. Pen registers recorded more email accounts, and agents followed up with preservation letters until search warrants could be issued. They watched Ivins walking erratically down the street, alone and talking to no one in particular. Ed Montooth and Lieber began to worry about a deterioration of Ivins's mental state. The pressure of the investigation, his impending retirement, an uncertain future, mounting legal bills, altered medications during and after his four-week detoxification—any, maybe all, might account for the odd behavior. They wondered if he had already returned to his decade-long habit of drinking vodka and mixing it with Ambien, Lunesta, and Unisom. Colleagues at USAMRIID had told the task force that the habit dated back to the mid-1990s when his depression became severe. With sufficient liquor and sleep aids, he would send increasingly bizarre email messages until sleep took over. Waking up, he ingested more alcohol to the point he would call in sick rather than go to work. At times, he awoke with car keys in hand, but no memory of driving or leaving the house. Recently, a fellow scientist reported asking Ivins if the "other Bruce"—the one self-described in late-night emails—could have sent the attack letters. Ivins became ambivalent, neither denying nor getting mad. The colleague described that when Ivins interacted with the FBI, he would change demeanors. At times he assumed a wounded puppy dog approach, yet in other instances, he adopted a seemingly devious, baiting, and secretive posture—a tactic his attorney advised against.[3] Confidential sources relayed that Ivins had a new therapist and attended a counseling group. He anticipated seeing a different psychiatrist in the near future and claimed to enjoy a renewed sobriety.

Montooth doubted Ivins's claims. In the household trash near the end of June, the surveillance team had recovered prescriptions for sedatives written by a doctor who was neither Ivins's psychiatrist nor primary care physician. The task force also suspected Ivins of habitually obtaining drugs illegally. A forged slip in the name of his current psychiatrist, prescribing medication used to combat attention deficit disorder, had been recovered during a trash run earlier in the year.[4]

As July began its second week, a confidential source at USAMRIID telephoned the task force. Ivins had threatened coworkers with veiled comments, talking to himself, saying the words *dimed me out*. He seemed to spend his entire day plotting revenge. A supervisor told one employee who had become frightened to hide in the biocontainment laboratory, knowing that Ivins had been barred from entering. Weighing the risks of having their source's identity revealed against allowing Ivins to act on his plan, Lieber contacted Ivins's attorney. She told him of Ivins's recent bizarre actions and now this latest development. She urged the attorney to intercede.

Three days later, Montooth's telephone rang. FBI Headquarters had just received a call. Frederick detectives had escorted a scientist from USAMRIID. As they led the man away, he had ranted on and on about being involved with the FBI. Agents in the Hoover Building looked up the name and realized the police had detained the subject of a major investigation—Amerithrax—Bruce Edwards Ivins. Ivins's therapist had given a statement to the police, certifying that Ivins had mental disorders and presented a danger to himself and others. Frederick detectives filed a petition for emergency evaluation—a public document—and took Ivins to Frederick Memorial Hospital. In the petition, the task force found the name and address of Jean C. Duley, Ivins's new therapist.

At Memorial, two physicians, according to state law, evaluated Ivins. Their findings would determine if they released or ordered him held. An angry Ivins confronted the doctors. He answered their questions in a loud voice, the words coming quickly, gesturing in rapid movements. He rambled about going to death row and that he was now "under arrest," "held against my will," "incarcerated" in a psych hospital. Time and again he railed to hospital staff that now the FBI would be able to see notes of past therapy sessions, review his doctors' observations, read about past deeds, admissions he made in confidence. The two psychiatrists finished evaluating and contacted the noted Sheppard and Enoch Pratt Hospital[5] to request a bed. They would hold Ivins for further examination.

Two task force agents arrived at the offices of Comprehensive Counseling Associates—just beyond the rear gate of Fort Detrick—unannounced. They walked quietly up to the receptionist, showing their credentials for a brief moment. "We would like to speak with Ms. Jean Duley, please."

As the three talked, Duley took the agents back in time to early spring, when she had counseled Ivins on substance abuse dangers and he joined her group therapy sessions. He had shown her notes carried in his wallet: a written recipe for suicide, the amount of alcohol and pills needed to kill a man weighing 150 pounds. She described the events of three days ago and what had prompted her to call the Frederick police. She had begun her evening counseling session, and Ivins arrived as he had done for the past month. But this time he acted differently. He was agitated and abrupt. When it became his turn to talk, he let loose a barrage. He told the group that the government would indict him for the anthrax attacks and it made him angry; mad at coworkers who had gotten him into trouble, FBI agents who made it worse, the entire US government. And he did not plan on going to death row.

He had said, "I know how to murder and not make a mess. Other people made a mess."

He described a hit list: people at work and an FBI agent. His son would soon bring him a Glock pistol from North Carolina and a 22-caliber rifle. He already had a bulletproof vest and plenty of ammunition.

He smiled. "I'll shoot the ones at work who wronged me. I'm not going down for capital murder. I'm going to get them all."

One member stood and walked out of the room. Another in the group asked, "If you are innocent, then why are you doing, planning to do that?"

Duley had waited for Ivins to answer, but he only grinned.

The two agents reported back to Montooth and the task force. If Ivins did have a list, they needed to find it. Several of his coworkers had been helping the investigation, providing updates on his activities and comments—potential witnesses to be protected at all costs. Pulling out last fall's search warrants and affidavits, the task force added Duley's information and rushed before a magistrate. This time they would not look for anthrax and related bacteria, or Federal Eagle envelopes and tape, or addresses of grade schools in New Jersey. They would be after a new gun, rounds of ammunition, and the list of coworkers hated and feared by Ivins. On July 12, the task force split up and delivered the warrants. They again entered the Ivinses' residence; they towed his red van and blue Saturn and Honda sedan to a secure garage. A postal inspector drove north of Baltimore to Sheppard Hospital.

From a closet in the house, they retrieved gunpowder and a high-quality ballistic vest along with hand-made, duct-taped body armor. In an upstairs bedroom, they found 22-caliber bullets in a plastic bag. Under a bedroom dresser, boxes of nine millimeter and 40-caliber rounds, magazines loaded with more nine millimeter, .40, and .22—and on the kitchen table lay a hand-written note about counselor Jean Duley.[6] At the hospital Ivins remained calm and quiet as he handed over his wallet and clothes, but there was no list.

Two days later, the task force served a warrant to the commander of US-AMRIID as they had seven months ago and again searched through Ivins's office and clothes lockers, his computers and drives—but again, no list appeared. The task force began to wonder if Ivins was planning a siege that he would not survive, the improvised body armor only delaying the inevitable as he settled decade-old grudges and avenged perceived wrongs.

Three days after her interview, Duley telephoned the agents with new information. For the first time, she had read Ivins's complete file at Comprehensive Counseling. It dated back to the millennial year, and the contents shocked her. Ivins's counselor from eight years ago, Judith McLean, had left copious notes.[7, 8] She described shocking details of her discussions with Ivins: a chronicle of bomb-making plans, plotting to use cyanide and kill the dog belonging to a neighbor he felt disparaged by, driving to visit a woman in upstate New York with a bottle of wine spiked with poison. McLean's notes described how the woman's competitive nature on the soccer field annoyed him, and he had decided she needed killing and he was the one to do it.

Duley now feared Ivins. In addition to discovering the information in Ivins's file, he had contacted her three times since his commitment. On the first night, between 4:00 and 5:00 a.m., he left two messages on her telephone. He blamed her for destroying the client relationship; her lapse would allow the FBI to read his files and learn of his private past. The next day Ivins telephoned again. He relayed the same message. He still blamed her and claimed the FBI would be able to look at Comprehensive Counseling's file, the one containing his secrets.

The task force quickly located McLean. She now lived in Pennsylvania, just beyond the Maryland border. And she clearly remembered Bruce Ivins. He had begun therapy sessions with her in June 2000. He had described how he would like to take revenge on individuals that had bothered him during his childhood in Ohio. How he had vandalized property years ago and carried a gun on the University of Cincinnati campus during his college and graduate school days, and that he had shot the gun at a wall and clock, imagining them to be people, not inanimate objects.

He confided in her how he was taken with a woman thirty years his junior. The woman had worked for him until the end of the summer in 1999, when she left for medical school in upstate New York. It upset Ivins. He felt a deep attachment to the student, but she did not return the affection, nor did she always respond to his many email messages. He had sent her packages containing gifts, without his name or a return address, using mailboxes in locations away from his home and work to further disguise his identity. But her disinterest angered him, and he had devised a plan to poison a wine bottle and pay her a visit. McLean told Ivins that she felt it her duty to report his plan to the authorities, and before he left she made him promise that he would abandon the idea and not do anything to harm the woman and he had agreed.[9] However, she still contacted the police, but they told her they could do nothing since she knew neither the woman's name nor location. It was not enough for them to act.[10]

The next week, Ivins had appeared for his fourth session with McLean. He had told her that he did make the drive to New York with the poisoned wine, but ultimately returned without opening the bottle. Once there, Ivins aborted the plan—the woman had injured herself during a soccer match, but her team had still won and Ivins changed his mind. After the two visited, he drove back to Frederick with the bottle of wine and poison intact.[11] The revelation shocked McLean. She reminded Ivins of his promise and told him that she had called the police. McLean recalled Ivins's extreme reaction, his cold hostility, and how he had accused McLean, telling her, "You betrayed my trust."[12] The two agreed changing counselors or a move into group therapy sessions would be best.[13]

While the agents interviewed Duley and located McLean, other Amerithrax members responded to a request from Fort Detrick's Provost Marshal Office. The director of emergency services and the chief of law enforcement for the base had tried to get agreement from the army's judge advocate general to bar Ivins from the property. They showed the judge advocate the commitment order outlining Ivins's threats, but it was not enough. Did the FBI have any information they could share that would bolster the case with the advocate general? Yes, they had recovered several handguns from Ivins's residence last November, and just this past week they had also gotten a bulletproof vest and hundreds of rounds of ammunition from his house. They knew Ivins's son had purchased Glock pistols, and Ivins expected to get one of them. Armed with this new information from the FBI, the provost's representatives now thought they had enough to keep Ivins off their base. They would also work to get his secret-level security clearance suspended.[14]

By the third day in Sheppard, Ivins had begun to pull himself together. Without the cloud of prescription sleeping drugs mixed with a dozen shots of vodka, he realized he must get out.[15] He filled out self-evaluation forms disclaiming violence, convinced the staff psychiatrists he was no longer a threat to himself and others—never had been—he needed to get out. He signed himself in voluntarily, switching his status from mandatory confinement and changing the criteria that would dictate his release.[16] If his attorney was correct, he would soon be indicted and jailed. Bail would be unlikely. The window to carry out his plan—to circumvent the government bearing down on him and eliminate a trial that would publicly label him a demonic terrorist, ending with a trip to the death chamber—would be closed for good. He would finally be outsmarted, his secrets revealed.[17]

During the second week at Sheppard Pratt, the doctors continued their evaluation. Ivins denied there ever having been a hit list. He had no intention of harming anyone, not at work, nor himself. The doctors found him stable, deemed he had been in a transient frame of mind when the police committed him, but the rage had moved on. He could leave if he wanted.

Ivins had not convinced everyone. Duley talked to his physician at Sheppard, arguing that a commitment hearing was needed. Attorney Lieber also talked with a lawyer at Sheppard Pratt, confirming Duley's assertions and requesting Ivins stay confined. Ivins's attorney contended the opposite,[18] agreeing with the psychiatrists that his client posed no danger. As he had for many years, Ivins again presented himself to those nearby as meek, mild, and well intentioned. The hospital authorities decided he was free to go. The morning of July 24, his wife picked Ivins up and dropped him off at their house, then went on to work. In Frederick District Court, a judge granted Jean Duley a restraining order before the day was out. Amerithrax resumed surveillance.

Three nights later, at 10:30 p.m., the task force watched the small house on Military Road, just over one hundred yards from the fence surrounding Fort Detrick. Ivins's red van and blue Honda Civic were parked outside. The agents and postal inspectors could see no lights inside and nothing seemed to be moving. It had been dark for over an hour. They mentally prepared for another long, hot, humid night.

Almost three hours had passed when a siren pierced the summer air. Red flashing lights quickly followed. As the small team watched, a fire truck roared down the street, straight toward their parked cars, braking to a stop in front of the Ivinses' residence. A police cruiser appeared from behind. Inside their cars they listened to a radio tuned to the frequency used by the Frederick Police. The dispatcher mentioned the address where they sat, followed by the reason for the emergency—an unresponsive male identified as Bruce Ivins. Ivins had been found on the bathroom floor lying in pools of urine; near him lay an empty container with remnants of orange liquid. His wife was telling the responding officers that Ivins abused pills, but she could account for all his prescriptions. The last time she had seen him that night, he was sleeping in bed, but when she checked on him two hours later, she found him like this.

Within minutes, the paramedics had Ivins on a stretcher and into an ambulance on his way to Frederick Memorial Hospital[19]—the second time in less than three weeks. Cold and clammy, blisters forming on his skin, heart racing, his lungs struggled for air. Quickly, the paramedics clamped an oxygen mask across his face—he would soon be intubated with a breathing tube down his throat. In front of the screaming ambulance, a Frederick Police car led the way lit by lights and sirens. Ivins's wife trailed further back in her small blue Civic. The surveillance team followed.

As the paramedics wheeled Ivins's stretcher through the emergency room doors, an agent and postal inspector remained in the parking lot and conferred with the responding officer. He agreed to keep them updated. Fifteen minutes later, the team learned Ivins still lived and had been admitted. They would have to wait to learn the details of what was happening inside.

The hospital moved Ivins to the intensive care unit and began an intravenous line for medications to raise his blood pressure. Doctors suspected an overdose and ordered blood tests. Skin tears, known as pressure ulcers—caused by flesh compressed between bone and hard surfaces during states of profound motionless—suggested he had taken enormous amounts of sleep aids, perhaps Valium as suggested by his wife earlier in March,[20] Ambien, or an antihistamine, such as Benadryl, or a combination. The blood work included a check for acetaminophen, the active component of Tylenol. Acetaminophen toxicity accounts for the highest number of calls to the nation's poison control centers. By itself, Tylenol poisoning can be a painful way to die as abdominal pain, diarrhea, and vomiting rack the body. But heavy doses of sleeping aids would sedate the victim while the liver and kidney deteriorate, muscles break down, and the brain swells with liquid. The Frederick Memorial staff began an intravenous drip of N-acetyl-cysteine, the antidote for Tylenol overdosing.[21]

Within hours the hospital laboratory reported their testing and confirmed suspicions. Ivins had extraordinarily high levels of acetaminophen in his blood. In his urine they found evidence of diazepam, the active component of Valium. But acetaminophen and diazepam metabolize at different rates.

Valium acts quickly as a sedative, reducing tension and anxiety and inducing relaxation. The effects will last for hours as the drug is converted into three components, which the kidney excretes into the urine. In a few days, the metabolites disappear. In contrast, Tylenol must first be processed in the liver before becoming toxic, a progression that takes time. Hepatic cytochrome enzymes convert the acetaminophen to a poison; the antidote, N-acetyl-cysteine, acts to convert the toxin to innocuous metabolites also expelled by the kidneys. The antidote is most effective, however, if given within eight hours, and complicating matters, cytochrome activity in alcoholics can be elevated, accelerating the conversion of Tylenol to a poison.[22]

By midmorning, the diazepam began to wear off, and a nurse noticed he had regained consciousness and movement of his head and arms. She walked to his side and looked down. "Did you try to commit suicide?"

Ivins nodded slowly, *Yes.* He struggled and pulled at the tubes entering his body. The staff gently tied his arms and ankles to the bed. Throughout the day and into early evening he opened his eyes when a nurse called his name and moved a foot when asked. A check of his simple cognitive function, estimated by eye movement and motor function, indicated normal brain activity.

Ivins had left an advance directive; there would be no aggressive treatment if the doctors pronounced his condition grave. Subsequent blood work and vital signs indicated severe organ damage. His wife directed an end to hemodialysis; natural wastes were now poisoning his body. A doctor discussed liver transplantation as an option—again she refused, citing Ivins's advance orders and instructed there should be no resuscitation if his heart arrested.[23] A ventilator continued to help him breathe, and medication maintained blood pressure.

The next day, Ivins turned for the worst. His organ function worsened as his liver and kidneys failed and blood pressure grew tenuous. Bacteria, common *Escherichia coli*, a normal component of healthy digestive systems, now multiplied in Ivins's veins, sending his body into septic shock, further destroying its ability to maintain arterial pressure. Loss of eye movement and motor function indicated a rapid decline in brain activity. His wife ordered an end to life support—removal of the ventilator and assisted breathing; cessation of blood pressure drugs.[24] As he lay there, midway through his third day in the intensive care unit, a little over an hour before noon, Ivins's heart arrested. In going, he stole the opportunity for the United States and its justice system to examine our evidence and judge him for the first lethal act of biological terrorism unleashed upon the people of the United States.

24

Epilogue
2008 and Beyond

By November, the Frederick City Police Department made it official: Dr. Bruce Edwards Ivins had deliberately killed himself. With Ivins's death, proving his guilt before a court of law would not be possible, and we realized that doubt would always linger in some minds. But the totality of evidence could not be ignored: Ivins was the anthrax mailer and a serial killer. His motive? For those who investigated the attacks, we are in agreement: the troubled anthrax vaccine and the looming potential of shutting down anthrax research at USAMRIID, bringing an end to his professional life's work, coupled with an increasingly troubled mind pushed him to murder, using the weapon he understood best. But personally, I do not think he anticipated killing postal workers, and when he did, he stopped mailing his deadly letters. I also believe he anticipated being the go-to guy for the FBI and our developing forensics. But if that was his plan, it did not work out. We continued to work with John Ezzell, who, in the three to four years preceding the attacks had developed a microbial forensic laboratory with strong quality assurance. Ivins's lab was simply too "dirty"; the potential for contaminating our evidence with his spore preparations too great.

Today, our country still feels the effects of the anthrax attacks. The air sampling system that the Pentagon and Secret Service put in place immediately after 9/11 has evolved into the Department of Homeland Security's BioWatch Program, found today in thirty urban areas.[1] The original system, called BASIS and designed by the Department of Energy, relied on stationary air samplers, manual removal and transport of the collection filters, and finally testing by the polymerase chain reaction using probes and primers specific for a panel of potential biological warfare agents—anthrax at the top of the list. The Department of Energy had intended the 2002 Winter Olympics in Salt Lake City as its inaugural deployment, and I had been briefed on the system's capabilities during my trips to Salt Lake in preparation for the Hazmat Response Unit's deployment during the Winter Games. I found BASIS unwieldy. The PCR analysis was technically cumbersome. Two technicians, confined to a small portable lab, soaked filters, loaded small tubes, and added PCR reagents for hours on end. It must have been mind numbing. I could not imagine how they continued without a complaint. The managers of BASIS also had no operational plan if the system gave a positive alarm, but I knew that the FBI, perhaps me, would be expected to respond.[2]

But after deploying BASIS earlier than anticipated in response to 9/11,[3] the Department of Energy corrected the shortcomings. By mid-2002, an operational plan had been written and the rate of false alarms was null.[4] Further, the PCR reaction was on its way to being automated. Energy's BASIS also become the forerunner of the US Postal System's Biohazard Detection System (BDS). After the deaths of four of its postal workers, Postal reacted. By February 2002, its engineering division identified technologies required for a robust screening system, and by September, they had tested over twenty of them. The system utilized the same core technology developed for BASIS. The Postal Service chose Northrop Grumman as its prime contractor, and Northrop selected the best tools available in the private sector—acquiring technologies from top companies such as Cepheid and Midwest Research Institute. By 2006, over three hundred postal facilities counted BDS in their security posture.[5, 6]

Following 9/11 and the anthrax attacks, Congress acted quickly. On October 26, 2001, President Bush signed into law the Uniting and Strengthening America by Providing Appropriate Tools Required to Intercept and Obstruct Terrorism Act; today we know it as simply the Patriot Act. It included provisions that strengthened 1996's Antiterrorism and Effective Death Penalty Act requirement for facilities wishing to transfer or receive biological select agents to register with the CDC. The Patriot Act put requirements in place for the appropriate use of select agents and which persons could be restricted from working with them.

By June 2002, Congress had passed the Public Health Security Bioterrorism Preparedness and Response Act. This legislation required all facilities that possessed select agents to register, rather than if they only planned to transfer microbes and toxins as the 1996 legislation called for; it also expanded regulatory authority to the USDA, in addition to the CDC. It provided for training, safety, and security measures, and mandated that the Department of Justice conduct a database check for all persons handling select agents. The latter provision, termed a Security Risk Assessment (SRA), was delegated to the FBI's Criminal Justice Information Services Division (CJIS) in West Virginia.[7] It would include a fingerprint check, criminal history query, and disclosure of illegal drug use and mental health history. As of September 2009, 208 persons have been denied access from over thirty-two thousand names submitted to CJIS.[8]

Individual agencies have also established their own Personnel Reliability Programs (PRP) in addition to the mandated SRA. The Department of Defense modeled their Biological PRP of 2006 after their decades-old Nuclear PRP. The Department also instituted a dual-entry rule—at least two people must be in a high-containment biology lab at one time. The two-person rule is augmented by use of Closed Camera TV monitoring.

While he didn't personally benefit, Ivins's mailing of live anthrax spores did spur an expansion of anthrax and select agent research. This is exemplified by the increase in the number of high-containment labs, biosafety level (BSL) -3 and -4—either operational or in the planning stages—since 2001.[9] In 1990, two BSL-4 labs existed in the United States, both on the East Coast; one at the CDC in Atlanta and the second at the US Army Medical Research Institute of Infectious Diseases on Fort Detrick. By year 2000, the number had not changed. But eleven years later, by 2011, the BSL-4 labs had grown to thirteen located around the country.[10] The number of BSL-3 labs and individuals approved to work in high-level biological containment paralleled this increase. The increase in the number of containment labs and people working with select biological agents can be viewed as both a benefit—more resources in place for an emergency response to a biological attack—but also a much larger and diverse pool from which another insider threat might emerge.

The threat from the ranks of biologists with laboratory access became very real to Pentagon and White House officials after Ivins's suicide in July 2008. On August 8, the District of Columbia's US attorney held a press conference and announced that Dr. Bruce E. Ivins, winner of the Decoration of Exceptional Civilian Service,[11] the highest Defense Department civilian honor, had mailed the anthrax letters. Identifying Bruce Ivins as the anthrax killer resulted in a flurry of activity at the highest levels of government. Before August ended, the secretary of the army formed a task force to study the state of biosurety[12] in its research facilities. A month later the Executive Office of the President asked the National Science Advisory Board for Biosecurity, a group originally chartered in 2004, for recommendations on personnel reliability programs for those with access to select agents.[13] Also that month, the CDC's Division of Select Agents and Toxins began a two-week inspection of USAMRIID. In October, the White House's Office of Science and Technology solicited recommendations for improvements to the biological personnel reliability programs already in place. In January 2009, President

Bush signed Executive Order 13486, calling for a federal Working Group
to bring recommendations for Strengthening Laboratory Biosecurity in the
United States.[14] The American Association for the Advancement of Science
and the National Academy of Sciences also formed committees in early 2009
to examine biosecurity.

Prevention of future biological attacks has become the mission for the
FBI's Weapons of Mass Destruction Directorate. The various Headquarters entities supporting investigations of WMD during 2001—biological,
chemical, nuclear, and radiological—have been codified into a single WMD
Directorate. The WMDD has worked extensively since its founding in 2006
to form partnerships with federal and private entities. The relationships that
the Directorate has built with commercial suppliers of synthetic DNA and
nonprofit organizations that offer hands-on experience in biotechnology, such
as Genspace, as well as its membership on biosurety committees such as the
National Science Advisory Board for Biosecurity and the Federal Experts
Security Advisory Panel—represent a proactive stance against bioterrorism,
in contrast to the reactive position we found ourselves in on October 4, 2001.

The FBI Laboratory has also taken a progressive approach. In 2002, it
formed the Chemical Biological Sciences Unit.[15] Based at Quantico, the new
unit was created as a response to our lack of validated forensic techniques
for the mailed anthrax. The Laboratory has also formed partnerships with
experts from outside labs such as Homeland Security's new 160,000-square-
foot National Bioforensic Analysis Center on the grounds of Fort Detrick. In
October and November 2001, we struggled to carry out traditional forensics,
such a latent fingerprint examinations, on evidence heavily contaminated
with anthrax spores. None of our forensic examiners were immunized against
anthrax, nor were they trained to handle hazardous materials.

Today, the FBI has its Hazardous Evidence Analysis Team (HEAT). The
Laboratory staffs HEAT with forensic examiners trained to handle hazardous biological materials. They stand ready to deploy to partner labs that
operate BSL-3 and -4 containment facilities; either the new National Bioforensic Center in the case of suspected human pathogen contamination or
the Plum Island Animal Disease Center if the suspect pathogen is specific
for animals.[16]

The FBI has taken a rigorous stance with regard to prevention of biological
terrorism. But what if it did happen today? What if anthrax spores suddenly
appeared in the mail? The expansion of facilities working on select agents
coupled with the increase in numbers of individuals with access make the
universe of possible suspects much larger than it was in the fall of 2001. But
I believe this is offset by the leaps technology has taken in the past fifteen
years, specifically in the field of DNA sequencing,[17] and something the bio-

tech community calls bioinformatics. To convince myself that I was up to speed, I reached out to Greg Meyers.

Greg had left American International Biotechnology, LLC (AIB) in late 2015 to help Tom Reynolds with a new startup venture: NEXT Molecular Analytics.[18] At NEXT, Tom has the role of president, and Greg is the chief operating officer. As COO, he oversees the company's technical capabilities, with next generation DNA sequencing being at the forefront. I placed a call to NEXT Molecular.

"Hello, Greg, how are you? Do you have a minute to talk?"

"Sure. We're doing fine, how are you?

"Good. I wanted to ask you about next gen sequencing and how our cost and timeline would be different from back in 2001 to 2002; if the anthrax attacks happened today."

"Right, it's something I've thought about. What percent of the spores were the morphs? They were around 5 to 10 percent of the total, correct?"

"Yes," I answered. "Pat Worsham estimated the A morphologies made up 1 to 2 percent of the total colonies; B at 1 percent, and E at 5 percent. She picked just under four hundred random colonies to get those estimates."[19]

"Next gen sequencing could easily identify the morphology mutants at those levels. There have been claims of identifying unique sequences in the 0.1 percent range in mixed viral or bacterial cultures. And, it would take us maybe five days, tops."

I found Greg's estimates of what we could do with today's technology amazing. "Wow, back in 2001 to 2002, it took Pat Worsham months of culturing and checking controls to locate the morphs, and then four months for us to identify the B mutation in the DNA using whole genome sequencing; eight months for the A mutation. And that was at tenfold coverage" (coverage refers to each nucleotide being sequenced ten different times to ensure no errors).

"Today, we could find the DNA mutations at five-hundred- to one-thousand-fold coverage, probably for a cost of under $5,000, in five days. The labor-intensive part is analyzing the data. We now have access to free-ware and would send the data to a bioinformatist to put the wild type and morph genomes together. We would just send the data via the Cloud," Greg said.

"That is amazing. Back in 2002, I used to estimate it was costing us close to half-a-million dollars to sequence the original 1981 Ames at tenfold. It took two months to get a draft sequence and six months to get the sequence with complete accuracy. We could also screen the Ames Repository using next gen, rather than TaqMan, couldn't we? How much could we do it for today? I estimate we collected approximately 1,070 samples of Ames, although that number varies slightly in different publications."

Without hesitation, Greg offered, "It would take a day or two, about $200 per sample, each in duplicate," he continued. "The tricky part would be getting it accepted in court. I think next gen sequencing has only been introduced in a courtroom in three or four cases."

Even with today's powerful advances in molecular biology and DNA/RNA sequencing, the same hurdle would face us today as nine years earlier, had we attempted to enter the Ames DNA sequencing and repository screening in court. In order to successfully use evidence in the federal judiciary, we would first have to demonstrate the validity of the chosen technique—that it is testable and has undergone peer review, show the use of control standards, and that the error rate is known and the scientific community has accepted the technique.[20]

The use of next generation DNA sequencing, also called massively parallel sequencing, deep sequencing, and (ultra) high-throughput sequencing, became commercially available in 2005.[21] At the time, our counterparts at the FBI Laboratory suggested that we switch gears and take advantage of this new technology, which they referred to as DNA chip technology, a reference to the small tilelike sequencing platforms on which next gen sequencing technology relied. But I resisted. We had our first match of the mailed spores with the RMR-1029 preparation in May 2004, and the task force had immediately begun to broaden the investigation of Ivins while evaluating Steve Hatfill's access to Ivins's spore prep. We were aware that a match of the mailed Ames to any repository sample would not be proof, but it definitely pointed us in a direction. Proof beyond a reasonable doubt would require old-fashioned detective work developing multiple lines of corroborative evidence. So, I stuck by our commitment; we would continue screening the repository using the TaqMan protocol rather than switch to new technology requiring additional time to contract, develop controls, and validate. Scott Stanley and Rick Langham supported me. I realized our stance might cause hard feelings with our Quantico partners, but using TaqMan had given us our biggest lead to date.

The National Research Council's critique of our work also suggested we should have turned to next gen sequencing. In their 2011 final report, the Council wrote, "Thus, while it was not feasible at the start of the investigation, investigators should have subsequently examined the value from a forensic perspective of 'deep sequencing' of key samples."[22]

Perhaps, but I believe the approach we used to be valid. In 2004, before early next gen sequencing systems became available, our genetic screening directed us to Dr. Bruce Ivins. He stalked women whom he felt had betrayed him; he held grudges for decades. As he aged, his psychosis drew him to serial murder. What trigger would set him off to begin mailing spores again we did not know, but in 2005, we could not take the chance by delaying to explore a new technology.

On Amerithrax, we gathered together in January 2011 for the last time. Director Mueller had received a draft of the National Research Council's review of our science and passed it on to Ed Montooth, who immediately called all hands. The report contained omissions and errors, and we had one last chance to make comments before it became public. The Council took our additions and corrections to heart and published their final report in February. At that, the Amerithrax Task Force disbanded.

Today, we have all moved on. I retired from the FBI in the fall of 2011 to become director of security at American International Biotechnology in Richmond, Virginia. American International had been Commonwealth Biotechnologies, where Tom Reynolds and Greg Meyers had done such a great job of testing our repository of Ames samples. Dr. David Bostwick, a native of Baltimore, a medical alumni of the Mayo Clinic and leading expert on prostate cancer and its pathology, bought the assets of CBI and transformed them into AIB, with the goal of becoming a leader in genetic testing using the power of next generation DNA sequencing.

As for the rest of the team, Terry Kerns left the Hazmat Response Unit at Quantico and took a position as the FBI Laboratory's liaison officer in Homeland Security's Domestic Nuclear Detection Office in Washington, DC. Scott Stanley finished up a stint as a behavioral profiler and chief of Behavioral Analysis Unit-1 in Quantico, and he opted to go back to the street, as part of Jim Rice's former National Capital Response Squad in the Washington Field Office. Jim retired shortly after I did and took a job as inspector for Intelligence and Counterterrorism with the Amtrak Police. Of the two Hazmat officers that went with me to Ground Zero and helped throughout the Amerithrax investigation, Steve Rhea is finally retired and now finds himself busier than ever caring for his cherished grandchildren. Mike Cook resigned from the Hazardous Materials Response Unit and the FBI and returned to his native Colorado where he took a job in Denver as special agent and section chief in the Environmental Protection Agency's Office of Criminal Enforcement. John Ezzell, a true country gentleman, retired and returned to his native North Carolina. Sadly, he succumbed to complications from Parkinson's disease in 2015. Doug Beecher, still with the FBI Laboratory, married a prominent Capitol Hill attorney and lobbyist. At least one sitting US Senator attended the ceremony. Rich Meyer retired from the CDC and remained in Atlanta, moving into a penthouse condominium looking over the city. Today he consults on bioweapons detection for the Department of Homeland Security. The

Postal Service recognized the work and commitment Tom Dellafera had contributed during the Amerithrax investigation and promoted him to the ranks of the federal Senior Executive Service. Paul Keim remains at picturesque Northern Arizona University where he is a Regent's Professor of Biology and holds the Cowden Endowed Chair in Microbiology; occasionally he finds time for a rafting trip down the Grand Canyon.

Ed Montooth also retired and moved to the private sector as chief security officer for the highly respected DuPont Company. Vince Lisi became a legal attaché in a Middle Eastern US Embassy. Director Mueller then promoted Vince to special agent in charge of the Boston Division, the same office where I began my career. At the Department of Justice, Rachel Lieber prepared a summary of the investigation and our evidence against Ivins. The Department released her report in February 2010, and shortly after that, Justice announced the case closed.

At the end of 2013, Terry L. Kerns successfully competed for what I thought was the best job in the Bureau—commute, lifestyle, and most importantly, the work—she would supervise a Joint Terrorism Task Force investigating domestic terrorism for the FBI's Las Vegas Division. Bomb technicians, the WMD program, skilled FBI agents, top intel analysts, and some of the best Las Vegas Metro Police detectives would staff her squad—adopting both a proactive and reactive posture against those with an inclination to harm Las Vegas citizens and visitors.

In May 2014, Terry returned to Stafford, Virginia, and we married. I left my security job at American International Biotech and followed her out to Las Vegas. The weather here is great. We found a nice home with a fantastic view of the city's northern valley. The mountains of the Sheep Range and majestic Gass Peak frame the backdrop under a brilliant blue sky. Two small rescues—a good-natured beagle-Jack Russell mix and a somewhat high-strung miniature pinscher—round out our household.

Notes

CHAPTER 1

1. The Centers for Disease Control is now known as the Centers for Disease Control and Prevention. Congress directed the renaming in 1992 but mandated that the acronym CDC remain.

2. Before either the North or South World Trade Center Tower collapsed on September 11, the Federal Aviation Administration (FAA) had banned all commercial and private flights over, and to, the United States. However, nonmilitary air traffic was still allowed on a case-by-case basis with FAA authorization.

3. After the attacks, ironworkers across New York City ceased work and as a group went to the Twin Towers site to assist. Many Local 40 members went without pay in those initial weeks of the crisis. Their experiences are described by Damon DiMarco, "Ground Zero and the Volunteers, Tony Rasemus," in *Tower Stories: An Oral History of 9/11*, 2nd edition (Santa Monica, CA: Santa Monica Press, 2007), 300–9. The ironworkers' sacrifices following 9/11 are also documented by Tommy Harris Jr., *Through the Eyes of the Ironworkers: A Photographic Salute to the World Trade Center Heroes of Local 40* (Silver Spring, MD: Beckham Publications, 2008), and in Rachel Maguire's documentary *Metal of Honor: The Ironworkers of 9/11* (Chicago: Naja Productions, 2006), running time: 75 minutes.

4. Douglas H. Hamilton, "The Epidemic Intelligence Service: The Centers for Disease Control and Prevention's Disease Detectives," *AMA Journal of Ethics* 8 (2006): 261–64.

5. Speculation that the hijackers carried secondary bombs, possibly biological, is described by the National Commission on Terrorist Attacks upon the United States, *The 9/11 Report*, Chairman Thomas H. Kean and Vice Chairman Lee H. Hamilton (New York: St. Martin's Paperbacks, 2004), 3–70.

6. Erik A. Henchal, Colonel, US Army (ret.), supervised the Special Pathogens Branch at USAMRIID and ensured that laboratory facilities of the highest sterility were used to test the air samples; personal communication to author, August 2012.

7. For the entire citation of Bruce E. Ivins's email in its context, see David Willman, *The Mirage Man: Bruce Ivins, the Anthrax Attacks, and America's Rush to War* (New York: Bantam Books, 2011), 79–80.

8. Initially impromptu, onsite memorial services became more formalized in the weeks that followed and continued over the course of the 9/11 rescue and recovery efforts. See DiMarco, "Ground Zero and the Volunteers, Bobbie-Jo Randolph," 325–39, and Maguire, *Metal of Honor*.

CHAPTER 2

1. Maureen Stevens provided public health officials with a detailed summary of her husband's daily pursuits leading up to his hospitalization, as did his American Media coworkers. See Leonard A. Cole, *The Anthrax Letters: A Medical Detective Story* (Washington, DC: Joseph Henry Press, 2003), 1–25.

2. Richard Preston, *The Demon in the Freezer: A True Story* (New York: Random House, 2002), 3–9, also describes the activities of Florida anthrax victims Robert Stevens and Ernesto Blanco before their illnesses.

3. *Bacillus anthracis* is the name of the bacteria that causes the disease anthrax, a noncontagious disease. The name *anthrax* is derived from the Greek word for "coal," in recognition of the deep black skin lesions that manifest in the cutaneous form. Scientific convention calls for the genus (*Bacillus*) and species (*anthracis*) to be italicized. Throughout this book, the bacterial species, *anthracis*, and *anthrax* are used interchangeably.

4. The 1957 outbreak of inhalational and cutaneous anthrax involved nine combing, carding, and weaving workers from Manchester, New Hampshire. See Philip S. Brachman, Arnold F. Kaufmann, and Frederic G. Dalldorf, "Industrial Inhalational Anthrax," *Bacteriological Reviews* 30 (1966): 646–57.

5. For an excellent summary of anthrax hoaxes, see W. Seth Carus, *Bioterrorism and Biocrimes: The Illicit Use of Biological Agents since 1900* (Washington, DC: Center for Counterproliferation Research, National Defense University, 2001 revised), 122–50.

6. Arthur M. Friedlander, "Anthrax," in *Medical Aspects of Chemical and Biological Warfare*, ed. F. R. Sidell, E. T. Takafuji, and D. R. Franz (Washington, DC: TMM Publications, Borden Institute, 1997), 467–78, presents an excellent review of the etiology of anthrax infections.

7. Paul Keim and colleagues studied the genetics of the *Bacillus anthracis* released by Aum Shinrikyo, confirming cult members' trial testimony about the strain source. See Hiroshi Takahashi et al., "*Bacillus anthracis* Bioterrorism Incident, Kameido, Tokyo, 1993," *Emerging Infectious Diseases* 10, no. 1 (2004): 117–20.

8. Between 1990 through 1995, Aum Shinrikyo carried out seventeen chemical and biological attacks for purposes ranging from assassination to mass murder. See

"Chronology of Aum Shinrikyo's CBW Activities," Monterey WMD Terrorism Database (Monterey Institute of International Studies, 2001). Former secretary of the navy Richard Danzig and colleagues published a sixty-one-page summary of Aum Shinrikyo's activities. The study was the result of interviews of Aum members incarcerated at the Tokyo Detention Center. See Richard Danzig et al., *Aum Shinrikyo: Insights into How Terrorists Develop Biological and Chemical Weapons* (Washington, DC: Center for a New American Security, 2012), accessed March 17, 2017, https://www.cnas.org/publications/reports/aum-shinrikyo-second-edition-english.

9. The spelling of the Al-Qaeda leader's name is found as both *Osama bin Laden* and *Usama bin Laden. Usama* is the spelling found in most FBI documents. See https://www.fbi.gov/news/stories/bin-laden-killed, accessed March 17, 2017, and *FBI Ten Most Wanted Fugitive* poster of June 1999, revised November 2001.

10. Mark Caro analyzed the divergent ways American Media Incorporated's publications reported news and events following the attacks of September 11, 2001. See Mark Caro, "Now That the Tabloids Have Become the News, Where Do They Go from Here?" *Chicago Tribune*, October 16, 2001.

11. The renting of apartments to the al-Qaeda hijackers by Michael Irish's spouse is described in detail by Cole, *The Anthrax Letters*, 42–45.

CHAPTER 3

1. Prior to 1999, the FBI had recruited and hired individuals with microbiology degrees and expertise, but these people moved into other areas of science and forensics within the Bureau. Doug Beecher would be the first of two hired specifically as an FBI career microbiologist, with the goal of creating a new field of microbial forensics. The other full-time microbiologist I hired during the 1999 to 2000 time frame was Doug Anders.

2. The Laboratory Response Network is generally credited as the concept of Scott Lillibridge, a US Public Health Service physician assigned to the CDC during the latter 1990s, and FBI Laboratory Division deputy assistant director Randall Murch (ret.). During January 20–22, 1999, the CDC and the Association of Public Health Laboratories hosted an interagency meeting of national experts and state laboratory public health leaders, "Meeting to Determine Specific Core Capacities of Public Health Laboratories for Bioterrorism Threat Agents," in Atlanta, Georgia; memorandum of Stephen A. Morse, dated January 1999. The meeting, where I represented the FBI, would frame the mission of the network and begin drafting standardized protocols for testing suspected biological threat agents. During those three days, I made the specific request that ricin toxin be included in the first set of test protocols. At the time, ricin possession and its potential use as a weapon comprised a number of cases that the FBI's Hazardous Materials Response Unit encountered.

3. Variable Number Tandem Repeat.

4. Alex R. Hoffmaster described the reduction, begun in the 1980s, of anthrax research at the CDC and the goal of the US Army, through its leading institution, USAMRIID, assuming an expanded role. At the same time, the CDC would maintain

its large collection of anthrax isolates. This collection contained isolates distinct from those found in Keim's reference collection of anthrax strains. Keim's collection was obtained from a collection originally begun by Martin Hugh-Jones at Louisiana State University; personal communications to author, November 2012.

5. The details of the discussions between Paul Keim, Richard Meyer, and Douglas Beecher can also be read for more detail in the *Frontline* interview, Sarah Moughty, "Paul Keim: We Were Surprised It Was the Ames Strain" (Public Broadcasting Service, October 10, 2011), accessed March 17, 2017, http://www.pbs.org/wgbh/frontline/article/paul-keim-we-were-surprised-it-was-the-ames-strain/. Richard Meyer also provided details in personal communications to author, August and November 2012.

6. Paul Keim, personal communication to author, August 2012.

7. Chung Marston, CDC, personal communication to author, November 2012.

8. Tularemia disease is an exception; it is spread through the air, and small outbreaks can occur in rabbit populations.

9. Segaran Pillai, personal communication to author, August 2012.

10. Segaran Pillai tested once for the bacteria's main genomic DNA, a double strand of five million nucleic acids pairs, and twice again for two smaller strands of nucleic acid pairs—the bacteria's satellite, or plasmid DNAs. All three DNA strands were necessary for the anthrax to be lethal. The two small plasmid DNAs contained the information to produce the bacteria's deadly toxins; if one plasmid were missing, the anthrax would still live but could no longer produce a complete toxin molecule.

11. Spreadsheet and records of Alex R. Hoffmaster, dated November 2001.

12. Photograph, dated October 8, 2001, 6:30 p.m., of Multiple-Locus Variable Analysis electrophoresis comparing Stevens's spinal isolate, an isolate from Stevens's computer keyboard, and a known isolate of the Ames strain of anthrax. The photograph was on display in the Centers for Disease Control and Prevention Visitor Center Museum, Fall 2012.

13. In 1996, subsequent to testimony before the Senate Judiciary Committee, the Select Agent Transfer Regulations were enacted requiring the Centers for Disease Control and Prevention to maintain records of all shipments and transfers of anthrax; Stephen A. Morse, personal communication to author, November 2012.

CHAPTER 4

1. Gary C. Schroen, *First In—An Insider's Account of How the CIA Spearheaded the War on Terror in Afghanistan* (New York: Ballantine Books, 2005), 153–54.

2. Gina Kolata, "Florida Man Is Hospitalized with Pulmonary Anthrax," *New York Times*, October 5, 2001.

3. David W. Sifton, ed., *Physicians' Desk Reference*, 55th edition (Montvale, NJ: Medical Economics, 2001).

4. Steve Abrams, Boca Raton councilman and former mayor of Boca Raton, personal communication to author, August 2012.

5. The accession number is an internal tracking number assigned by the Florida State Public Health Bureau of Laboratory in Miami and is not meant to denote a chronological or quantitative value; spreadsheet titled "Non-FBI Nasal Swabs," *Bureau of Labs–Miami*, October 8–9, 2001, 60 pages.

6. Segaran Pillai, personal communication to author, August 2012.

7. Pillai, August 2012.

8. Ali Khan, personal communication to author, November 2012.

9. Stephen A. Morse and Richard B. Kellogg, personal communications to author, November 2012.

10. Stephen A. Morse and Richard B. Kellogg, personal communications to author, November 2012.

11. An immunoassay is a test to measure the presence and/or concentration of an analyte. The analyte can be large proteins, such as those on the outside of a virus particle or anthrax spore. The principle component of the assay is an antibody that has been carefully selected to specifically bind the analyte at low concentration with high fidelity. Immunoassays can be designed to detect target analytes in a wide range of sample types, including serum, plasma, whole blood, urine, or suspicious, unidentified powders. In Meyer's test, his antibodies were coupled with a small molecule that fluoresced when the antibody bound the analyte, in this case, anthrax spores.

12. Stephen A. Morse et al., "Detecting Biothreat Agents: The Laboratory Response Network," *ASM News* 69 (2003): 433–37.

13. Steven A. Morse and Richard F. Meyer, personal communications to author, November 2012.

14. Richard F. Meyer, personal communication to author, November 2012.

CHAPTER 5

1. Spreadsheet titled "Specimens Collected by FBI from AMI Building," *Bureau of Labs–Miami*, October 5–26, 2001, 5 pages.

2. See chapter 2, endnote 3, for an explanation of cutaneous anthrax.

3. Daniel B. Jernigan et al., "Investigation of Bioterrorism-Related Anthrax, United States, 2001: Epidemiologic Findings," *Emerging Infectious Diseases* 8, no. 10 (2002): 1019–28.

4. Organic insecticide powders composed of dried *Bacillus thuringiensis* bacterial spores are described in chapter 6.

5. PCR is the acronym for Polymerase Chain Reaction, a rapid and extremely sensitive DNA test. The inventors of the Polymerase Chain Reaction were the recipients of the Nobel Prize in Medicine in 1993. The Polymerase Chain Reaction is described in detail in chapter 14.

6. The construction and use of gloveboxes is detailed in chapter 10.

7. Richard F. Meyer, personal communication to author, September and November, 2012.

8. Alex A. Hoffmaster et al., "Molecular Subtyping of *Bacillus anthracis* and the 2001 Bioterrorism-Associated Anthrax Outbreak, United States," *Emerging Infectious Diseases* 8, no. 10 (2002): 1111–16.

9. Marc S. Traeger et al., "First Case of Bioterrorism-Related Inhalational Anthrax in the United States, Palm Beach County, Florida, 2001," *Emerging Infectious Diseases* 8, no. 10 (2002): 1029–34.

10. A thorough discussion of Blanco's test results and his clinical symptomology can be found in Leonard A. Cole, *The Anthrax Letters: A Medical Detective Story* (Washington, DC: Joseph Henry Press, 2003), 22–32. Cole's book details the early days of the investigation.

11. Meyer, August and November 2012.

12. Ernesto Blanco's diagnosis resulted in a formal change of the Centers for Disease Control and Prevention definition for clinical anthrax disease. For a description of anthrax definitions pre- and post-Blanco's diagnosis, see Jernigan, "Investigation of Bioterrorism-Related Anthrax," 1020.

CHAPTER 6

1. Senator Tom Daschle discusses the events of Friday, October 12, 2001, and the days that followed in Tom Daschle with Michael D'Orso, *Like No Other Time: The 107th Congress and The Two Years That Changed America* (New York: Random House, 2003), 247–51.

2. CBS News, "Feds Would Have Shot Down Pa. Jet," and NBC News, "*Meet the Press*: Dick Cheney," September 16, 2001.

3. Accessed March 18, 2017, https://www.congress.gov/bill/107th-congress/house-bill/3162.

4. *Frontline* interview of Grant Leslie, "Exclusive: The Intern Who Opened an Anthrax Letter" (Public Broadcasting Station, October 10, 2011), accessed March 18, 2017, http://www.pbs.org/wgbh/frontline/article/exclusive-the-intern-who-opened-an-anthrax-letter/.

5. SMART (sensitive membrane antigen rapid test) ticket is a registered trademark of New Horizons Diagnostics Corporation (NHDC). The tests are known generically as Hand-held Immunochromaticassays or Hand-held Immunoassays and are discussed later in this chapter. In 2001, the tests were available commercially from NHDC and Tetracore, Incorporated. They also were available to select US government entities from the US Navy's Naval Medical Research Center.

6. James Rice, personal communication to author, February 2013.

7. Scott Stanley was an FBI special agent and Gary Vienna was a US Capitol Police special agent; both were assigned to the FBI's Joint Terrorism Task Force in October 2001.

8. John F. Eisold, Rear Admiral, US Navy (ret.), personal communication to author, February 2013.

9. Norman Lee, Lieutenant Commander (Oct. 2001), US Navy (ret.), personal communication to author, February 2013.

10. Whitney S. Cranshaw, *"Bacillus thuringiensis,* Colorado State University Extension Fact Sheet" (1999): No. 5.556, accessed March 18, 2017, http://www.ext .colostate.edu/pubs/insect/05556.html.

11. *Bacillus thuringiensis,* May 2014.

12. Scott Stanley's deployments are described in more detail in chapter 9.

13. Upon their arrival at Senator Daschle's office, Scott Stanley and Gary Vienna also conducted their own field tests for anthrax. Stanley had brought the FBI's own hand-held immunoassay strips, and using a weak salt solution, he made a series of dilutions from the powder in Daschle's office according to the protocol he had developed three years ago for the FBI's Hazardous Materials Response Unit. Each of the seven strips to which he applied diluted powder turned bright red. These results, coupled with the pungent odor in the office, told Stanley that this time it was not a hoax.

14. Rice, February 2013.

15. *BA* is one of the acronyms used to refer to *Bacillus anthracis.*

16. Eisold, February 2013.

17. *Doxy* is a common acronym for the antibiotic doxycycline. It is effective against a range of infectious bacteria, including *Bacillus anthracis.* For a discussion of the use of doxycycline for treatment of inhalational exposure to *Bacillus anthracis,* see Department of Health and Human Services, *Biological Threats and Terrorism: Assessing the Science and Response Capabilities: Workshop Summary,* ed. Stacey L. Knobler, Adel A. F. Mahmoud, and Leslie A. Pray (Washington, DC: National Academies Press, 2002), Appendix E, 244–51.

18. During October 2001, a lethal dose of anthrax for a healthy human was estimated to be eight thousand to ten thousand spores.

19. Eisold, February 2013.

20. Segaran Pillai, personal communication to author, August 2012.

21. Pillai, August 2012.

22. Leonard A. Cole, *The Anthrax Letters: A Medical Detective Story* (Washington, DC: Joseph Henry Press, 2003), 75.

23. One published account lists George Fairfax as a pseudonym. See Daschle, *Like No Other Time,* 292.

CHAPTER 7

1. Tom Daschle with Michael D'Orso, *Like No Other Time: The 107th Congress and The Two Years That Changed America* (New York: Random House, 2003), 285–86.

2. Qieth McQureerier was first publicly identified with his permission in Leonard A. Cole, *The Anthrax Letters: A Medical Detective Story* (Washington, DC: Joseph Henry Press, 2003), 59–68.

3. By the end of October 2001, anthrax contamination had been found in multiple buildings in the Capitol Hill area: the Hart, Dirksen, and Russell Senate office buildings, the Ford and Longworth House office buildings, the US Supreme Court mail facility, and the Library of Congress. Outside Capitol Hill, but still in the Washington,

DC, area, anthrax was found in the CIA mailroom, the Department of State mailroom, and Dulles Post Office in Sterling, Virginia, the US Capitol Police mail facility on P Street, the Pentagon Post Office, the Friendship post office, Southwest Station, the Brentwood mail facility, a Department of Justice building in Landover, Maryland, and an off-site mailroom serving the US Supreme Court. Anthrax contamination was documented in forty-two buildings as far away as Florida, Connecticut, Indiana, and Missouri. See Ketra Schmitt and Nicholas A. Zacchia, "Total Decontamination Cost of the Anthrax Letter Attacks," *Biosecurity and Bioterrorism: Biodefense Strategy, Practice, and Science* 10 (2012): 98–107, accessed online March 23, 2017, http://online.liebertpub.com/doi/abs/10.1089/bsp.2010.0053.

4. See chapter 11 for Dean Fetterolf's expanding role in the investigation.

5. Frederick T. Carson, "Some Observations on Determining the Size of Pores in Paper," *Journal of Research of the National Bureau of Standards* 24 (1940): 435–42.

6. Paper is produced from wood fibers. The wood is heated in a process producing pulp, and the pulp is cleaned with bleach, then spread on large, chromed rollers and pressed dry. The result is a thin mat of fibers laid at random over each in all directions. A comprehensive description of the history and processes of papermaking can be found in Nicolas A. Basbanes, *On Paper: The Everything of Its Two-Thousand-Year History* (New York: Alfred A. Knopf, 2013).

7. A micron (μm), is a measurement of length commonly used in science. It is 1/1000 of a millimeter in length, equivalent to 1/25,000 inch.

8. Most measurements of dried *anthracis* spores find a diameter of one-and-one-half microns and a length of approximately two microns.

9. Amido Black, also known as Naphthol Blue Black, is a powdered dye used to stain proteins that have been subjected to electrophoresis or bound to nitrocellulose strips. An individual molecule has a molecular weight (mass) of 616.49 daltons.

10. Each letter has been estimated to contain between 0.8 to 1.0 gram of material. The concentration of spores in the Daschle and Leahy letters was estimated at 2x10E12 spores per gram, and the concentration of spores in the *New York Post* and Brokaw letters was estimated at 2x10E11 per gram. See National Research Council, *Review of the Scientific Approach Used during the FBI's Investigation of the 2001 Anthrax Attacks*, ed. Alice P. Gast et al. (Washington, DC: National Academies Press, 2011), 75–78.

11. Spreadsheet titled "Sample Identification Record," *PathCon Laboratories*, October 18, 2001, 4 pages.

12. Accessed March 21, 2017, https://www.justice.gov/archive/ag/speeches/2001/agcrisisremarks10_16.htm.

13. The investigations of the September 11, 2001, attacks had been given major case status using the codenames of TRADEBOM for the New York City attacks and PENTBOMB for the attack on the Pentagon.

14. Garrett M. Graff, *The Threat Matrix: The FBI at War in the Age of Global Terror* (New York: Little, Brown and Company, 2011); see also citations within.

15. While several books have been published on the infamous serial bomb mailer, Theodore Kaczynski, codenamed Unabomber, an excellent version was recently published by three FBI agents (retired) who worked on the case during the time of its solution; see Jim Freeman, Terry D. Turchie, and Donald Max Noel, *Unabomber:*

How the FBI Broke Its Own Rules to Capture the Terrorist Ted Kaczynski (Palisades, NY: History Publishing Company, 2014).

CHAPTER 8

1. It has been estimated that decontamination alone for all affected buildings cost $320 million. See Ketra Schmitt and Nicholas A. Zacchia, "Total Decontamination Cost of the Anthrax Letter Attacks," *Biosecurity and Bioterrorism: Biodefense Strategy, Practice, and Science* 10 (2012): 98–107, accessed online March 23, 2017, http://online.liebertpub.com/doi/abs/10.1089/bsp.2010.0053.

2. The question of Iraq being behind the anthrax attacks was very much on the minds of those in charge of national security, especially the White House. At the end of October 2001, I received a call from Captain James Burans, commander of the US Naval Medical Research Unit in Lima, Peru. I had worked with Burans when he headed up a biological defense laboratory at the Naval Medical Research Center in Silver Spring and I was assigned to the Hazardous Materials Response Unit. Burans had also been on UN inspections in Iraq and examined the anthrax powder produced there. The Iraqis had included the clay additive bentonite in their production process, and Burans had observed the finished product. He offered to assist us, and we accepted. He would find no bentonite in our anthrax.

3. The number of mailboxes that could have been used to send the letters to the Trenton Processing and Distribution Center in Hamilton, New Jersey, eventually totaled 625 at 525 addresses in seven counties.

4. V. Tuborsky, "Small-Scale Processing of Microbial Pesticides," *FAO Agricultural Services Bulletin No. 96* (1992), accessed April 2, 2017, http://www.fao.org/docrep/t0533e/t0533e03.htm; see also Jean-Francois Charles, Armelle Delécluse, and Christina Nielsen-le Roux, ed., *Entomopathogenic Bacteria: From Laboratory to Field Applications* (Boston: Kluwer Academic Publishers, 2000).

5. Richard F. Meyer, personal communication to author, September and November 2012.

6. Arthur Eberhart, personal communication to author, April 2013.

7. *HEPA* is an acronym for "High-Efficiency Particulate Air."

8. Douglas J. Beecher, "Forensic Application of Microbiological Culture Analysis to Identify Mail Intentionally Contaminated with *Bacillus anthracis* Spores," *Applied and Environmental Microbiology* 72 (2006): 5304–10.

9. David M. Lesak, *Hazardous Materials: Strategies and Tactics* (Upper Saddle River, NJ: Brady/Prentice Hall, 1999), Appendix B, 417–35.

10. Steve Rhea's operations plan used soap and water rather than dilute bleach. The EPA initially disagreed with this approach, but Rhea remained with his original plan; Steven Rhea, personal communication to author, March 2013.

11. Personal observation by author; between November 6 and 14, 2001, I stopped at the warehouse for a briefing. Doug Beecher and Steve Rhea explained their operation in detail, including the offers of assistance from the various FBI units and resources stationed at Quantico.

12. The FBI's Hostage Rescue Team (HRT) of tactical operators originated in 1983 with the goal of deploying to the 1984 Los Angeles Summer Olympics. HRT's capabilities equaled or surpassed those of any other tactical law enforcement team in the United States, and it is extremely selective in its membership. Special agent applicants had to excel during an intensive two-week selection, followed by a four-month probationary period under the close scrutiny of senior team members. Extreme physical and mental toughness are prerequisite. See Sean Joyce, deputy director of the FBI and former HRT operator, at: https://www.fbi.gov/news/stories, *Hostage Rescue Team: The Crucible of Selection*, February 1, 2013, accessed March 23, 2017.

13. Beecher, "Forensic Application of Microbiological Culture Analysis," 5307.

14. Richard Preston first interviewed Steven Hatfill in 1999, at which time Hatfill made many of the claims subsequently reported as false in Preston's 2002 book of narrative nonfiction: Richard Preston, *The Demon in the Freezer* (New York: Random House, 2002), 203–8. In *The Demon*, Preston describes both Hatfill's resume and the Rhodesian anthrax outbreak. Hatfill's resume can also be found in its entirety on Ed Lake's Internet site, accessed April 2, 2017, http://www.anthraxinvestigation.com/hatfill.pdf.

CHAPTER 9

1. Richard H. Cummings, *Cold War Radio: The Dangerous History of American Broadcasting in Europe, 1950–1989* (Jefferson, NC: McFarland & Company, 2009), 71–74, accessed March 26, 2017, Google Books.

2. Oleg Kalugin, *Spymaster: My Thirty-Two Years in Intelligence and Espionage against the West* (New York: Basic Books, 2009), 203–12.

3. A discussion of the use of ricin as a weapon of mass destruction is presented in L. J. Schep et al., "Ricin as a Weapon of Mass Terror—Separating Fact from Fiction," *Environmental International* 35, no. 8 (2009): 1267–71.

4. Ricin is a single protein, made up of two separate and distinct peptide chains, each chain the product of a different gene. The two peptides combine after their synthesis to form a single, dimeric protein molecule.

5. Ryuichi Hirota et al., "The Silicon Layer Supports Acid Resistance of *Bacillus cereus* Spores," *Journal of Bacteriology* 192, no. 1 (2010): 111–16, and references within.

6. Later that week I inquired where the term *Person of Interest* originated, a phrase unfamiliar to me after eleven years in the FBI. The explanation: There had been discussion about what to call the people (and one organization) on the growing list of individuals being reported to the FBI and fitting the profile of the mailer. At the time, however, none of those on the list fit the definition of "Suspect" (reasonable suspicion of guilt existed) or that of "Subject" (probable cause of guilt). At one point during the discussion, a voice yelled from the back of the classroom, "They're persons of interest!" and the term stuck. The term was first used during the investigation of Richard Jewell in connection with the Centennial Park bombing during the 1996 Summer Olympics.

7. Del Jones, "Muslim CEOs of U.S. Firms Fight Terrorism, Stop Evil," *USA Today*, Money Section, May 18, 2004.

8. Jim Freeman, Terry D. Turchie, and Donald Max Noel, *Unabomber: How the FBI Broke Its Own Rules to Capture the Terrorist Ted Kaczynski* (Palisades, NY: History Publishing Company, 2014).

9. Amerithrax Press Briefing, "Linguistic/Behavioral Briefing Points," Critical Incident Response Group, November 9, 2001.

10. The full assessment lists six linguistic characteristics.

11. Gary Matsumoto, "The Pentagon's Toxic Secret," *Vanity Fair*, May 1999, 82–98.

12. B. E. Ivins et al., Patent publication Number US6387665B1, May 14, 2002 (filed March 7, 2000).

13. FBI Vault, November 19, 2001, FBI interview of Bruce Ivins, Fort Detrick, Maryland, accessed March 26, 2017, https://vault.fbi.gov, part 29.

14. After a thorough investigation, no evidence was found to associate Joseph Farchaus with any of the anthrax letters, and his name was removed from the persons of interest list. Farchaus was first publicly identified by Jack Dolan, "Anthrax Probe Remains Slow Go; Experts Speculate in FBI's Thrust," *Hartford Courant*, March 4, 2002, and further discussed by David Willman, *The Mirage Man: Bruce Ivins, the Anthrax Attacks, and America's Rush to War* (New York: Bantam Books, 2011), 132–33.

15. Paul Keim, personal communication to author, August 2012.

16. K. S. Griffith et al., "Bioterrorism-Related Inhalational Anthrax in an Elderly Woman, Connecticut, 2001," *Emerging Infectious Diseases* 9, no. 6 (2003): 681–88.

17. T. H. Holtz et al., "Isolated Case of Bioterrorism-Related Inhalational Anthrax, New York City, 2001," *Emerging Infectious Diseases* 9, no. 6 (2003): 689–96.

18. The agent requested anonymity for this book.

19. The Institute for Genomic Research (TIGR) did not have a biosafety laboratory certified to handle live *Bacillus anthracis* and could only work with inert DNA, necessitating that DNA be isolated from live *B. anthracis* at an alternate laboratory and shipped to TIGR.

CHAPTER 10

1. Accessed April 2, 2017, http://www.company7.com/library/staticmaster/AlphaIonization.p.pdf, and http://www.company7.com/staticmaster/products/static maser.html.

2. Robert William Reid, *Marie Curie* (New York: Saturday Review Press, 1974).

3. Reid, *Marie Curie*. Born Maria Salomea Skłodowska in Poland, Curie immigrated to Paris in 1891 and studied at the Sorbonne (the University of Paris), where she was known as Marie. Married to Pierre Curie in 1895, she then used the name Marie Skłodowska Curie.

4. Bill Bryson, *A Short History of Nearly Everything* (New York: Broadway Books, 2003), 74.

5. Eoin O'Carroll, "Marie Curie: Why Her Papers Are Still Radioactive," *Christian Science Monitor*, November 7, 2011.

6. Dominick Murphy, inspector, New Scotland Yard, presentation at MidAtlantic Intelligence and Law Enforcement Training Seminar, Annapolis, MD, June 25, 2013.

7. Final Report, January 2016, accessed April 3, 2017, www.litvinenkoinquiry .com, 39.

8. *ECL*, enhanced chemilluminescence, is an antibody-based test for confirming *B. anthracis* identity. The test was developed by Dr. Richard F. Meyer at the CDC and transferred to Dr. John Ezzell's lab for use as part of the National Laboratory Response Network test protocols.

9. Rosa Grenha et al., "Structural Characterization of *SpoOE*-like Protein-aspartic Acid Phosphatases That Regulate Sporulation in *Bacilli*," *Journal of Biological Chemistry* 281, no. 49 (2006): 37993–8003.

10. *Bact Division* is an acronym commonly used for the Bacteriology Division at USAMRIID.

11. P. L. Worsham and M. R. Sowers, "Isolation of an Asporogenic (*SpoOA*) Protective Antigen-Producing strain of *Bacillus anthracis*," *Canadian Journal of Microbiology* 45, no. 1 (1999): 1–8.

12. See chapter 11 for rationale to code samples given to outside collaborators.

13. The Leahy letter had been folded in a configuration used by pharmacists. The configuration is designed so the folds will contain pills being dispensed by a druggist.

14. Actual amount of powder collected from the Leahy letter was 0.9 grams.

15. Both the Daschle and Leahy letters were photocopies; the original was never located.

16. In 2003, the Laboratory Division relocated from the third floor of the J. Edgar Hoover Building to Quantico, Virginia. However, pursuant to an agreement with the US Marine Corps, there would be no anthrax, nor any hazardous evidence—biological, chemical, or radiological—coming through, or on, Marine Corps Base Quantico.

17. This is for the most common form of DNA, B-DNA. Other less common forms, such as A-DNA and Z-DNA, have different geometries.

18. DNA plasmids are explained in more detail in chapter 11.

19. FBI Vault, FD-302, August 15, 2003, file 279A-WF-222936, sub-302, accessed April 3, 2017, https://vault.fbi.gov.

CHAPTER 11

1. *QC* is an acronym commonly used for "quality control."

2. *MIPR* is the acronym for Military Interdepartmental Purchase Request. Verbally, in government circles, the acronym is used as both a verb and noun. It is a vehicle for transferring funds between government agencies, often pursuant to a preexisting Memorandum of Agreement.

3. Paul Keim, personal communication to author, July 2013.

4. Radiation can cause damage to DNA in a number of ways. These include inducing breaks in one or both of the phosphate backbones, chemically altering the structure of the individual nucleotide bases (A, C, G, T), and breaking the hydrogen bonds responsible for the pairing of bases (A-T and C-G). DNA structure is discussed in chapter 10.

5. The Laboratory reviewed photographs of the letters and preliminarily determined that all the four recovered anthrax letters were photocopies and they had been trimmed to an irregular size on one to three sides. See US Department of Justice, *Amerithrax Investigative Summary*, February 19, 2010, 13; accessed April 6, 2017, https://www.justice.gov/archive/amerithrax/docs/amx-investigative-summary.pdf.

6. When I began my FBI career, FBI latent fingerprint examiners required a minimum of sixteen identifiable points to conclude an identical match between a person and a latent print. Less than sixteen identifiable points in a latent print can still provide lead value.

7. Also found three trash marks on the Daschle and Leahy letters; identical on each of the letters. See chapter 12 for additional details.

8. *Bacillus anthracis* DNA consists of a 5.3 million base pair (bp) genomic molecule and two smaller plasmid molecules: pOX1 (181,677 bp) and pOX2 (94,829 bp). pOX1 encodes three proteins necessary for lethality: protective antigen, lethal factor, and edema factor. pOX2 encodes a protein capsule that protects the bacteria from the mammalian immune system.

9. *TIGR* is an acronym for The Institute for Genomic Research. See chapter 9.

10. For more information on foraminifera use in ocean geological research, see http://www.ldeo.columbia.edu/core-repository/collections#ocean, accessed April 6, 2017.

11. The New Jersey Public Health Laboratory had agreed to analyze the samples using Laboratory Response Network protocols.

12. Hatfill's resume can also be found in its entirety on Ed Lake's Internet site, accessed April 2, 2017, http://www.anthraxinvestigation.com/hatfill.pdf.

13. Richard Preston, *The Demon in the Freezer* (New York: Random House, 2002), 115.

14. The FBI maintained a small two-man Resident Agency in Frederick, Maryland, approximately one mile from USAMRIID. The office had been there before 9/11 and the anthrax attacks.

15. FBI Vault, January 23 and 29, 2002, FBI interviews of Bruce Ivins, Fort Detrick, Maryland, accessed March 26, 2017, https://vault.fbi.gov.

16. FBI Vault, January 23 and 29, 2002.

17. As with Joseph Farchaus (see chapter 8 endnotes), following a thorough investigation, no evidence was found to link Gregory Knudson to any of the anthrax letters.

CHAPTER 12

1. Described in US Department of Justice, *Amerithrax Investigative Summary*, February 19, 2010, 13; accessed April 6, 2017, https://www.justice.gov/archive/amerithrax/docs/amx-investigative-summary.pdf.

2. Ideally, a direct search of each laboratory would have been preferred. But in early 2002, we had insufficient probable cause to search any of the sixteen laboratories containing Ames. Further, we had no indication that any of them might try to obstruct a submission of Ames, thus we relied on the subpoena process.

3. "Chapel Hill" refers to the University of North Carolina's main campus in Chapel Hill, North Carolina, where Ivins conducted postgraduate research following his doctoral work at the University of Cincinnati. See also David Willman, *The Mirage Man: Bruce Ivins, the Anthrax Attacks, and America's Rush to War* (New York: Bantam Books, 2011), 18.

4. *RIID* is a shortened version of the acronym USAMRIID.

5. The antigen looked for was for protective antigen.

6. Steven J. Hatfill, *Emergence* (Frederick, MD: unpublished, 1998).

7. Holly Tucker, *Blood Work: A Tale of Medicine and Murder in the Scientific Revolution* (New York: Norton, 2011), 37–57.

8. Daniel Defoe, *A Journal of the Plague Year* (Mineola, NY: Dover Publications, 2001).

9. Phil Gyford, *The Diary of Samuel Pepys: Daily Entries from 17th Century London Diary*, accessed April 6, 2017, http://www.pepysdiary.com/encyclopedia/301/.

10. Tucker, *Blood Work*, 37–57.

11. Rex A. Stockham, Dennis L. Slavin, and William Kift, "Specialized Use of Human Scent in Criminal Investigations," *Forensic Science Communications* 6, no. 3 (2004): accessed online April 7, 2017.

12. Original Stasi scent jars are on display in the International Spy Museum, 800 F Street, N.W., Washington, DC.

13. Kristie Macrakis, *Seduced by Secrets: Inside the Stasi's Spy-Tech World* (New York: Cambridge University Press, 2008).

14. Macrakis, *Seduced by Secrets*.

15. Brian A. Eckenrode et al., "Performance Evaluation of the Scent Transfer Unit (STU-100) for Organic Compound Collection and Release," *Journal of Forensic Science* 51, no. 4 (2006): 780–89.

16. Only 622 boxes were tested for anthrax; three had been removed and placed out of service by the postal service before the teams could do the sampling.

CHAPTER 13

1. See chapter 10 for original sequencing strategy.

2. National Research Council, *Review of the Scientific Approach Used during the FBI's Investigation of the 2001 Anthrax Attacks*, ed. Alice P. Gast et al. (Washington, DC: National Academies Press, 2011), 114.

3. The use of bloodhounds Knight, Tinkerbelle, and Lucy has also been described by David Willman, *The Mirage Man: Bruce Ivins, the Anthrax Attacks, and America's Rush to War* (New York: Bantam Books, 2011), 171, and Robert Graysmith, *Amerithrax: The Hunt for the Anthrax Killer* (New York: Berkley Books, 2003), 363–66. In addition, retired assistant director in charge Van Harp names the bloodhounds

in his civil suit deposition, September 22, 2005, pages 416–18; accessed March 17, 2017, http://mrmc.amedd.army.mil/index.cfm?pageid=foia_reading_room.overview#. The FBI's Human Scent Canine program manager, SSA Rex A. Stockham, discusses the scent and alert protocol used in Amerithrax in his civil suit deposition, May 9, 2006, 19–198; Ibid.

On November 6, 2015, I submitted a request pursuant to the Freedom of Information Act for any documents relating to human scent canines in Amerithrax. The FBI's Records Management Division denied the request. An appeal was filed with the Department of Justice (DOJ) on January 14, 2016. Inexplicably, the appeal was also denied, the reason being, "the FBI could locate no indexed references to human-scent canines within the Amerithrax investigation records." Thus, all information cited in the text is from my memory and could not be corroborated with documentation; some of which I drafted during my tenure on Amerithrax.

4. This breach of John Ezzell's security procedures is explained fully by Willman, *Mirage Man*, 109–11.

5. The potential alert on Ivins's residence by the bloodhound is identified as a "positive hit" in the FBI Vault, December 4, 2004 Electronic Communication (EC), accessed March 27, 2017, vault.fbi.gov, part 54, 112. The EC is a summary of the investigation of Ivins.

6. Michael A. Lang, "Ice Diving," *DAN: The Magazine of Diver Alert Network*, accessed April 7, 2017, http://www.alertdiver.com/Ice-Diving.

7. Walt Hendrick and Andrea Zaferes, *Ice Diving Operations* (Tulsa, OK: PennWell Books, 2003).

8. 10-4; Radio code (ten-codes or ten-signals) for "Understood—Okay."

9. We had enlisted the help of the local Red Cross chapter while dive operations took place. The Red Cross agreed to erect tents and provide hot coffee, sport drinks, and hot food to anyone involved in the operations.

10. My experience identifying deer trails came from years of successful whitetail deer hunting on my family's farm in New Jersey.

CHAPTER 14

1. A recent study of chemical and biological weapon use during the Rhodesian war of 1975–1980 concludes that the anthrax outbreak (1978–1980) was a natural occurrence exacerbated by the collapse of the nation's veterinary services as the conflict intensified. See Glenn Cross, *Dirty War: Rhodesia and Chemical Biological Warfare, 1975–1980* (West Midlands, England: Helion & Company, 2017), 175–210.

2. P. F. Fellows et al., "Efficacy of a Human Anthrax Vaccine in Guinea Pigs, Rabbits, and Rhesus Macaques against Challenge by *Bacillus anthracis* Isolates of Diverse Geographic Origin," *Vaccine* 19 (2001): 3241–47.

3. The anthrax vaccine approved for human use in 2001 activates the immune system specifically against toxins produced by *B. anthracis* following spore germination. Adjuvants stimulate an immune reaction in various ways, one being activation of macrophage cells—the cells responsible for carrying spores to the lymph nodes.

4. Bruce E. Ivins et al., "Immunization against Anthrax with *Bacillus anthracis* Protective Antigen Combined with Adjuvants," *Infection and Immunity* 60, no. 2 (1992): 662–68.

5. FBI Vault, April 2003 FBI interviews of USAMRIID employees, Fort Detrick, Maryland, accessed April 8, 2017, https://vault.fbi.gov, parts 32 and 42.

6. In particular, a small freeze dryer on a rolling cart remained in the hallway outside Ivins's containment lab, and I noticed it during my many visits to see John Ezzell, Pat Worsham, or Commander Ed Eitzen. The lyophilizer was assigned to John Ezzell's property sheet but was available for USAMRIID community use.

7. Fellows, "Efficacy of a Human Anthrax," 3241–47; Ivins, "Immunization against Anthrax," 662–68.

8. FBI Vault, September 10, 2004, interview of Bruce E. Ivins, part 30.

9. The complete list of samples and the labeling codes used are in National Research Council, *Review of the Scientific Approach Used during the FBI's Investigation of the 2001 Anthrax Attacks*, ed. Alice P. Gast et al. (Washington, DC: National Academies Press, 2011), Table 5-2, 115.

10. GB11 (A from *Post*), GB15 (A from Daschle), GB18 (C from Leahy).

11. The National Research Council review indicates that the B-variant from the Daschle letter was not sequenced, but Keim did confirm the T to C change in the Daschle B-variant using PCR and sequencing the amplicon fragment; see National Research Council, *Review of the Scientific Approach Used during the FBI's Investigation*, 115.

12. R. E. Chance and B. H. Frank, "Research, Development, Production, and Safety of Biosynthetic Human Insulin," *Diabetes Care* 16, suppl. 3 (1993): 133–42.

13. Paul Berg and Maxine F. Singer, "The Recombinant DNA Controversy: Twenty Years Later," *Proceedings of the National Academy of Sciences* 92 (1995): 9011–13.

14. Arghya Ray and Bengt Norden, "Peptide Nucleic Acid (PNA): Its Medical and Biotechnical Applications and Promise for the Future," *FASEB Journal* 14, no. 9 (2000): 1041–60.

15. R. Saiki et al., "Enzymatic Amplification of Beta-Globin Genomic Sequences and Restriction Site Analysis for Diagnosis of Sickle Cell Anemia," *Science* 239, no. 4732 (1985): 1350–54.

16. Detection of the B-mutation in a TaqMan PCR assay can also be accomplished by making a primer strand specific for the thymine to cytosine mutation, rather than the fluorescent third fragment (probe). See National Research Council, *Review of the Scientific Approach Used during the FBI's Investigation*, Box 5-3, 106.

17. In June 2003, I also assisted in an ambitious project. We drained the Whiskey Springs Pond where the Sterilite box had been recovered. While demonstrating the lengths that the FBI will go to solve a crime, I have not included details of the operation due to nothing of evidentiary value being found.

18. D. A. Rasko et al., "*Bacillus anthrax* Comparative Genome Analysis in Support of the Amerithrax Investigation," *Proceedings of the National Academy of Sciences* 108, no. 12 (2011): 5027–32.

CHAPTER 15

1. As mentioned in chapter 14, the name *TaqMan* is derived from the video game Pac-Man, which was combined with *Taq*, an acronym for the heat-stable DNA polymerase isolated from the bacteria *Thermus aquaticus* and used in PCR. Accessed April 8, 2017. See http://www.thermofisher.com/us/en/home/life-science/pcr/real -time-pcr/real-time-pcr-assays.htmlT.

2. The number of laboratories that submitted samples to the FBI's Ames Repository has been inaccurately reported over time. The National Research Council's 2011 report (page 29) states eighteen labs in the United States and two foreign labs. This is incorrect; it was sixteen domestic and three foreign. (If the two labs at Porton Down are considered independent of each other, then the number of foreign labs is four.) The Department of Justice's February 2010 report (page 24) states fifteen domestic and three foreign labs were issued subpoenas. We never issued subpoenas to non-US labs as these labs would be under no legal obligation to comply. We either used a verbal or informal written request, or relied on the Mutual Legal Assistance Treaty process.

3. Peter M. Hammond and Gradon B. Carter, *From Biological Warfare to Healthcare, Porton Down, 1940–2000* (New York: Palgrave Macmillan, 2002), 3–16.

4. David Ride, *In Defence of Landscape, An Archaeology of Porton Down* (Stroud, Gloucestershire: Tempus Publishing Ltd., 2006), 145–52.

5. Hammond and Carter, *From Biological Warfare to Healthcare*, 4–18.

6. Theodore Rosebury, *Experimental Air-Borne Infection* (Baltimore: The Wilkens & Wilkens Company, 1947).

7. Tim Brooks was the director of Public Health Affairs in the United Kingdom's Health Protection Agency located at Porton Down.

8. We also collected Ames anthrax from a laboratory in Sweden and from the Defence Research and Development Canada, Alberta. At the University of New Mexico, we found a FedEx shipping label that had been prepared for a shipment of Ames to the Institut Pasteur in Paris, but after further investigation, we discovered that the Ames sample(s) had never been sent.

9. Detection of heme and/or agar in the mailed spores would have indicated growth on solid agar culture plates, not liquid broth; liquid broth was the prevailing theory at the time. Heme, a multiring chemical compound responsible for transporting oxygen in red blood cells, arises from the breakdown of red blood cells in agar using blood as a nutrient for *B. anthracis* growth.

10. FBI Vault, 2003 FBI interviews of Bruce Ivins, accessed April 8, 2017, https://vault.fbi.gov.

11. FBI Vault, 2003 FBI interviews of Bruce Ivins.

12. Special Agent Darin Steele conducted two consent searches, one in October and a second, much more extensive one, in December 2003. Four samples were collected from Ivins in October and forty-one in December. Two Amerithrax special agents assisted Steele in the December search.

CHAPTER 16

1. PowerPoint presentation by Tom Reynolds, "Review of the Microbial Forensics in the Amerithrax Investigation" (American International Biotechnologies, LLC, 2011).

2. Riegel Paper Corporation of Milford, New Jersey. I worked there in 1973 and 1974. During the fall of 1974, the employees, members of the United Paperworkers International Union (I was a member also, but now away at college), struck for wages and conditions. The strike was bitter. Fights broke out as truck drivers attempted to cross the union line. The paper mill's managers maintained a minimum of operations, but the membership stayed out four months and Riegel Paper lost customers. After the strike, the company was forced to lay off all but its most senior workers. I returned during winter break and met with three high school friends in the mill's back parking lot. All four of us had worked together on the warehouse floor; now they were being laid off. Frank P., my best buddy, summed it up, "Scott, we struck ourselves out of a job."
The mill was bought and sold several times after that until it closed for good in 2003. Today, after too many chemical spills, the mill has been added to the federal Superfund National Priorities List and is considered one of the most hazardous sites in New Jersey.

3. US Department of Justice, *Amerithrax Investigative Summary*, February 19, 2010, 51–56, accessed April 6, 2017, https://www.justice.gov/archive/amerithrax/docs/amx-investigative-summary.pdf.

4. Envelopes were also shipped as groups of five, sealed in cellophane. The banded envelopes were held together, five at a time, with a white paper band; their production totaled 5.8 million.

5. US Department of Justice, *Amerithrax Investigative Summary*, 51–56.

6. Shortly after Tom Dellafera and I returned to Washington, DC, the Ohio Beltway sniper was arrested. The bloodhounds that we had used at the Catoctin Mountains had gone to Ohio to assist in the manhunt. Together with Bob Roth, I listened on a speaker telephone in Roth's office as the dog's FBI manager described their work. While the manhunt was underway, the dogs trailed to a house one mile distant from where the sniper was being arrested. We stared at the floor without a word—the Ohio operation confirmed what we had been suspecting about their reliability. We would not use the bloodhounds again during the anthrax investigation.

7. US Department of Justice, *Amerithrax Investigative Summary*, 54–55.

8. Experiments would be performed by the FBI laboratory to determine the likelihood of A, D, and E variant sampling errors; see National Research Council, *Review of the Scientific Approach Used during the FBI's Investigation of the 2001 Anthrax Attacks*, ed. Alice P. Gast et al. (Washington, DC: National Academies Press, 2011), 143.

9. During the latter part of the investigation, a legal representative of each submitting domestic laboratory would be called to swear before a grand jury that, according

to the FBI's protocol, their facility had faithfully searched and submitted all samples of Ames in their possession; failure to answer honestly before the grand jury could result in criminal sanction. In 2002, we did not have sufficient probable cause or the resources to search sixteen laboratories across the country.

CHAPTER 17

1. While in the Mideast, I had little communication with the Amerithrax Task Force at the Washington Field Office. While I was deployed, computers were limited in supply, and those that were available had sporadic connections to the Internet.

2. E. E. Zumbrun et al., "A Characterization of Aerosolized Sudan Virus Infection in African Green Monkeys, Cynomolgus Macaques, and Rhesus Macaques," *Viruses* 4, no. 10 (2002): 2115–36.

3. *Mics* is pronounced "mikes."

4. We also located many samples of *B. anthracis* with no strain designation; these were sent to Paul Keim for identification.

5. PowerPoint presentation by Tom Reynolds (Commonwealth Biotechnologies, Incorporated, 2004).

6. *FBIR* is an acronym for Federal Bureau of Investigation Repository.

7. For FBIR code numbers, see National Research Council, *Review of the Scientific Approach Used during the FBI's Investigation of the 2001 Anthrax Attacks*, ed. Alice P. Gast et al. (Washington, DC: National Academies Press, 2011), Table C-1, 187.

8. A table listing ten samples testing positive for mutations A1, A3, and D is shown in National Research Council, *Review of the Scientific Approach Used during the FBI's Investigation*, Table 6-3, 134. A table of matches using FBIR numbers can also be found on Ed Lake's Internet site, accessed April 8, 2017, http://www.anthrax investigation.com, posted on May 18, 2014.

9. *GLP* is an acronym for Good Laboratory Practice.

10. See also US District Court deposition of Kristie M. Friend, June 9, 2011, page 121, accessed April 8, 2017, http://mrmc.amedd.army.mil/content/foia_reading _room/Depositions/Friend%20Deposition_Redacted.pdf.

11. Notebook, March 17, 1998, page 74, signed by Bruce Ivins; see US Department of Justice, *Amerithrax Investigative Summary*, February 19, 2010, accessed April 6, 2017, https://www.justice.gov/archive/amerithrax/docs/amx-investigative -summary.pdf, attachment F.

12. US Department of Justice, *Amerithrax Investigative Summary*, 26–27.

13. See chapter 15 for origin of RMR-1030.

14. Ibid; Ivins's contribution to RMR-1029 was 15 percent of the spores; The US Department of Justice, *Amerithrax*, footnote 9, page 27. See also National Research Council, *Review of the Scientific Approaches Used during the FBI's Investigation*, for concentration and volume of RMR-1029, page 77, and an estimate of the total percentage of A-mutations, page 114.

CHAPTER 18

1. Paul Keim et al., "The International *Bacillus anthracis, B. cereus,* and *B. thuringiensis* Conference, Bacillus-ACT05," *Journal of Bacteriology* 188, no. 10 (2006): 3433–41.

2. Alice Gregory, "A Brief History of the Zoot Suit: Unraveling the Jazzy Life of a Snazzy Style," *Smithsonian Magazine,* April 2016, accessed April 9, 2017, http://www.smithsonianmag.com/arts-culture/brief-history-zoot-suit-180958507/.

3. US Department of Justice, *Amerithrax Investigative Summary,* February 19, 2010, 13, accessed April 6, 2017, https://www.justice.gov/archive/amerithrax/docs/amx-investigative-summary.pdf.

4. See chapter 13 for background on carbon-14 testing.

5. See chapter 15.

6. Hatfill's resume can be found in its entirety on Ed Lake's Internet site, accessed April 2, 2017, http://www.anthraxinvestigation.com/hatfill.pdf.

7. Richard Preston, *The Demon in the Freezer* (New York: Random House, 2002), 203–8.

8. Rebecca Skloot, *The Immortal Life of Henrietta Lacks* (New York: Random House, 2010).

9. Preston, *The Demon in the Freezer,* 115.

10. Described in chapter 1.

11. Night hours are defined as after 6:00 p.m. and before 1:00 a.m. There were entries between 1:00 a.m. and 6:00 a.m. See US Department of Justice, *Amerithrax Investigative Summary,* 31, and Appendix H.

12. For entry/exit records, see Mrmc.amedd.army.mil/index.cfm?pageid=foia_reading_room.overview#, accessed April 9, 2017, and US Department of Justice, *Amerithrax Investigative Summary,* 29–33.

CHAPTER 19

1. Originally, the total production runs were fifty-seven (chapter 6), but with the elimination of envelopes printed with old ink and the envelopes produced after the first mailing in September 2001, the number of runs potentially producing the attack envelopes was thirty-seven, producing thirty-one million envelopes.

2. USSS History, https://www.secretservice.gov/about/history/events, accessed April 9, 2017.

3. Nicholas A. Basbanes, *On Paper: The Everything of Its Two-Thousand-Year History* (New York: Alfred A. Knopf, 2013), 107.

4. Basbanes, *On Paper,* 96–114.

5. USSS History, https://www.secretservice.gov/about/history/events, accessed April 9, 2017.

6. ViveBerlin.com, https://viveberlin.wordpress.com/2012/08/17/stories-of-sachsenhausen-the-counterfeit-operation, accessed April 9, 2017.

7. Basbanes, *On Paper*, 96–114.

8. US Department of Justice, *Amerithrax Investigative Summary*, February 19, 2010, 51–56, accessed April 6, 2017, https://www.justice.gov/archive/amerithrax/docs/amx-investigative-summary.pdf.

9. US Department of Justice, *Amerithrax Investigative Summary*.

10. Gerald M. LaPorte, Joseph C. Stephens, and Amanda K. Beuchel, "The Examination of Commercial Printing Defects to Assess Common Origin, Batch Variation, and Error Rate," *Journal of Forensic Science* 55, no. 1 (2010): 136–40.

11. A field office undergoes inspection, on average, every three years. The Washington Field Office, Amerithrax included, was inspected in 2003 and again in 2006.

12. Every FBI squad has a permanent supervisory special agent who manages squad activities. One of the squad's special agents is designated as the primary, or principle relief supervisor, who oversees the squad in the absence of the permanent supervisor.

CHAPTER 20

1. Harry R. Weber, "Former Olympic Park Guard Jewell Dies," *Associated Press* in *Washington Post*, August 30, 2007.

2. Eric R. Rudolph, *Between the Lines of Drift: The Memoirs of a Militant* (Lulu Press, 2013), accessed April 9, 2017, https://www.armyofgod.com/EricLinesOfDrift1_18_15.pdf.

3. A Gannett Company, WGRZ, "Jewell Finally Honored as a Hero," August 2, 2006, accessed April 9, 2017, https://archive.fo/iFgIg.

4. Today, the CART program has grown to five hundred agents and examiners. Assigned to a network of Regional Computer Forensic Laboratories around the country, they interrogate all types of computer-related items—laptop, desktop, notebook and tablet computers, thumb and flash drives and digital video discs (DVDs), digital cameras, and cell phones. They provide a training course in basic forensic interrogation of digital media, enabling street agents to safely collect and conduct basic examinations without risking damage. They support investigations of financial crime, violent crime, potential breaches of national security, instances of child pornography, and terrorist money laundering; in year 2012 alone, CART performed over thirteen thousand digital forensic examinations and lent assistance in over ten thousand cases. Accessed April 9, 2017, https://www.fbi.gov/investigate/cyber.

5. Special Agent Richard Langham took over coordination of the AMX-2 genetics projects when Special Agent Scott Stanley was promoted to supervisor in the Behavioral Analysis Units, Critical Incident Response Group.

6. *Bacillus subtilis* is considered nonpathogenic and can be worked with at the FBI Laboratory on the Quantico Marine Corps base, in contrast to its lethal cousin, *Bacillus anthracis*.

7. John G. Holt, *Bergey's Manual of Systematic Bacteriology, 1st Edition, Volume 2*, ed. David Hendricks Bergey, John G. Holt, and Noel R. Krieg (Baltimore: Williams & Wilkins, 1986).

8. A sampling of well-known genus members include *Bacillus anthracis* and *Bacillus subtilis* (also called *B. globigii* or sometimes *B. atophaeus), Bacillus cereus* and *B. licheniformis, B. thuringiensis, B. amyloliquefacieus, B. mycoides, B. pumilus, B. megaterium, B. circulans,* and *B. fusiformis.*

9. See chapter 1.

10. See chapter 6.

11. My first science research project, conducted at the Argonne National Laboratory's off-campus study program while a college senior, was studying chromosome replication in *Bacillus subtilis.*

12. Students and technicians would devote a week's labor to isolating pure preparations of restriction enzymes until they became commercially available. One project assigned to me as a first-year graduate student at the University of Michigan was the preparation of large amounts of Bam H1 restriction enzyme. Today, the enzyme is commercially available from dozens of companies.

13. *Bergey's Manual of Systematic Bacteriology, 2nd Edition, Volume 3*, ed. Paul Vos et al. (New York: Springer-Verlag, 2009).

14. Kenneth Todar, *Todar's Online Textbook of Bacteriology*, accessed April 9, 2017, http://textbookofbacteriology.net/Bacillus.html.

15. As with genus and species names, scientific convention also calls for the names of genes to be italicized.

16. National Research Council, *Review of the Scientific Approach Used during the FBI's Investigation of the 2001 Anthrax Attacks*, ed. Alice P. Gast, et al. (Washington, DC: National Academies Press, 2011), 104–6, 121–22.

CHAPTER 21

1. Accessed April 10, 2017, http://uscode.house.gov/view.xhtml?path=/prelim@title18/part2/chapter206&edition=prelim.

2. In addition to the contents of Bruce Ivins's work computer, we also had contents from a personal computer, taken in March 2005. Inspector Rick Lambert interviewed Ivins at this time and had received Ivins's permission to copy Ivins's computer.

3. Gregory Saathoff, chair, et al., *The Amerithrax Case: Report of the Expert Behavioral Analysis Panel* (Vienna, VA: Research Strategies Network, unsealed and redacted, 2011), 68.

4. David Willman, *The Mirage Man: Bruce Ivins, the Anthrax Attacks, and America's Rush to War* (New York: Bantam Books, 2011), 65.

5. Willman, *The Mirage Man*, 62.

6. Willman, *The Mirage Man*, page 63, and US Department of Justice, *Amerithrax Investigative Summary*, February 19, 2010, 45; accessed April 6, 2017, https://www.justice.gov/archive/amerithrax/docs/amx-investigative-summary.pdf.

7. The therapist, Judith McLean, did contact police during the summer of 2000 after Ivins revealed his plot to poison Mara Linscott; however, the police did not feel that she had enough information for them to act on. During March 2001, in an email

message to Linscott, Ivins refers to his therapist wanting to have him jailed but does not give a reason why. See Willman, *Mirage Man*, 61–69.

8. Saathoff, *The Amerithrax Case*, 71.

9. DOJ AMX Investigative Summary, February 19, 2010, page 46.

10. Saathoff, *The Amerithrax Case*, 71.

11. Saathoff, *The Amerithrax Case*, 78.

12. Willman, *Mirage Man*, 73.

13. Willman, *Mirage Man*, 289 and throughout.

14. FBI Vault, Electronic Communication, April 4, 2005, accessed April 3, 2017, https://vault.fbi.gov, part 47.

15. Accessed April 10, 2017, http://www.hhs.gov/ocr/privacy/hipaa/understand ing/summary/privacysummary.pdf.

16. Ivins's drug use is described in detail by Willman, *Mirage Man*, 62–69, 220–316.

17. Saathoff, *The Amerithrax Case*, 85.

18. PowerPoint presentations, June 2014, by the *Expert Behavioral Analysis Panel* at American Red Cross Headquarters (Research Strategies Network).

19. US Department of Justice, *Amerithrax Investigative Summary*, 44–45.

20. Saathoff, *The Amerithrax Case*, 71.

21. FBI Vault, November 1, 2007. FBI interview of Bruce Ivins, Frederick, MD, serial 172.

22. FBI Vault, November 1, 2007.

23. FBI Vault, November 1, 2007, serial 223.

CHAPTER 22

1. FBI Vault, November 13, 2007, FBI review summary of items seized on November 13, 2007, Frederick, MD, accessed March 26, 2017, https://vault.fbi.gov, subfile BEI, serial 149.

2. FBI Vault, November 6, 2017, serial 153.

3. FBI Vault, January 15, 2008, interview of USAMRIID employees, sub-USAMRIID, serial 1785.

4. FBI Vault.

5. FBI Vault, March 31, 2005, FBI interview of Bruce Ivins, sub-BEI, serial 53.

6. February 22, 2008, Application and Affidavit Search Warrant 08-124-M-01, US District Court for the District of Columbia Search Warrant, accessed April 10, 2017, https://www.justice.gov/archive/amerithrax/docs/08-124-m-01.pdf.

7. *Frontline* interview, *Nancy Haigwood: I Had a Gut Feeling It Was Bruce* (Public Broadcasting Station, October 10, 2011), accessed April 10, 2017, http://www.pbs .org/wgbh/frontline/article/nancy-haigwood-i-had-a-gut-feeling-it-was-bruce/.

8. FBI Vault, February 12, 2008, FBI interview of Kappa Kappa Gamma member, sub-BEI, serial 214.

9. February 22, 2008, Application and Affidavit Search Warrant 08-124-M-01.

10. February 22, 2008, Application and Affidavit Search Warrant 08-124-M-01.

11. "MSN Online Services, Where to Serve Criminal Legal Process," Microsoft, April 2005 revision, accessed April 10, 2017, https://info.publicintelligence.net/MSN-Compliance.pdf.

12. *Frontline* interview, *Edward Montooth: The Mandate Was to Look at the Case with Fresh Eyes* (Public Broadcasting Station, October 10, 2011).

13. Sketch can be seen in US Department of Justice, *Amerithrax Investigative Summary*, February 19, 2010, Appendix K; accessed April 6, 2017, https://www.justice.gov/archive/amerithrax/docs/amx-investigative-summary.pdf; a second and similar sketch can be seen in Appendix M.

14. *Frontline* interview, *Rachel Lieber: The Case against Dr. Bruce Ivins* (Public Broadcasting Station, October 10, 2011).

15. Photograph can be seen in US Department of Justice, *Amerithrax Investigative Summary*, February 19, 2010, Appendix L.

16. FBI Vault, February 14, 2008, FBI interview of Bruce E. Ivins, sub-BEI, serial 198.

17. *Frontline, Rachel Lieber* (Public Broadcasting Station, October 10, 2011).

18. Gregory Saathoff, chair, et al., *The Amerithrax Case: Report of the Expert Behavioral Analysis Panel* (Vienna, VA: Research Strategies Network, unsealed and redacted, 2011), 93.

19. The anthrax that Dr. Bruce Ivins spilled was an attenuated vaccine strain, but still subject to USAMRIID's safety reporting requirements.

20. FBI Vault, March 26, 2008, FBI interview of a Confidential Human Source, CHS, sub-BEI, serial 231.

21. FBI Vault, March 28, 2008, FBI report of March 19, 2008 emergency call transcript, sub-BEI, serial 232.

22. Frontline, *Rachel Lieber* and *Ed Montooth* (Public Broadcasting Station, October 10, 2011).

CHAPTER 23

1. FBI Vault, FD-302, June 26, 2008, file 279A-WF-222936, accessed March 26, 2017, https://vault.fbi.gov, sub-BEI, serial 284.

2. *Frontline* interview of Rachel Lieber, *Rachel Lieber: The Case against Dr. Bruce Ivins* (Public Broadcasting Station, October 10, 2011).

3. FBI Vault, FD-302, June 5, 2008, file 279A-WF-222936, sub-BEI, serial 287.

4. Gregory Saathoff, chair, et al., *The Amerithrax Case: Report of the Expert Behavioral Analysis Panel* (Vienna, VA: Research Strategies Network, unsealed and redacted, 2011), 93. See also chapter 22.

5. Built in 1862 as Sheppard Asylum, the institution was designated a historic landmark in 1971, accessed April 10, 2017, https://www.nps.gov/nhl/.

6. FBI Vault, FD-597, July 12, 2008, Receipt for Property, file 279A-WF-222936.

7. Saathoff, *The Amerithrax Case*, 75.

8. David Willman, *The Mirage Man: Bruce Ivins, the Anthrax Attacks, and America's Rush to War* (New York: Bantam Books, 2011), 62–69.

9. Willman, *The Mirage Man*.

10. Saathoff, *The Amerithrax Case*, 73.

11. There are two written versions of Ivins's trip to Linscott's soccer game; See Saathoff, *The Amerithrax Case*, 66, and Edward G. Lake, *A Crime Unlike Any Other: What the Facts Say about Dr. Bruce Edwards Ivins and the Anthrax Attacks of 2001* (Racine, WI: Edward G. Lake, 2012), 44.

12. Willman, *The Mirage Man*, 66.

13. Judith McLean felt strongly enough about the danger Ivins represented that she resigned her position at Comprehensive Counseling Associates.

14. FBI Vault, FD-302, July 17, 2008, file 279A-WF-222936, sub-BEI, serial 324.

15. Saathoff, *The Amerithrax Case*, 135.

16. Lake, *A Crime Unlike Any Other*, 331.

17. Saathoff, *The Amerithrax Case*, 107–36.

18. Saathoff, *The Amerithrax Case*, 104.

19. FBI Vault, FD-302, July 26–27, 2008 Surveillance Log, file 279A-WF-222936, sub-BEI, serial 357.

20. Willman, *The Mirage Man*, 412n.

21. Lake, *A Crime Unlike Any Other*, 340.

22. On July 31, 2008, task force members searched the Ivinses' household trash. They found two empty containers of Tylenol PM and a store receipt for the same, dated July 24, 2008; see Saathoff, *The Amerithrax Case*, 106. Tylenol PM contains the sedative diphenhydramine. The Tylenol likely worked in combination with any Valium taken by Bruce Ivins during July 26–27, 2008.

23. Willman, *The Mirage Man*, 319.

24. Jeanne Guillemin, *American Anthrax: Fear, Crime, and the Investigation of the Nation's Deadliest Bioterror Attack* (New York: Times Books, Henry Holt and Company, 2011), 239.

EPILOGUE

1. David Willman, "U.S. System to Detect Bioterrorism Can't Be Counted On, Government Watchdog Finds," *Los Angeles Times*, November 23, 2015.

2. The Department of Energy, using its Los Alamos and Lawrence Livermore National Laboratories, designed its Biological Aerosol Sentry and Information System (BASIS) for air monitoring at the 2002 Winter Olympics in Salt Lake City, but the threat of a secondary biological attack by al-Qaeda following 9/11 stepped up the inaugural deployment of BASIS to fall 2001 in and around the US Capital region. The system also monitored air in New York City's Yankee Stadium during three games of the delayed 2001 World Series.

3. "Lab's Work Provides BASIS for Biodetection," Lawrence Livermore National Laboratory, accessed May 5, 2017, www.llnl.gov/news/labs-work-provides-basis-biodetection.

4. By 2015, however, the effectiveness of the BioWatch system had become controversial amid claims of a number of false alarms and a lack of specifications for operation. See Willman, "U.S. System to Detect Bioterrorism," and references therein.

5. "How the Biohazard Detection System Was Developed," National Association of Letter Carriers, accessed April 29, 2017, www.nalc.org/workplace-issues/body/BDSDev.pdf.

6. "Bio-Hazard Detection System (BDS) Exercise at Columbia Mail Processing and Distribution Center," US Postal Service, accessed April 29, 2017, about.usps.com/news/state-releases/sc/2013/sc_2013_0911.htm.

7. "Backgrounder: The Select Agent Rule, December 9, 2002," Centers for Disease Control and Prevention, accessed May 25, 2017, https://www.cdc.gov/media/pressrel/b021210.htm.

8. Brian J. Gorman and J. Corey Creek, "Risk and Reliability of Laboratory Personnel," *Biosecurity Commons Review*, ed. Brian J. Gorman (Towson, MD: Towson University, 2010), 29, accessed May 17, 2017, https://www.scribd.com/document/30902475/Bio-Security-Commons-AR-May-2010.

9. For purposes here, a biosafety level-3 laboratory is where work is performed with biological agents that may cause serious disease through the inhalation route. A biosafety level-4 laboratory is for work with biological agents that pose a high risk of aerosol-transmitted disease that is frequently fatal and there are no vaccines or treatment. See, L. Casey Chosewood and Deborah E. Wilson, ed., *Biosafety in Microbiological and Biomedical Laboratories* (Washington: US Government Printing Office, 2009), 38–45.

10. National Research Council, *Biosecurity Challenges of the Global Expansion of High-Containment Biological Laboratories: Summary of a Workshop*, ed. Alison K. Hottes, Benjamin Rusek, and Fran Sharples (Washington, DC: National Academies Press, 2012).

11. In March 2003, Bruce E. Ivins and two colleagues at USAMRIID received the Department of Defense's Decoration for Exceptional Civilian Service in recognition of their efforts in solving technical problems with the anthrax vaccine's manufacture.

12. For purposes here, the term *biosurety* will mean the combination of security, safety, biological agent accountability, and personnel reliability needed to prevent unauthorized access to select agents of bioterrorism.

13. Brian J. Gorman and J. Corey Creek, "Risk and Reliability of Laboratory Personnel," *Biosecurity Commons Review*, 35.

14. For a detailed discussion and summary of the various biosurety committee findings and recommendations, see Brian J. Gorman, ed., *Biosecurity Commons Review*, 28–48, accessed May 17, 2017, https://www.scribd.com/document/30902475/Bio-Security-Commons-AR-May-2010.

15. As of May 2017, the Chemical Biological Sciences Unit has been renamed the Scientific Response and Analysis Unit.

16. For a thorough analysis of the consequences of the 2001 anthrax attacks and our readiness as a country twelve years later, see Vahid Majidi, *A Spore on the Grassy Knoll: An Insider's Account of the 2001 Anthrax Mailings* (Lexington, KY: Vahid Majidi, 2013), 163–96.

17. "An Introduction to Next-Generation Technology," Illumina, Inc., accessed May 13, 2017, https://www.illumina.com/content/dam/illumina-marketing/documents/products/illumina_sequencing_introduction.pdf.

18. Tom Reynolds, Robert B. Harris, and Greg Meyers started NEXT Molecular Analytics in October 2015. All three had been senior executives at American International Biotechnology, LLC before leaving to form NEXT Molecular Analytics.

19. For estimates of morphology variants in the mailed spores, see National Research Council, *Review of the Scientific Approach Used during the FBI's Investigation of the 2001 Anthrax Attacks*, ed. Alice P. Gast et al. (Washington, DC: National Academies Press, 2011), 149–50.

20. Kristen French, "The Path to Legal Standing: Next-Generation Sequencing May Have to Overcome a Few Hurdles," accessed June 11, 2017, http://protomag.com/articles/the-path-to-legal-standing.

21. C. Bertelli and G. Greub, "Rapid Bacterial Genome Sequencing: Methods and Application in Clinical Microbiology," *Clinical Microbiology and Infection* 19 (2013): 803–13.

22. National Research Council, *Review of the Scientific Approach Used during the FBI's Investigation of the 2001 Anthrax Attacks*, 149–50.

Selected Bibliography

Basbanes, Nicolas A. *On Paper: The Everything of Its Two-Thousand-Year History.* New York: Alfred A. Knopf, 2013.

Beecher, Douglas J. "Forensic Application of Microbiological Culture Analysis to Identify Mail Intentionally Contaminated with *Bacillus anthracis* Spores." *Applied and Environmental Microbiology* 72, no. 8 (2006): 5304–10.

Berg, Paul, and Maxine F. Singer. "The Recombinant DNA Controversy: Twenty Years Later." *Proceedings of the National Academy of Sciences* 92, no. 20 (1995): 9011–13.

Brachman, Philip S., Arnold F. Kaufmann, and Frederic G. Dalldorf. "Industrial Inhalational Anthrax." *Bacteriological Reviews* 30, no. 3 (1966): 646–57.

Bryson, Bill. *A Short History of Nearly Everything.* New York: Broadway Books, 2003.

Caro, Mark. "Now That the Tabloids Have Become the News, Where Do They Go from Here?" *Chicago Tribune*, October 16, 2001.

Carson, Frederick T. "Some Observations on Determining the Size of Pores in Paper." *Journal of Research of the National Bureau of Standards* 24 (1940): 435–42.

Carus, W. Seth. *Bioterrorism and Biocrimes: The Illicit Use of Biological Agents since 1900.* Washington, DC: Center for Counterproliferation Research, National Defense University, 2001 revised.

Chance, R. E., and B. H. Frank. "Research, Development, Production, and Safety of Biosynthetic Human Insulin." *Diabetes Care* 16, suppl. 3 (1993): 133–42.

Charles, Jean-Francois, Armelle Delecluse, and Christina Nielsen-le Roux, editors. *Entomopathogenic Bacteria: From Laboratory to Field Applications.* Boston: Kluwer Academic Publishers, 2000.

Cole, Leonard A. *The Anthrax Letters: A Medical Detective Story.* Washington, DC: Joseph Henry Press, 2003.

Colwell, Rita R., and Sharon Bertsch McGrayne. *What I Really Think: A Feminist's View of Research Science.* New York: Simon & Schuster, in preparation.

Cranshaw, Whitney S. *"Bacillus thuringiensis."* Colorado State University Cooperative Extension Fact Sheet (1999): No. 5.556. Accessed March 18, 2017. http://www.ext.colostate.edu/pubs/insect/05556.html.

Cross, Glenn. *Dirty War: Rhodesia and Chemical Biological Warfare 1975–1980.* West Midlands, England: Helion & Company, 2017.

Cummings, Richard D. *Cold War Radio: The Dangerous History of American Broadcasting in Europe, 1950–1989.* Jefferson, NC: McFarland & Company, 2009.

Danzig, Richard, et al. *Aum Shinrikyo: Insights into How Terrorists Develop Biological and Chemical Weapons* (2nd edition). Washington, DC: Center for a New American Security, 2012.

Daschle, Tom, with Michael D'Orso. *Like No Other Time: The Two Years That Changed America Forever.* New York: Random House, 2003.

Defoe, Daniel. *A Journal of the Plague Year.* Mineola, NY: Dover Publications, 2001.

Department of Health and Human Services. *Biological Threats and Terrorism: Assessing the Science and Response Capabilities: Workshop Summary,* edited by Stacey L. Knobler, Adel A. F. Mahmoud, and Leslie A. Pray. Washington, DC: National Academy Press, 2002.

DiMarco, Damon. *Tower Stories: An Oral History of 9/11* (2nd edition). Santa Monica, CA: Santa Monica Press, 2007.

Dolan, Jack. "Anthrax Probe Remains Slow Go; Experts Speculate in FBI's Thrust." *Hartford Courant,* March 4, 2002.

Eckenrode, Brian A., et al. "Performance Evaluation of the Scent Transfer Unit (STU-100) for Organic Compound Collection and Release." *Journal of Forensic Science* 51, no. 4 (2006): 780–89.

Fellows, P. F., et al. "Efficacy of a Human Anthrax Vaccine in Guinea Pigs, Rabbits, and Rhesus Macaques against Challenge by *Bacillus anthracis* Isolates of Diverse Geographic Origin." *Vaccine* 19 (2001): 3241–47.

Freeman, Jim, Terry D. Turchie, and Donald Max Noel. *Unabomber: How the FBI Broke Its Own Rules to Capture the Terrorist Ted Kaczynski.* Palisades, NY: History Publishing Company, 2014.

Friedlander, Arthur M. "Anthrax." In *Medical Aspects of Chemical and Biological Warfare,* edited by F. R. Sidell, E. T. Takafuji, and D. R. Franz, 467–78. Washington, DC: TMM Publications, Borden Institute, 1997.

Graff, Garrett M. *The Threat Matrix: The FBI at War in the Age of Global Terror.* New York: Little, Brown and Company, 2011.

Graysmith, Robert. *Amerithrax: The Hunt for the Anthrax Killer.* New York: Berkley Books, 2003.

Gregory, Alice. "A Brief History of the Zoot Suit: Unraveling the Jazzy Life of a Snazzy Style." *Smithsonian Magazine,* April 2016. Accessed April 9, 2017. http://www.smithsonianmag.com/arts-culture/brief-history-zoot-suit-180958507/.

Grenha, Rosa, et al. "Structural Characterization of SpoOE-Like Protein-aspartic Acid Phosphatases That Regulate Sporulation in Bacilli." *Journal of Biological Chemistry* 281, no. 49 (2006): 37993–8003.

Griffith, K. S., et al. "Bioterrorism-Related Inhalational Anthrax in an Elderly Woman, Connecticut, 2001." *Emerging Infectious Diseases* 9, no. 6 (2003): 681–88.

Guillemin, Jeanne. *American Anthrax: Fear, Crime, and the Investigation of the Nation's Deadliest Bioterror Attack*. New York: Times Books, Henry Holt and Company, 2011.

Gyford, Phil. *The Diary of Samuel Pepys: Daily Entries from 17th Century London Diary*. Accessed April 6, 2017. http://www.pepysdiary.com/encyclopedia/301/.

Hamilton, Douglas H. "The Epidemic Intelligence Service: The Centers for Disease Control and Prevention's Disease Detectives." *AMA Journal of Ethics* 8 (2006): 261–64.

Hammond, Peter M., and Gradon B. Carter. *From Biological Warfare to Healthcare, Porton Down, 1940–2000*. New York: Palgrave Macmillan, 2002.

Harris, Jr., Tommy. *Through the Eyes of the Ironworkers: A Photographic Salute to the World Trade Center Heroes of Local 40*. Silver Spring. MD: Beckham Publications, 2008.

Hendrick, Walt, and Andrea Zaferes. *Ice Diving Operations*. Tulsa, OK: PennWell Books, 2003.

Hirota, Ryuichi, et al. "The Silicon Layer Supports Acid Resistance of *Bacillus cereus* Spores." *Journal of Bacteriology* 192, no. 1 (2010): 111–16.

Hoffmaster, Alex A., et al. "Molecular Subtyping of *Bacillus anthracis* and the 2001 Bioterrorism-Associated Anthrax Outbreak, United States." *Emerging Infectious Diseases* 8, no. 10 (2002): 1111–16.

Holt, John G. *Bergey's Manual of Systematic Bacteriology, 1st Edition, Volume 2*, edited by David Hendricks Bergey, John G. Holt, and Noel R. Krieg. Baltimore: Williams & Wilkins, 1986.

Holtz, T. H., et al. "Isolated Case of Bioterrorism-Related Inhalational Anthrax, New York City, 2001." *Emerging Infectious Diseases* 9, no. 6 (2003): 689–96.

Ivins, Bruce E., et al. "Immunization against Anthrax with *Bacillus anthracis* Protective Antigen Combined with Adjuvants." *Infection and Immunity* 60, no. 2 (1992): 662–68.

Jernigan, Daniel B., et al. "Investigation of Bioterrorism-Related Anthrax, United States, 2001: Epidemiologic Findings." *Emerging Infectious Diseases* 8, no. 10 (2002): 1019–28.

Jones, Del. "Muslim CEOs of U.S. Firms Fight Terrorism, 'Stop Evil.'" *USA Today*, Money Section, May 18, 2004.

Kalugin, Oleg. *Spymaster: My Thirty-Two Years in Intelligence and Espionage against the West*. New York: Basic Books, 2009.

Keim, Paul, et al. "The International *Bacillus anthracis*, *B. cereus*, and *B. thuringiensis* Conference, 'Bacillus-ACT05.'" *Journal of Bacteriology* 188, no. 10 (2006): 3433–41.

Kolata, Gina. "Florida Man Is Hospitalized with Pulmonary Anthrax." *New York Times*, October 5, 2001.

Lake, Edward G. *Analyzing the Anthrax Attacks: The First 3 Years*. Racine, WI: Edward G. Lake, 2005.

Lake, Edward G. *A Crime Unlike Any Other: What the Facts Say about Dr. Bruce Edwards Ivins and the Anthrax Attacks of 2001*. Racine, WI: Edward G. Lake, 2012.

Lake, Edward G. "Analyzing the Anthrax Attacks (2009–2014 edition)." Accessed April 18, 2017. http://www.anthraxinvestigation.com.

Lang, Michael A. "Ice Diving." *DAN: The Magazine of Diver Alert Network.* Accessed April 7, 2017. http://www.alertdiver.com/Ice-Diving.

LaPorte, Gerald M., Joseph C. Stephens, and Amanda K. Beuchel. "The Examination of Commercial Printing Defects to Assess Common Origin, Batch Variation, and Error Rate." *Journal of Forensic Science* 55, no. 1 (2010): 136–40.

Lesak, David M. *Hazardous Materials: Strategies and Tactics.* Upper Saddle River, NJ: Brady/Prentice Hall, 1999.

Macrakis, Kristie. *Seduced by Secrets: Inside the Stasi's Spy-Tech World.* New York: Cambridge University Press, 2008.

Maguire, Rachel. *Metal of Honor: The Ironworkers of 9/11.* [Film]. Chicago: Naja Productions, 2006, running time: 75 minutes.

Majidi, Vahid. *A Spore on the Grassy Knoll: An Insider's Account of the 2001 Anthrax Mailings.* Lexington, KY: Vahid Majidi, 2013.

Matsumoto, Gary. "The Pentagon's Toxic Secret." *Vanity Fair*, May 1999.

Microsoft Corporation. "MSN Online Services, Where to Serve Criminal Legal Process." April 2005 revision. Accessed April 10, 2017. https://info.publicintelligence.net/MSN-Compliance.pdf.

Monterey Institute of International Studies. "Chronology of Aum Shinrikyo's CBW Activities." 2001. Accessed April 18, 2017. https://www.nonproliferation.org/wp-content/uploads/2016/06/aum_chrn.pdf.

Morse, Stephen A., et al. "Detecting Biothreat Agents: The Laboratory Response Network." *ASM News* 69, no. 9 (2003): 433–37.

National Commission on Terrorist Attacks upon the United States. *The 9/11 Report.* Chairman Thomas H. Kean and Vice Chairman Lee H. Hamilton. New York: St. Martins Paperbacks, 2004.

National Research Council. *Review of the Scientific Approach Used during the FBI's Investigation of the 2001 Anthrax Attacks*, edited by Alice P. Gast et al. Washington, DC: National Academy Press, 2011.

O'Carroll, Eoin. "Marie Curie: Why Her Papers Are Still Radioactive." *Christian Science Monitor*, November 7, 2011.

Preston, Richard. *The Demon in the Freezer: A True Story.* New York: Random House, 2002.

Rasko, D. A., et al. "*Bacillus anthracis* Comparative Genome Analysis in Support of the Amerithrax Investigation." *Proceedings of the National Academy of Sciences* 108, no. 12 (2011): 5027–32.

Ravel, J., et al. "The Complete Genome Sequence of *Bacillus anthracis* Ames 'Ancestor.'" *Journal of Bacteriology* 191, no. 1 (2009): 445–46.

Ray, Arghya, and Bengt Norden. "Peptide Nucleic Acid (PNA): Its Medical and Biotechnical Applications and Promise for the Future." *FASEB Journal* 14, no. 9 (2000): 1041–60.

Reid, Robert William. *Marie Curie.* New York: Saturday Review Press, 1974.

Ride, David. *In Defence of Landscape, An Archaeology of Porton Down.* Stroud, Gloucestershire: Tempus Publishing Ltd., 2006.

Rosebury, Theodore. *Experimental Air-Borne Infection.* Baltimore: The Wilkens & Wilkens Company, 1947.

Saathoff, Gregory, et al. *The Amerithrax Case: Report of the Expert Behavioral Analysis Panel.* Vienna, VA: Research Strategies Network, unsealed and redacted edition, 2011.

Saiki, R., et al. "Enzymatic Amplification of Beta-Globin Genomic Sequences and Restriction Site Analysis for Diagnosis of Sickle Cell Anemia." *Science* 230, no. 4732 (1985): 1350–54.

Schep, L. J., W. A. Temple, G. A. Butt, and M. D. Beasley. "Ricin as a Weapon of Mass Terror—Separating Fact from Fiction." *Environmental International* 35, no. 8 (2009): 1267–71.

Schmitt, Ketra, and Nicholas A. Zacchia. "Total Decontamination Cost of the Anthrax Letter Attacks." *Biosecurity and Bioterrorism: Biodefense Strategy, Practice, and Science* 10 (2012): 98–107. Accessed March 23, 2017. http://online.liebertpub.com/doi/abs/10.1089/bsp.2010.0053.

Schroen, Gary C. *First In: An Insider's Account of How the CIA Spearheaded the War on Terror in Afghanistan.* New York: Presidio Press, Ballantine Books, 2005.

Sifton, David W., ed. *Physicians' Desk Reference, 55th edition.* Montvale, NJ: Medical Economics, 2001.

Skloot, Rebecca. *The Immortal Life of Henrietta Lacks.* New York: Random House, 2010.

Stockham, Rex A., Dennis L. Slavin, and William Kift. "Specialized Use of Human Scent in Criminal Investigations." *Forensic Science Communications* 6, no. 3 (2004). Accessed online April 7, 2017.

Taborsky, V. "Small-Scale Processing of Microbial Pesticides." *FAO Agricultural Services Bulletin No. 96* (1992). Accessed April 2, 2017. http://www.fao.org/docrep/t0533e/t0533e03.htm.

Takahashi, Hiroshi, et al. "*Bacillus anthracis* Bioterrorism Incident, Kameido, Tokyo, 1993." *Emerging Infectious Diseases* 10, no. 1 (2004): 117–120.

Thompson, Marilyn W. *The Killer Strain: Anthrax and a Government Exposed.* New York: HarperCollins, 2003.

Todar, Kenneth. *Todar's Online Textbook of Bacteriology.* Accessed April 9, 2017. http://textbookofbacteriology.net/Bacillus.html.

Traeger, Marc S., et al. "First Case of Bioterrorism-Related Inhalational Anthrax in the United States, Palm Beach County, Florida, 2001." *Emerging Infectious Diseases* 8, no. 10 (2002): 1029–34.

Tucker, Holly. *Blood Work: A Tale of Medicine and Murder in the Scientific Revolution.* New York: Norton, 2011.

United States Department of Justice. *Amerithrax Investigative Summary.* February 19, 2010. Accessed April 6, 2017. https://www.justice.gov/archive/amerithrax/docs/amx-investigative-summary.pdf.

Warrick, Joby. "Trail of Odd Anthrax Cells Led FBI to Army Scientist." *Washington Post,* October 27, 2008.

Weber, Harry R. "Former Olympic Park Guard Jewell Dies." *Associated Press* in *Washington Post,* August 30, 2007.

Willman, David. *The Mirage Man: Bruce Ivins, the Anthrax Attacks, and America's Rush to War.* New York: Bantam Books, 2011.

Willman, David. "U.S. System to Detect Bioterrorism Can't Be Counted On, Government Watchdog Finds." *Los Angeles Times*, November 23, 2015.

Worsham, P. L., and M. R. Sowers. "Isolation of an Asporogenic (SpoOA) Protective Antigen-Producing Strain of *Bacillus anthracis*." *Canadian Journal of Microbiology* 45, no. 1 (1999): 1–8.

Zumbrun, E. E., et al. "A Characterization of Aerosolized Sudan Virus Infection in African Green Monkeys, Cynomolgus Macaques, and Rhesus Macaques." *Viruses* 4, no. 10 (2002): 2115–36.

Index

Zimbabwe strain, 16, 101. *See also* Ames strain
antibiotic, 12, 26, 29, 32, 45, 54-55, 58, 69, 106, 180-81, 188, 225n17
Argonne National Laboratory, 240n11
Armed Forces Radiology Research Institute (AFRRI), 67, 96, 104
Ashcroft, John, 63
Asilomar Grounds, Monterey Peninsula, 130
Association of Public Health Laboratories, 221n2
Atomic Weapons Establishment (United Kingdom), 86
Atta, Mohamed, 7
Aum Shinrikyo, 13, 220nn7-8
Automated Fingerprint Identification System (AFIS), 67, 97

B4 containment, 163, 213
Bacillus ACT 2005, 160
Bacillus amyloliquefacieus, 180, 240n8
Bacillus anthracis. See anthrax; Ames strain
Bacillus cereus, 160, 180, 240n8
Bacillus licheniformis, 180, 240n8
Bacillus megaterium, 180, 240n8
Bacillus subtilis, 179-83, 190-91, 239n6, 240nn8-11; fermentation of, 179, 182; *sboA* gene, 181; subtilosin A, 181; repository, 181
Bacillus thuringiensis (Bt), 47-48, 68, 127, 160, 180, 223n4, 225n11, 240n8; CRY protein(s), 47; DNA, 47; Israelensis strain, 47, 127; Kurstaki strain, 47
bacitracin, 180
bacteriophage, 129
Baltimore Sun, 123, 193
barcode(s), 54, 102
Battelle Memorial Institute, 152, 154, 157, 162, 172, 198
Beecher, Douglas, 15-17, 19-21, 26-27, 70, 72-74, 90-91, 101-2, 161, 217, 221n1, 222n5, 227n11

bentonite, 227n2
Bergey's Manual of Systemic Bacteriology, 180
Biohazard Detection System (BDS), 212
Biological Aerosol Sentry and Information System (BASIS), 211-12, 243n2
biological safety cabinet, 71, 73, 102-3, 107, 117
biological terrorism (bioterrorism), 6, 8, 16, 25, 31-33, 48, 57, 89, 104, 112, 160, 210, 212, 214, 244n12
biological weapon (bioweapon), 6, 13, 15, 48, 68, 75, 78, 104-5, 128, 185, 233n1
BioPort, Inc., 29, 80-82
biosafety level (BSL), 33, 104, 131, 140, 163, 193, 213-14, 244n9
biotechnology, 2, 126, 129-30, 214
bin Laden, Osama, 6-7, 14, 22, 221n9
Birmingham, Alabama, 93
BioWatch Program, 211, 244n4
Black Death. *See* plague, bubonic
Blanco, Ernesto, 9-10, 12-13, 18, 23, 31-32, 40-41, 220n2, 224nn10-12
bloodhounds. *See* dogs
Boca Raton, City of, Florida, 7, 9, 12, 14, 18-19, 22, 26-27, 30, 33, 35, 54, 57, 70, 74, 91, 222n4
Boca Raton Fire Department, 27-28
Boston University, 44
botulism, 153
Bostwick, David, 217
Brentwood Processing and Distribution Center, 55, 57-59, 61-63, 65-66, 72, 80, 97, 144-45, 226n3
Brokaw, Tom, 35-37, 194; letter and envelope to, 37, 39-40, 54, 56-58, 61, 97, 101, 114, 147, 160, 164, 169; spore powder, 37-40, 61, 70, 179, 181; *anthracis* isolated, 37-38, 57, 226n10
Brooks, Tim, 235n7
Budowle, Bruce, 97-99, 141
Bulgarian Secret Police, 78-79

About the Author

Scott Decker retired as a special agent with the Federal Bureau of Investigation after a career investigating everything from stolen property to international terrorism. He spent the first seven years of his law enforcement career on the Boston Division's Bank Robbery Task Force. From there he was promoted to the FBI Laboratory's new Hazardous Materials Response Unit. On September 12, 2001, he led a team of FBI Hazmat officers to Ground Zero where they established a command post at the edge of the fallen World Trade Center buildings. He returned from New York to head up a squad of agents—each with an advanced degree in science—at the Washington Field Office where they coordinated the forensic components of the 2001 anthrax attack investigation. In 2009, he and his fellow investigators were awarded the FBI Director's Award for Outstanding Scientific Advancement. Decker completed a National Institutes of Health Postdoctoral Fellowship at Harvard Medical School (Biological Chemistry), and he holds a PhD and MSc in Human Genetics from the University of Michigan and a BSc in Zoology from the University of Rhode Island.

Decker is a contributing author to an anthology of stories about gallantry, *I Pledge Allegiance . . . : Stories of Valor, Heroism and Patriotism*, by the Wednesday Warrior Writers of Las Vegas (2nd Edition, 2017). *Recounting the Anthrax Attacks: Terror, the Amerithrax Task Force and the Evolution of Forensics in the FBI* is his first full-length book. He lives in southern Nevada with his wife, Terry L. Kerns, and a good-natured beagle mix and an overly protective miniature pinscher.

www.ingramcontent.com/pod-product-compliance
Lightning Source LLC
Chambersburg PA
CBHW031211240326
R18026300002B/R180263PG41599CBX00018B/5